Understanding Computation

Tom Stuart

O'REILLY®

Beijing · Cambridge · Farnham · Köln · Sebastopol · Tokyo

Understanding Computation

by Tom Stuart

Copyright © 2013 Tom Stuart. All rights reserved.
Printed in the United States of America.

Published by O'Reilly Media, Inc., 1005 Gravenstein Highway North, Sebastopol, CA 95472.

O'Reilly books may be purchased for educational, business, or sales promotional use. Online editions are also available for most titles (*http://my.safaribooksonline.com*). For more information, contact our corporate/institutional sales department: 800-998-9938 or *corporate@oreilly.com*.

Editors: Mike Loukides and Nathan Jepson
Production Editor: Christopher Hearse
Copyeditor: Rachel Leach
Proofreader: Linley Dolby

Indexer: Lucie Haskins
Cover Designer: Randy Comer
Interior Designer: David Futato
Illustrator: Rebecca Demarest

May 2013:   First Edition.

Revision History for the First Edition:

2013-05-10   First release
2013-05-31   Second release

See *http://oreilly.com/catalog/errata.csp?isbn=9781449329273* for release details.

ISBN: 978-1-449-32927-3

[LSI]

1369775750

Table of Contents

Part II. Computation and Computability

Preface

Who Should Read This Book?

This book is for programmers who are curious about programming languages and the theory of computation, especially those who don't have a formal background in mathematics or computer science.

If you're interested in the mind-expanding parts of computer science that deal with programs, languages, and machines, but are discouraged by the mathematical language that's often used to explain them, this book is for you. Instead of complex notation we'll use working code to illustrate theoretical ideas and turn them into interactive experiments that you can explore at your own pace.

This book assumes that you know at least one modern programming language like Ruby, Python, JavaScript, Java, or C#. All of the code examples are in Ruby, but if you know another language you should still be able to follow along. However, this book *isn't* a guide to best practices in Ruby or object-oriented design. The code is intended to be clear and concise, but not necessarily to be easy to maintain; the goal is always to use Ruby to illustrate the computer science, not vice versa. It's also not a textbook or an encyclopedia, so instead of presenting formal arguments or watertight proofs, this book tries to break the ice on some interesting ideas and inspire you to learn about them in more depth.

Conventions Used in This Book

The following typographical conventions are used in this book:

Italic
> Indicates new terms, URLs, email addresses, filenames, and file extensions.

`Constant width`
> Used for program listings, as well as within paragraphs to refer to program elements such as variable or function names, databases, data types, environment variables, statements, and keywords.

Constant width bold

Shows commands or other text that should be typed literally by the user.

Constant width italic

Shows text that should be replaced with user-supplied values or by values determined by context.

This icon signifies a tip, suggestion, or general note.

This icon indicates a warning or caution.

Using Code Examples

This book is here to help you get your job done. In general, if this book includes code examples, you may use the code in your programs and documentation. You do not need to contact us for permission unless you're reproducing a significant portion of the code. For example, writing a program that uses several chunks of code from this book does not require permission. Selling or distributing a CD-ROM of examples from O'Reilly books does require permission. Answering a question by citing this book and quoting example code does not require permission. Incorporating a significant amount of example code from this book into your product's documentation does require permission.

We appreciate, but do not require, attribution. An attribution usually includes the title, author, publisher, and ISBN. For example: "*Understanding Computation* by Tom Stuart (O'Reilly). Copyright 2013 Tom Stuart, 978-1-4493-2927-3."

If you feel your use of code examples falls outside fair use or the permission given above, feel free to contact us at *permissions@oreilly.com*.

Safari® Books Online

Safari Safari Books Online (*www.safaribooksonline.com*) is an on-demand digital library that delivers expert content in both book and video form from the world's leading authors in technology and business.

Technology professionals, software developers, web designers, and business and creative professionals use Safari Books Online as their primary resource for research, problem solving, learning, and certification training.

Safari Books Online offers a range of product mixes and pricing programs for organizations, government agencies, and individuals. Subscribers have access to thousands of books, training videos, and prepublication manuscripts in one fully searchable database from publishers like O'Reilly Media, Prentice Hall Professional, Addison-Wesley Professional, Microsoft Press, Sams, Que, Peachpit Press, Focal Press, Cisco Press, John Wiley & Sons, Syngress, Morgan Kaufmann, IBM Redbooks, Packt, Adobe Press, FT Press, Apress, Manning, New Riders, McGraw-Hill, Jones & Bartlett, Course Technology, and dozens more. For more information about Safari Books Online, please visit us online.

How to Contact Us

Please address comments and questions concerning this book to the publisher:

O'Reilly Media, Inc.
1005 Gravenstein Highway North
Sebastopol, CA 95472
800-998-9938 (in the United States or Canada)
707-829-0515 (international or local)
707-829-0104 (fax)

We have a web page for this book, where we list errata, examples, and any additional information. You can access this page at *http://oreil.ly/understanding-computation*.

To comment or ask technical questions about this book, send email to *bookquestions@oreilly.com*.

For more information about our books, courses, conferences, and news, see our website at *http://www.oreilly.com*.

Find us on Facebook: *http://facebook.com/oreilly*

Follow us on Twitter: *http://twitter.com/oreillymedia*

Watch us on YouTube: *http://www.youtube.com/oreillymedia*

Acknowledgments

I'm grateful for the hospitality of Go Free Range (*http://gofreerange.com/*), who provided me with office space, friendly conversation, and tea throughout the writing of this book. Without their generous support, I'd definitely have gone a bit Jack Torrance.

Thank you to James Adam, Paul Battley, James Coglan, Peter Fletcher, Chris Lowis, and Murray Steele for their feedback on early drafts, and to Gabriel Kerneis and Alex Stangl for their technical reviews. This book has been immeasurably improved by their thoughtful contributions. I'd also like to thank Alan Mycroft from the University of Cambridge for all the knowledge and encouragement he supplied.

Many people from O'Reilly helped shepherd this project to completion, but I'm especially grateful to Mike Loukides and Simon St.Laurent for their early enthusiasm and faith in the idea, to Nathan Jepson for his advice on how to turn the idea into an actual book, and to Sanders Kleinfeld for humoring my relentless quest for perfect syntax highlighting.

Thank you to my parents for giving an annoying child the means, motive, and opportunity to spend all his time mucking about with computers; and to Leila, for patiently reminding me, every time I forgot how the job should be done, to keep putting one damn word after another. I got there in the end.

## CHAPTER 1

Just Enough Ruby

The code in this book is written in Ruby, a programming language that was designed to be simple, friendly, and fun. I've chosen it because of its clarity and flexibility, but nothing in the book relies on special features of Ruby, so you should be able to translate the code examples into whatever language you prefer—especially another dynamic language like Python or JavaScript—if that helps to make the ideas clearer.

All of the example code is compatible with both Ruby 2.0 and Ruby 1.9. You can find out more about Ruby, and download an official implementation, at the official Ruby website (*http://www.ruby-lang.org/*).

Let's take a quick tour of Ruby's features. We'll concentrate on the parts of the language that are used in this book; if you want to learn more, O'Reilly's *The Ruby Programming Language* is a good place to start.

If you already know Ruby, you can safely skip to Chapter 2 without missing anything.

Interactive Ruby Shell

One of Ruby's friendliest features is its interactive console, *IRB*, which lets us enter pieces of Ruby code and immediately see the results. In this book, we'll use IRB extensively to interact with the code we're writing and explore how it works.

You can run IRB on your development machine by typing **irb** at the command line. IRB shows a >> prompt when it expects you to provide a Ruby expression. After you type an expression and hit Enter, the code gets evaluated, and the result is shown at a => prompt:

```
$ irb --simple-prompt
>> 1 + 2
=> 3
```

```
>> 'hello world'.length
=> 11
```

Whenever we see these >> and => prompts in the book, we're interacting with IRB. To make longer code listings easier to read, they'll be shown without the prompts, but we'll still assume that the code in these listings has been typed or pasted into IRB. So once the book has shown some Ruby code like this…

```
x = 2
y = 3
z = x + y
```

…then we'll be able to play with its results in IRB:

```
>> x * y * z
=> 30
```

Values

Ruby is an *expression-oriented* language: every valid piece of code produces a value when it's executed. Here's a quick overview of the different kinds of Ruby value.

Basic Data

As we'd expect, Ruby supports Booleans, numbers, and strings, all of which come with the usual operations:

```
>> (true && false) || true
=> true
>> (3 + 3) * (14 / 2)
=> 42
>> 'hello' + ' world'
=> "hello world"
>> 'hello world'.slice(6)
=> "w"
```

A Ruby *symbol* is a lightweight, immutable value representing a name. Symbols are widely used in Ruby as simpler and less memory-intensive alternatives to strings, most often as keys in hashes (see "Data Structures" on page 3). Symbol literals are written with a colon at the beginning:

```
>> :my_symbol
=> :my_symbol
>> :my_symbol == :my_symbol
=> true
>> :my_symbol == :another_symbol
=> false
```

The special value nil is used to indicate the absence of any useful value:

```
>> 'hello world'.slice(11)
=> nil
```

Data Structures

Ruby array literals are written as a comma-separated list of values surrounded by square brackets:

```
>> numbers = ['zero', 'one', 'two']
=> ["zero", "one", "two"]
>> numbers[1]
=> "one"
>> numbers.push('three', 'four')
=> ["zero", "one", "two", "three", "four"]
>> numbers
=> ["zero", "one", "two", "three", "four"]
>> numbers.drop(2)
=> ["two", "three", "four"]
```

A *range* represents a collection of values between a minimum and a maximum. Ranges are written by putting a pair of dots between two values:

```
>> ages = 18..30
=> 18..30
>> ages.entries
=> [18, 19, 20, 21, 22, 23, 24, 25, 26, 27, 28, 29, 30]
>> ages.include?(25)
=> true
>> ages.include?(33)
=> false
```

A *hash* is a collection in which every value is associated with a key; some programming languages call this data structure a "map," "dictionary," or "associative array." A hash literal is written as a comma-separated list of *key* => *value* pairs inside curly brackets:

```
>> fruit = { 'a' => 'apple', 'b' => 'banana', 'c' => 'coconut' }
=> {"a"=>"apple", "b"=>"banana", "c"=>"coconut"}
>> fruit['b']
=> "banana"
>> fruit['d'] = 'date'
=> "date"
>> fruit
=> {"a"=>"apple", "b"=>"banana", "c"=>"coconut", "d"=>"date"}
```

Hashes often have symbols as keys, so Ruby provides an alternative *key*: *value* syntax for writing key-value pairs where the key is a symbol. This is more compact than the *key* => *value* syntax and looks a lot like the popular JSON format for JavaScript objects:

```
>> dimensions = { width: 1000, height: 2250, depth: 250 }
=> {:width=>1000, :height=>2250, :depth=>250}
>> dimensions[:depth]
=> 250
```

Procs

A *proc* is an unevaluated chunk of Ruby code that can be passed around and evaluated on demand; other languages call this an "anonymous function" or "lambda." There are several ways of writing a proc literal, the most compact of which is the -> *argu ments { body }* syntax:

```
>> multiply = -> x, y { x * y }
=> #<Proc (lambda)>
>> multiply.call(6, 9)
=> 54
>> multiply.call(2, 3)
=> 6
```

As well as the .call syntax, procs can be called by using square brackets:

```
>> multiply[3, 4]
=> 12
```

Control Flow

Ruby has if, case, and while expressions, which work in the usual way:

```
>> if 2 < 3
     'less'
   else
     'more'
   end
=> "less"
>> quantify =
     -> number {
       case number
       when 1
         'one'
       when 2
         'a couple'
       else
         'many'
       end
     }
=> #<Proc (lambda)>
>> quantify.call(2)
=> "a couple"
>> quantify.call(10)
=> "many"
>> x = 1
=> 1
>> while x < 1000
     x = x * 2
   end
=> nil
>> x
=> 1024
```

Objects and Methods

Ruby looks like other dynamic programming languages but it's unusual in an important way: every value is an *object*, and objects communicate by sending *messages* to each other.[1] Each object has its own collection of *methods* that determine how it responds to particular messages.

A message has a name and, optionally, some arguments. When an object receives a message, its corresponding method is executed with the arguments from the message. This is how all work gets done in Ruby; even 1 + 2 means "send the object 1 a message called + with the argument 2," and the object 1 has a #+ method for handling that message.

We can define our own methods with the def keyword:

```
>> o = Object.new
=> #<Object>
>> def o.add(x, y)
     x + y
   end
=> nil
>> o.add(2, 3)
=> 5
```

Here we're making a new object by sending the new message to a special built-in object called Object; once the new object's been created, we define an #add method on it. The #add method adds its two arguments together and returns the result—an explicit return isn't necessary, because the value of the last expression to be executed in a method is automatically returned. When we send that object the add message with 2 and 3 as arguments, its #add method is executed and we get back the answer we wanted.

We'll usually send a message to an object by writing the receiving object and the message name separated by a dot (e.g., o.add), but Ruby always keeps track of the *current object* (called self) and will allow us to send a message to that object by writing a message name on its own, leaving the receiver implicit. For example, inside a method definition the current object is always the object that received the message that caused the method to execute, so within a particular object's method, we can send other messages to the same object without referring to it explicitly:

```
>> def o.add_twice(x, y)
     add(x, y) + add(x, y)
   end
=> nil
>> o.add_twice(2, 3)
=> 10
```

---

1. This style comes from the Smalltalk programming language, which had a direct influence on the design of Ruby.

Notice that we can send the add message to o from within the #add_twice method by writing add(x, y) instead of o.add(x, y), because o is the object that the add_twice message was sent to.

Outside of any method definition, the current object is a special top-level object called main, and any messages that don't specify a receiver are sent to it; similarly, any method definitions that don't specify an object will be made available through main:

```
>> def multiply(a, b)
     a * b
   end
=> nil
>> multiply(2, 3)
=> 6
```

Classes and Modules

It's convenient to be able to share method definitions between many objects. In Ruby, we can put method definitions inside a *class*, then create new objects by sending the new message to that class. The objects we get back are *instances* of the class and incorporate its methods. For example:

```
>> class Calculator
     def divide(x, y)
       x / y
     end
   end
=> nil
>> c = Calculator.new
=> #<Calculator>
>> c.class
=> Calculator
>> c.divide(10, 2)
=> 5
```

Note that defining a method inside a class definition adds the method to instances of that class, not to main:

```
>> divide(10, 2)
NoMethodError: undefined method `divide' for main:Object
```

One class can bring in another class's method definitions through *inheritance*:

```
>> class MultiplyingCalculator < Calculator
     def multiply(x, y)
       x * y
     end
   end
=> nil
>> mc = MultiplyingCalculator.new
=> #<MultiplyingCalculator>
>> mc.class
=> MultiplyingCalculator
>> mc.class.superclass
```

```
=> Calculator
>> mc.multiply(10, 2)
=> 20
>> mc.divide(10, 2)
=> 5
```

A method in a subclass can call a superclass method of the same name by using the super keyword:

```
>> class BinaryMultiplyingCalculator < MultiplyingCalculator
     def multiply(x, y)
       result = super(x, y)
       result.to_s(2)
     end
   end
=> nil
>> bmc = BinaryMultiplyingCalculator.new
=> #<BinaryMultiplyingCalculator>
>> bmc.multiply(10, 2)
=> "10100"
```

Another way of sharing method definitions is to declare them in a *module*, which can then be included by any class:

```
>> module Addition
     def add(x, y)
       x + y
     end
   end
=> nil
>> class AddingCalculator
     include Addition
   end
=> AddingCalculator
>> ac = AddingCalculator.new
=> #<AddingCalculator>
>> ac.add(10, 2)
=> 12
```

Miscellaneous Features

Here's a grab bag of useful Ruby features that we'll need for the example code in this book.

Local Variables and Assignment

As we've already seen, Ruby lets us declare local variables just by assigning a value to them:

```
>> greeting = 'hello'
=> "hello"
>> greeting
=> "hello"
```

We can also use *parallel assignment* to assign values to several variables at once by breaking apart an array:

```
>> width, height, depth = [1000, 2250, 250]
=> [1000, 2250, 250]
>> height
=> 2250
```

String Interpolation

Strings can be single- or double-quoted. Ruby automatically performs *interpolation* on double-quoted strings, replacing any #{*expression*} with its result:

```
>> "hello #{'dlrow'.reverse}"
=> "hello world"
```

If an interpolated expression returns an object that isn't a string, that object is automatically sent a to_s message and is expected to return a string that can be used in its place. We can use this to control how interpolated objects appear:

```
>> o = Object.new
=> #<Object>
>> def o.to_s
     'a new object'
   end
=> nil
>> "here is #{o}"
=> "here is a new object"
```

Inspecting Objects

Something similar happens whenever IRB needs to display an object: the object is sent the inspect message and should return a string representation of itself. All objects in Ruby have sensible default implementations of #inspect, but by providing our own definition, we can control how an object appears on the console:

```
>> o = Object.new
=> #<Object>
>> def o.inspect
     '[my object]'
   end
=> nil
>> o
=> [my object]
```

Printing Strings

The #puts method is available to every Ruby object (including main), and can be used to print strings to standard output:

```
>> x = 128
=> 128
```

```
>> while x < 1000
     puts "x is #{x}"
     x = x * 2
   end
x is 128
x is 256
x is 512
=> nil
```

Variadic Methods

Method definitions can use the * operator to support a variable number of arguments:

```
>> def join_with_commas(*words)
     words.join(', ')
   end
=> nil
>> join_with_commas('one', 'two', 'three')
=> "one, two, three"
```

A method definition can't have more than one variable-length parameter, but normal parameters may appear on either side of it:

```
>> def join_with_commas(before, *words, after)
     before + words.join(', ') + after
   end
=> nil
>> join_with_commas('Testing: ', 'one', 'two', 'three', '.')
=> "Testing: one, two, three."
```

The * operator can also be used to treat each element of an array as a separate argument when sending a message:

```
>> arguments = ['Testing: ', 'one', 'two', 'three', '.']
=> ["Testing: ", "one", "two", "three", "."]
>> join_with_commas(*arguments)
=> "Testing: one, two, three."
```

And finally, * works in parallel assignment too:

```
>> before, *words, after = ['Testing: ', 'one', 'two', 'three', '.']
=> ["Testing: ", "one", "two", "three", "."]
>> before
=> "Testing: "
>> words
=> ["one", "two", "three"]
>> after
=> "."
```

Blocks

A *block* is a piece of Ruby code surrounded by do/end or curly brackets. Methods can take an implicit block argument and call the code in that block with the yield keyword:

```
>> def do_three_times
     yield
     yield
     yield
   end
=> nil
>> do_three_times { puts 'hello' }
hello
hello
hello
=> nil
```

Blocks can take arguments:

```
>> def do_three_times
     yield('first')
     yield('second')
     yield('third')
   end
=> nil
>> do_three_times { |n| puts "#{n}: hello" }
first: hello
second: hello
third: hello
=> nil
```

yield returns the result of executing the block:

```
>> def number_names
     [yield('one'), yield('two'), yield('three')].join(', ')
   end
=> nil
>> number_names { |name| name.upcase.reverse }
=> "ENO, OWT, EERHT"
```

Enumerable

Ruby has a built-in module called Enumerable that's included by Array, Hash, Range, and other classes that represent collections of values. Enumerable provides helpful methods for traversing, searching, and sorting collections, many of which expect to be called with a block. Usually the code in the block will be run against some or all values in the collection as part of whatever job the method does. For example:

```
>> (1..10).count { |number| number.even? }
=> 5
>> (1..10).select { |number| number.even? }
=> [2, 4, 6, 8, 10]
>> (1..10).any? { |number| number < 8 }
=> true
>> (1..10).all? { |number| number < 8 }
=> false
>> (1..5).each do |number|
     if number.even?
       puts "#{number} is even"
     else
```

```
      puts "#{number} is odd"
    end
  end
1 is odd
2 is even
3 is odd
4 is even
5 is odd
=> 1..5
>> (1..10).map { |number| number * 3 }
=> [3, 6, 9, 12, 15, 18, 21, 24, 27, 30]
```

It's common for the block to take one argument and send it one message with no arguments, so Ruby provides a &:*message* shorthand as a more concise way of writing the block { |object| object.*message* }:

```
>> (1..10).select(&:even?)
=> [2, 4, 6, 8, 10]
>> ['one', 'two', 'three'].map(&:upcase)
=> ["ONE", "TWO", "THREE"]
```

One of Enumerable's methods, #flat_map, can be used to evaluate an array-producing block for every value in a collection and concatenate the results:

```
>> ['one', 'two', 'three'].map(&:chars)
=> [["o", "n", "e"], ["t", "w", "o"], ["t", "h", "r", "e", "e"]]
>> ['one', 'two', 'three'].flat_map(&:chars)
=> ["o", "n", "e", "t", "w", "o", "t", "h", "r", "e", "e"]
```

Another useful method is #inject, which evaluates a block for every value in a collection and accumulates a final result:

```
>> (1..10).inject(0) { |result, number| result + number }
=> 55
>> (1..10).inject(1) { |result, number| result * number }
=> 3628800
>> ['one', 'two', 'three'].inject('Words:') { |result, word| "#{result} #{word}" }
=> "Words: one two three"
```

Struct

Struct is a special Ruby class whose job is to generate other classes. A class generated by Struct contains getter and setter methods for each of the attribute names passed into Struct.new. The conventional way to use a Struct-generated class is to subclass it; the subclass can be given a name, and it provides a convenient place to define any additional methods. For example, to make a class called Point with attributes called x and y, we can write:

```
class Point < Struct.new(:x, :y)
  def +(other_point)
    Point.new(x + other_point.x, y + other_point.y)
  end

  def inspect
```

```
    "#<Point (#{x}, #{y})>"
  end
end
```

Now we can create instances of Point, inspect them in IRB, and send them messages:

```
>> a = Point.new(2, 3)
=> #<Point (2, 3)>
>> b = Point.new(10, 20)
=> #<Point (10, 20)>
>> a + b
=> #<Point (12, 23)>
```

As well as whatever methods we define, a Point instance responds to the messages x and x= to get and set the value of its x attribute, and similarly for y and y=:

```
>> a.x
=> 2
>> a.x = 35
=> 35
>> a + b
=> #<Point (45, 23)>
```

Classes generated by Struct.new have other useful functionality, like an implementation of the equality method #==, which compares the attributes of two Structs to see if they're equal:

```
>> Point.new(4, 5) == Point.new(4, 5)
=> true
>> Point.new(4, 5) == Point.new(6, 7)
=> false
```

Monkey Patching

New methods can be added to an existing class or module at any time. This is a powerful feature, usually called *monkey patching*, which lets us extend the behavior of existing classes:

```
>> class Point
     def -(other_point)
       Point.new(x - other_point.x, y - other_point.y)
     end
   end
=> nil
>> Point.new(10, 15) - Point.new(1, 1)
=> #<Point (9, 14)>
```

We can even monkey patch Ruby's built-in classes:

```
>> class String
     def shout
       upcase + '!!!'
     end
   end
=> nil
```

```
>> 'hello world'.shout
=> "HELLO WORLD!!!"
```

Defining Constants

Ruby supports a special kind of variable, called a *constant*, which should not be reassigned once it's been created. (Ruby won't prevent a constant from being reassigned, but it will generate a warning so we know we're doing something bad.) Any variable whose name begins with a capital letter is a constant. New constants can be defined at the top level or within a class or module:

```
>> NUMBERS = [4, 8, 15, 16, 23, 42]
=> [4, 8, 15, 16, 23, 42]
>> class Greetings
     ENGLISH = 'hello'
     FRENCH  = 'bonjour'
     GERMAN  = 'guten Tag'
   end
=> "guten Tag"
>> NUMBERS.last
=> 42
>> Greetings::FRENCH
=> "bonjour"
```

Class and module names always begin with a capital letter, so class and module names are constants too.

Removing Constants

When we're exploring an idea with IRB it can be useful to ask Ruby to forget about a constant altogether, especially if that constant is the name of a class or module that we want to redefine from scratch instead of monkey patching its existing definition. A top-level constant can be removed by sending the `remove_const` message to `Object`, passing the constant's name as a symbol:

```
>> NUMBERS.last
=> 42
>> Object.send(:remove_const, :NUMBERS)
=> [4, 8, 15, 16, 23, 42]
>> NUMBERS.last
NameError: uninitialized constant NUMBERS
>> Greetings::GERMAN
=> "guten Tag"
>> Object.send(:remove_const, :Greetings)
=> Greetings
>> Greetings::GERMAN
NameError: uninitialized constant Greetings
```

We have to use `Object.send(:remove_const, :NAME)` instead of just `Object.remove_const(:NAME)`, because `remove_const` is a *private* method that ordinarily can only be called by sending a message from inside the `Object` class itself; using `Object.send` allows us to bypass this restriction temporarily.

## PART I

Programs and Machines

What is *computation*? The word itself means different things to different people, but everyone can agree that when a computer reads a program, runs that program, reads some input, and eventually produces some output, then some kind of computation has definitely happened. That gives us a decent starting point: computation is a name for *what a computer does*.

To create an environment where this familiar sort of computation can occur, we need three basic ingredients:

- A *machine* capable of performing the computation
- A *language* for writing instructions that the machine can understand
- A *program* written in that language, describing the exact computation that the machine should perform

So this part of the book is about machines, languages, and programs—what they are, how they behave, how we can model and study them, and how we can exploit them to get useful work done. By investigating these three ingredients, we can develop a better intuition for what computation is and how it happens.

In Chapter 2, we'll design and implement a toy programming language by exploring several different ways to specify its meaning. Understanding the meaning of a language is what allows us to take a lifeless piece of source code and animate it as a dynamic, executing process; each specification technique gives us a particular strategy for running a program, and we'll end up with several different ways of implementing the same language.

We'll see that programming is the art of assembling a precisely defined structure that can be dismantled, analyzed, and ultimately interpreted by a machine to create a computation. And more important, we'll discover that implementing programming languages is easy and fun: although parsing, interpretation, and compilation can seem intimidating, they're actually quite simple and enjoyable to play around with.

Programs aren't much use without machines to run them on, so in Chapter 3, we'll design very simple machines capable of performing basic, hardcoded tasks. From that humble foundation, we'll work our way up to more sophisticated machines in Chapter 4, and in Chapter 5, we'll see how to design a general-purpose computing device that can be controlled with software.

By the time we reach Part II, we'll have seen the full spectrum of computational power: some machines with very limited capabilities, others that are more useful but still frustratingly constrained, and finally, the most powerful machines that we know how to build.

## CHAPTER 2

The Meaning of Programs

*Don't think, feel! It is like a finger pointing away to the
moon. Don't concentrate on the finger or you will miss
all that heavenly glory.*

—Bruce Lee

Programming languages, and the programs we write in them, are fundamental to our
work as software engineers. We use them to clarify complex ideas to ourselves, communicate those ideas to each other, and, most important, implement those ideas inside
our computers. Just as human society couldn't operate without natural languages, so
the global community of programmers relies on programming languages to transmit
and implement our ideas, with each successful program forming part of a foundation
upon which the next layer of ideas can be built.

Programmers tend to be practical, pragmatic creatures. We often learn a new programming language by reading documentation, following tutorials, studying existing
programs, and tinkering with simple programs of our own, without giving much
thought to what those programs *mean*. Sometimes the learning process feels a lot like
trial and error: we try to understand a piece of a language by looking at examples and
documentation, then we try to write something in it, then everything blows up and we
have to go back and try again until we manage to assemble something that mostly
works. As computers and the systems they support become increasingly complex, it's
tempting to think of programs as opaque incantations that represent only themselves
and work only by chance.

But computer programming isn't really about *programs*, it's about *ideas*. A program is
a frozen representation of an idea, a snapshot of a structure that once existed in a
programmer's imagination. Programs are only worth writing because they have *meaning*. So what connects code to its meaning, and how can we be more concrete about
the meaning of a program than saying "it just does whatever it does"? In this chapter,
we're going to look at a few techniques for nailing down the meanings of computer
programs and see how to bring those dead snapshots to life.

The Meaning of "Meaning"

In linguistics, *semantics* is the study of the connection between words and their meanings: the word "dog" is an arrangement of shapes on a page, or a sequence of vibrations in the air caused by someone's vocal cords, which are very different things from an actual dog or the idea of dogs in general. Semantics is concerned with how these concrete signifiers relate to their abstract meanings, as well as the fundamental nature of the abstract meanings themselves.

In computer science, the field of *formal semantics* is concerned with finding ways of nailing down the elusive meanings of programs and using them to discover or prove interesting things about programming languages. Formal semantics has a wide spectrum of uses, from concrete applications like specifying new languages and devising compiler optimizations, to more abstract ones like constructing mathematical proofs of the correctness of programs.

To completely specify a programming language, we need to provide two things: a *syntax*, which describes what programs look like, and a semantics,[1] which describes what programs mean.

Plenty of languages don't have an official written specification, just a working interpreter or compiler. Ruby itself falls into this "specification by implementation" category: although there are plenty of books and tutorials about how Ruby is supposed to work, the ultimate source of all this information is Matz's Ruby Interpreter (MRI), the language's reference implementation. If any piece of Ruby documentation disagrees with the actual behavior of MRI, it's the documentation that's wrong; third-party Ruby implementations like JRuby, Rubinius, and MacRuby have to work hard to imitate the exact behavior of MRI so that they can usefully claim to be compatible with the Ruby language. Other languages like PHP and Perl 5 share this implementation-led approach to language definition.

Another way of describing a programming language is to write an official prose specification, usually in English. C++, Java, and ECMAScript (the standardized version of JavaScript) are examples of this approach: the languages are standardized in implementation-agnostic documents written by expert committees, and many compatible implementations of those standards exist. Specifying a language with an official document is more rigorous than relying on a reference implementation—design decisions are more likely to be the result of deliberate, rational choices, rather than accidental consequences of a particular implementation—but the specifications are often quite difficult to read, and it can be very hard to tell whether they contain any contradictions, omissions, or ambiguities. In particular there's no formal way to reason about an English-language specification; we just have to read it thoroughly, think about it a lot, and hope we've understood all the consequences.

---

1. In the context of programming language theory, the word *semantics* is usually treated as singular: we describe the meaning of a language by giving it *a semantics*.

A prose specification of Ruby 1.8.7 does exist, and has even been accepted as an ISO standard (ISO/IEC 30170).[2] MRI is still regarded as the canonical specification-by-implementation of the Ruby language, although the mruby project (*https://github.com/mruby/mruby*) is an attempt to build a lightweight, embeddable Ruby implementation that explicitly aims for compliance with the ISO standard rather than MRI compatibility.

A third alternative is to use the mathematical techniques of formal semantics to precisely describe the meaning of a programming language. The goal here is to be completely unambiguous, as well as to write the specification in a form that's suited to methodical analysis, or even *automated* analysis, so that it can be comprehensively checked for consistency, contradiction, or oversight. We'll look at these formal approaches to semantic specification after we've seen how syntax is handled.

Syntax

A conventional computer program is a long string of characters. Every programming language comes with a collection of rules that describe what kind of character strings may be considered valid programs in that language; these rules specify the language's *syntax*.

A language's syntax rules allow us to distinguish potentially valid programs like y = x + 1 from nonsensical ones like >/;x:1@4. They also provide useful information about how to read ambiguous programs: rules about operator precedence, for example, can automatically determine that 1 + 2 * 3 should be treated as though it had been written as 1 + (2 * 3), not as (1 + 2) * 3.

The intended use of a computer program is, of course, to be read by a computer, and reading programs requires a *parser*: a program that can read a character string representing a program, check it against the syntax rules to make sure it's valid, and turn it into a structured representation of that program suitable for further processing.

There are a variety of tools that can automatically turn a language's syntax rules into a parser. The details of how these rules are specified, and the techniques for turning them into usable parsers, are not the focus of this chapter—see "Implementing Parsers" on page 58 for a quick overview—but overall, a parser should read a string like y = x + 1 and turn it into an *abstract syntax tree* (AST), a representation of the source code that discards incidental detail like whitespace and focuses on the hierarchical structure of the program.

---

2. Although access to ISO/IEC 30170 costs money, an earlier draft of the same specification can be downloaded for free from *http://www.ipa.go.jp/osc/english/ruby/*.

In the end, syntax is only concerned with the surface appearance of programs, not with their meanings. It's possible for a program to be syntactically valid but not mean anything useful; for example, it might be that the program y = x + 1 doesn't make sense on its own because it doesn't say what x is beforehand, and the program z = true + 1 might turn out to be broken when we run it because it's trying to add a number to a Boolean value. (This depends, of course, on other properties of whichever programming language we're talking about.)

As we might expect, there is no "one true way" of explaining how the syntax of a programming language corresponds to an underlying meaning. In fact there are several different ways of talking concretely about what programs mean, all with different trade-offs between formality, abstraction, expressiveness, and practical efficiency. In the next few sections, we'll look at the main formal approaches and see how they relate to each other.

Operational Semantics

The most practical way to think about the meaning of a program is *what it does*—when we run the program, what do we expect to happen? How do different constructs in the programming language behave at run time, and what effect do they have when they're plugged together to make larger programs?

This is the basis of *operational semantics*, a way of capturing the meaning of a programming language by defining rules for how its programs execute on some kind of device. This device is often an *abstract machine*: an imaginary, idealized computer that is designed for the specific purpose of explaining how the language's programs will execute. Different kinds of programming language will usually require different designs of abstract machine in order to neatly capture their runtime behavior.

By giving an operational semantics, we can be quite rigorous and precise about the purpose of particular constructs in the language. Unlike a language specification written in English, which might contain hidden ambiguities and leave important edge cases uncovered, a formal operational specification will need to be explicit and unambiguous in order to convincingly communicate the language's behavior.

Small-Step Semantics

So, how can we design an abstract machine and use it to specify the operational semantics of a programming language? One way is to imagine a machine that evaluates a program by operating on its syntax directly, repeatedly *reducing* it in small steps, with each step bringing the program closer to its final result, whatever that turns out to mean.

These small-step reductions are similar to the way we are taught in school to evaluate algebraic expressions. For example, to evaluate (1 × 2) + (3 × 4), we know we should:

1. Perform the left-hand multiplication (1 × 2 becomes 2) and reduce the expression to 2 + (3 × 4)
2. Perform the right-hand multiplication (3 × 4 becomes 12) and reduce the expression to 2 + 12
3. Perform the addition (2 + 12 becomes 14) and end up with 14

We can think of 14 as the result because it can't be reduced any further by this process —we recognize 14 as a special kind of algebraic expression, a *value*, which has its own meaning and doesn't require any more work on our part.

This informal process can be turned into an operational semantics by writing down formal rules about how to proceed with each small reduction step. These rules themselves need to be written in some language (the *metalanguage*), which is usually mathematical notation.

In this chapter, we're going to explore the semantics of a toy programming language —let's call it SIMPLE.[3]

---

3. This can be an abbreviation for simple imperative language if you want it to be.

The mathematical description of SIMPLE's small-step semantics looks like this:

$$\frac{\langle e_1, \sigma \rangle \rightsquigarrow_e e_1'}{\langle e_1 + e_2, \sigma \rangle \rightsquigarrow_e e_1' + e_2} \qquad \frac{\langle e_2, \sigma \rangle \rightsquigarrow_e e_2'}{\langle v_1 + e_2, \sigma \rangle \rightsquigarrow_e v_1 + e_2'}$$

$$\frac{}{\langle n_1 + n_2, \sigma \rangle \rightsquigarrow_e n} \quad \text{if } n = n_1 + n_2$$

$$\frac{\langle e_1, \sigma \rangle \rightsquigarrow_e e_1'}{\langle e_1 * e_2, \sigma \rangle \rightsquigarrow_e e_1' * e_2} \qquad \frac{\langle e_2, \sigma \rangle \rightsquigarrow_e e_2'}{\langle v_1 * e_2, \sigma \rangle \rightsquigarrow_e v_1 * e_2'}$$

$$\frac{}{\langle n_1 * n_2, \sigma \rangle \rightsquigarrow_e n} \quad \text{if } n = n_1 \times n_2$$

$$\frac{\langle e_1, \sigma \rangle \rightsquigarrow_e e_1'}{\langle e_1 < e_2, \sigma \rangle \rightsquigarrow_e e_1' < e_2} \qquad \frac{\langle e_2, \sigma \rangle \rightsquigarrow_e e_2'}{\langle v_1 < e_2, \sigma \rangle \rightsquigarrow_e v_1 < e_2'}$$

$$\frac{}{\langle n_1 < n_2, \sigma \rangle \rightsquigarrow_e \text{true}} \quad \text{if } n_1 < n_2 \qquad \frac{}{\langle n_1 < n_2, \sigma \rangle \rightsquigarrow_e \text{false}} \quad \text{if } n_1 \geq n_2$$

$$\frac{}{\langle x, \sigma \rangle \rightsquigarrow_e \sigma(x)} \quad \text{if } x \in \text{dom}(\sigma)$$

$$\frac{\langle e, \sigma \rangle \rightsquigarrow_e e'}{\langle x = e, \sigma \rangle \rightsquigarrow_s \langle x = e', \sigma \rangle} \qquad \frac{}{\langle x = v, \sigma \rangle \rightsquigarrow_s \langle \text{do-nothing}. \sigma[x \mapsto v] \rangle}$$

$$\frac{\langle e, \sigma \rangle \rightsquigarrow_e e'}{\langle \text{if } (e) \ \{ \ s_1 \ \} \ \text{else} \ \{ \ s_2 \ \}, \sigma \rangle \rightsquigarrow_s \langle \text{if } (e') \ \{ \ s_1 \ \} \ \text{else} \ \{ \ s_2 \ \}, \sigma \rangle}$$

$$\frac{}{\langle \text{if } (\text{true}) \ \{ \ s_1 \ \} \ \text{else} \ \{ \ s_2 \ \}, \sigma \rangle \rightsquigarrow_s \langle s_1, \sigma \rangle} \qquad \frac{}{\langle \text{if } (\text{false}) \ \{ \ s_1 \ \} \ \text{else} \ \{ \ s_2 \ \}, \sigma \rangle \rightsquigarrow_s \langle s_2, \sigma \rangle}$$

$$\frac{\langle s_1, \sigma \rangle \rightsquigarrow_s \langle s_1', \sigma' \rangle}{\langle s_1 ; s_2, \sigma \rangle \rightsquigarrow_s \langle s_1' ; s_2. \sigma' \rangle} \qquad \frac{}{\langle \text{do-nothing}; s_2, \sigma \rangle \rightsquigarrow_s \langle s_2, \sigma \rangle}$$

$$\frac{}{\langle \text{while } (e) \ \{ \ s \ \}, \sigma \rangle \rightsquigarrow_s \langle \text{if } (e) \ \{ \ s; \text{while } (e) \ \{ \ s \ \} \ \} \ \text{else} \ \{ \ \text{do-nothing} \ \}, \sigma \rangle}$$

Mathematically speaking, this is a set of *inference rules* that defines a *reduction relation* on SIMPLE's abstract syntax trees. Practically speaking, it's a bunch of weird symbols that don't say anything intelligible about the meaning of computer programs.

Instead of trying to understand this formal notation directly, we're going to investigate how to write the same inference rules in Ruby. Using Ruby as the metalanguage is easier for a programmer to understand, and it gives us the added advantage of being able to execute the rules to see how they work.

We are *not* trying to describe the semantics of Simple by giving a "specification by implementation." Our main reason for describing the small-step semantics in Ruby instead of mathematical notation is to make the description easier for a human reader to digest. Ending up with an executable implementation of the language is just a nice bonus.

The big disadvantage of using Ruby is that it explains a simple language by using a more complicated one, which perhaps defeats the philosophical purpose. We should remember that the mathematical rules are the authoritative description of the semantics, and that we're just using Ruby to develop an understanding of what those rules mean.

Expressions

We'll start by looking at the semantics of Simple expressions. The rules will operate on the abstract syntax of these expressions, so we need to be able to represent Simple expressions as Ruby objects. One way of doing this is to define a Ruby class for each distinct kind of element from Simple's syntax—numbers, addition, multiplication, and so on—and then represent each expression as a tree of instances of these classes.

For example, here are the definitions of `Number`, `Add`, and `Multiply` classes:

```ruby
class Number < Struct.new(:value)
end

class Add < Struct.new(:left, :right)
end

class Multiply < Struct.new(:left, :right)
end
```

We can instantiate these classes to build abstract syntax trees by hand:

```ruby
>> Add.new(
     Multiply.new(Number.new(1), Number.new(2)),
     Multiply.new(Number.new(3), Number.new(4))
   )
=> #<struct Add
     left=#<struct Multiply
       left=#<struct Number value=1>,
       right=#<struct Number value=2>
     >,
     right=#<struct Multiply
       left=#<struct Number value=3>,
       right=#<struct Number value=4>
     >
   >
```

Eventually, of course, we want these trees to be built automatically by a parser. We'll see how to do that in "Implementing Parsers" on page 58.

The Number, Add, and Multiply classes inherit Struct's generic definition of #inspect, so the string representations of their instances in the IRB console contain a lot of unimportant detail. To make the content of an abstract syntax tree easier to see in IRB, we'll override #inspect on each class[4] so that it returns a custom string representation:

```ruby
class Number
  def to_s
    value.to_s
  end

  def inspect
    "«#{self}»"
  end
end

class Add
  def to_s
    "#{left} + #{right}"
  end

  def inspect
    "«#{self}»"
  end
end

class Multiply
  def to_s
    "#{left} * #{right}"
  end

  def inspect
    "«#{self}»"
  end
end
```

Now each abstract syntax tree will be shown in IRB as a short string of SIMPLE source code, surrounded by «guillemets» to distinguish it from a normal Ruby value:

```ruby
>> Add.new(
     Multiply.new(Number.new(1), Number.new(2)),
     Multiply.new(Number.new(3), Number.new(4))
   )
=> «1 * 2 + 3 * 4»
>> Number.new(5)
=> «5»
```

4. For the sake of simplicity, we'll resist the urge to extract common code into superclasses or modules.

Our rudimentary #to_s implementations don't take operator precedence into account, so sometimes their output is incorrect with respect to conventional precedence rules (e.g., * usually binds more tightly than +). Take this abstract syntax tree, for example:

```
>> Multiply.new(
     Number.new(1),
     Multiply.new(
       Add.new(Number.new(2), Number.new(3)),
       Number.new(4)
     )
   )
=> «1 * 2 + 3 * 4»
```

This tree represents «1 * (2 + 3) * 4», which is a different expression (with a different meaning) than «1 * 2 + 3 * 4», but its string representation doesn't reflect that.

This problem is serious but tangential to our discussion of semantics. To keep things simple, we'll temporarily ignore it and just avoid creating expressions that have an incorrect string representation. We'll implement a proper solution for another language in "Syntax" on page 80.

Now we can begin to implement a small-step operational semantics by defining methods that perform reductions on our abstract syntax trees—that is, code that can take an abstract syntax tree as input and produce a slightly reduced tree as output.

Before we can implement reduction itself, we need to be able to distinguish expressions that can be reduced from those that can't. Add and Multiply expressions are always reducible—each of them represents an operation, and can be turned into a result by performing the calculation corresponding to that operation—but a Number expression always represents a value, which can't be reduced to anything else.

In principle, we could tell these two kinds of expression apart with a single #reducible? predicate that returns true or false depending on the class of its argument:

```
def reducible?(expression)
  case expression
  when Number
    false
  when Add, Multiply
    true
  end
end
```

 In Ruby case statements, the control expression is matched against the cases by calling each case value's #=== method with the control expression's value as an argument. The implementation of #=== for class objects checks to see whether its argument is an instance of that class or one of its subclasses, so we can use the case *object* when *classname* syntax to match an object against a class.

However, it's generally considered bad form to write code like this in an object-oriented language;[5] when the behavior of some operation depends upon the class of its argument, the typical approach is to implement each per-class behavior as an instance method for that class, and let the language implicitly handle the job of deciding which of those methods to call instead of using an explicit case statement.

So instead, let's implement separate #reducible? methods for Number, Add, and Multiply:

```
class Number
  def reducible?
    false
  end
end

class Add
  def reducible?
    true
  end
end

class Multiply
  def reducible?
    true
  end
end
```

This gives us the behavior we want:

```
>> Number.new(1).reducible?
=> false
>> Add.new(Number.new(1), Number.new(2)).reducible?
=> true
```

We can now implement reduction for these expressions; as above, we'll do this by defining a #reduce method for Add and Multiply. There's no need to define Number#reduce, since numbers can't be reduced, so we'll just need to be careful not to call #reduce on an expression unless we know it's reducible.

So what are the rules for reducing an addition expression? If the left and right arguments are already numbers, then we can just add them together, but what if one or both of the arguments needs reducing? Since we're thinking about small steps, we need to decide which argument gets reduced first if they are both eligible for reduction.[6] A common strategy is to reduce the arguments in left-to-right order, in which case the rules will be:

• If the addition's left argument can be reduced, reduce the left argument.

---

5. Although this is pretty much exactly how we'd write #reducible? in a functional language like Haskell or ML.

6. At the moment, it doesn't make any difference *which* order we choose, but we can't avoid making the decision.

- If the addition's left argument can't be reduced but its right argument can, reduce the right argument.
- If neither argument can be reduced, they should both be numbers, so add them together.

The structure of these rules is characteristic of small-step operational semantics. Each rule provides a pattern for the kind of expression to which it applies—an addition with a reducible left argument, with a reducible right argument, and with two irreducible arguments respectively—and a description of how to build a new, reduced expression when that pattern matches. By choosing these particular rules, we're specifying that a SIMPLE addition expression uses left-to-right evaluation to reduce its arguments, as well as deciding how those arguments should be combined once they've been individually reduced.

We can translate these rules directly into an implementation of Add#reduce, and almost the same code will work for Multiply#reduce (remembering to multiply the arguments instead of adding them):

```ruby
class Add
  def reduce
    if left.reducible?
      Add.new(left.reduce, right)
    elsif right.reducible?
      Add.new(left, right.reduce)
    else
      Number.new(left.value + right.value)
    end
  end
end

class Multiply
  def reduce
    if left.reducible?
      Multiply.new(left.reduce, right)
    elsif right.reducible?
      Multiply.new(left, right.reduce)
    else
      Number.new(left.value * right.value)
    end
  end
end
```

 #reduce always builds a new expression rather than modifying an existing one.

Having implemented #reduce for these kinds of expressions, we can call it repeatedly to fully evaluate an expression via a series of small steps:

```
>> expression =
     Add.new(
       Multiply.new(Number.new(1), Number.new(2)),
       Multiply.new(Number.new(3), Number.new(4))
     )
=> «1 * 2 + 3 * 4»
>> expression.reducible?
=> true
>> expression = expression.reduce
=> «2 + 3 * 4»
>> expression.reducible?
=> true
>> expression = expression.reduce
=> «2 + 12»
>> expression.reducible?
=> true
>> expression = expression.reduce
=> «14»
>> expression.reducible?
=> false
```

 Notice that #reduce always turns one expression into another expression, which is exactly how the rules of small-step operational semantics should work. In particular, Add.new(Number.new(2), Number.new(12)).reduce returns Number.new(14), which represents a SIMPLE expression, rather than just 14, which is a Ruby number.

This separation between the SIMPLE language, whose semantics we are *specifying*, and the Ruby metalanguage, in which we are *writing the specification*, is easier to maintain when the two languages are obviously different—as is the case when the metalanguage is mathematical notation rather than a programming language—but here we need to be more careful because the two languages look very similar.

By maintaining a piece of state—the current expression—and repeatedly calling #reducible? and #reduce on it until we end up with a value, we're manually simulating the operation of an abstract machine for evaluating expressions. To save ourselves some effort, and to make the idea of the abstract machine more concrete, we can easily write some Ruby code that does the work for us. Let's wrap up that code and state together in a class and call it a *virtual machine*:

```ruby
class Machine < Struct.new(:expression)
  def step
    self.expression = expression.reduce
  end

  def run
    while expression.reducible?
      puts expression
      step
    end
```

```
    puts expression
  end
end
```

This allows us to instantiate a virtual machine with an expression, tell it to #run, and watch the steps of reduction unfold:

```
>> Machine.new(
     Add.new(
       Multiply.new(Number.new(1), Number.new(2)),
       Multiply.new(Number.new(3), Number.new(4))
     )
   ).run
1 * 2 + 3 * 4
2 + 3 * 4
2 + 12
14
=> nil
```

It isn't difficult to extend this implementation to support other simple values and operations: subtraction and division; Boolean true and false; Boolean and, or, and not; comparison operations for numbers that return Booleans; and so on. For example, here are implementations of Booleans and the less-than operator:

```
class Boolean < Struct.new(:value)
  def to_s
    value.to_s
  end

  def inspect
    "«#{self}»"
  end

  def reducible?
    false
  end
end

class LessThan < Struct.new(:left, :right)
  def to_s
    "#{left} < #{right}"
  end

  def inspect
    "«#{self}»"
  end

  def reducible?
    true
  end

  def reduce
    if left.reducible?
      LessThan.new(left.reduce, right)
    elsif right.reducible?
```

```
        LessThan.new(left, right.reduce)
      else
        Boolean.new(left.value < right.value)
      end
    end
  end
```

Again, this allows us to reduce a boolean expression in small steps:

```
>> Machine.new(
     LessThan.new(Number.new(5), Add.new(Number.new(2), Number.new(2)))
   ).run
5 < 2 + 2
5 < 4
false
=> nil
```

So far, so straightforward: we have begun to specify the operational semantics of a language by implementing a virtual machine that can evaluate it. At the moment the state of this virtual machine is just the current expression, and the behavior of the machine is described by a collection of rules that govern how that state changes when the machine runs. We've implemented the machine as a program that keeps track of the current expression and keeps reducing it, updating the expression as it goes, until no more reductions can be performed.

But this language of simple algebraic expressions isn't very interesting, and doesn't have many of the features that we expect from even the simplest programming language, so let's build it out to be more sophisticated and look more like a language in which we could write useful programs.

First off, there's something obviously missing from SIMPLE: variables. In any useful language, we'd expect to be able to talk about values using meaningful names rather than the literal values themselves. These names provide a layer of indirection so that the same code can be used to process many different values, including values that come from outside the program and therefore aren't even known when the code is written.

We can introduce a new class of expression, Variable, to represent variables in SIMPLE:

```
class Variable < Struct.new(:name)
  def to_s
    name.to_s
  end

  def inspect
    "«#{self}»"
  end

  def reducible?
    true
  end
end
```

To be able to reduce a variable, we need the abstract machine to store a mapping from variable names onto their values, an *environment*, as well as the current expression. In Ruby, we can implement this mapping as a hash, using symbols as keys and expression objects as values; for example, the hash { x: Number.new(2), y: Boolean.new(false) } is an environment that associates the variables x and y with a SIMPLE number and Boolean, respectively.

 For this language, the intention is for the environment to only map variable names onto irreducible values like Number.new(2), not onto reducible expressions like Add.new(Number.new(1), Number.new(2)). We'll take care to respect this constraint later when we write rules that change the contents of the environment.

Given an environment, we can easily implement Variable#reduce: it just looks up the variable's name in the environment and returns its value.

```
class Variable
  def reduce(environment)
    environment[name]
  end
end
```

Notice that we're now passing an environment argument into #reduce, so we'll need to revise the other expression classes' implementations of #reduce to both accept and provide this argument:

```
class Add
  def reduce(environment)
    if left.reducible?
      Add.new(left.reduce(environment), right)
    elsif right.reducible?
      Add.new(left, right.reduce(environment))
    else
      Number.new(left.value + right.value)
    end
  end
end

class Multiply
  def reduce(environment)
    if left.reducible?
      Multiply.new(left.reduce(environment), right)
    elsif right.reducible?
      Multiply.new(left, right.reduce(environment))
    else
      Number.new(left.value * right.value)
    end
  end
end

class LessThan
```

```
def reduce(environment)
  if left.reducible?
    LessThan.new(left.reduce(environment), right)
  elsif right.reducible?
    LessThan.new(left, right.reduce(environment))
  else
    Boolean.new(left.value < right.value)
  end
end
end
```

Once all the implementations of #reduce have been updated to support environments, we also need to redefine our virtual machine to maintain an environment and provide it to #reduce:

```
Object.send(:remove_const, :Machine) # forget about the old Machine class

class Machine < Struct.new(:expression, :environment)
  def step
    self.expression = expression.reduce(environment)
  end

  def run
    while expression.reducible?
      puts expression
      step
    end

    puts expression
  end
end
```

The machine's definition of #run remains unchanged, but it has a new `environment` attribute that is used by its new implementation of #step.

We can now perform reductions on expressions that contain variables, as long as we also supply an environment that contains the variables' values:

```
>> Machine.new(
    Add.new(Variable.new(:x), Variable.new(:y)),
    { x: Number.new(3), y: Number.new(4) }
  ).run
x + y
3 + y
3 + 4
7
=> nil
```

The introduction of an environment completes our operational semantics of expressions. We've designed an abstract machine that begins with an initial expression and environment, and then uses the current expression and environment to produce a new expression in each small reduction step, leaving the environment unchanged.

Statements

We can now look at implementing a different kind of program construct: *statements*. The purpose of an expression is to be evaluated to produce another expression; a statement, on the other hand, is evaluated to make some change to the state of the abstract machine. Our machine's only piece of state (aside from the current program) is the environment, so we'll allow SIMPLE statements to produce a new environment that can replace the current one.

The simplest possible statement is one that does nothing: it can't be reduced, so it can't have any effect on the environment. That's easy to implement:

```
class DoNothing ❶
  def to_s
    'do-nothing'
  end

  def inspect
    "«#{self}»"
  end

  def ==(other_statement) ❷
    other_statement.instance_of?(DoNothing)
  end

  def reducible?
    false
  end
end
```

❶ All of our other syntax classes inherit from a Struct class, but DoNothing doesn't inherit from anything. This is because DoNothing doesn't have any attributes, and unfortunately, Struct.new doesn't let us pass an empty list of attribute names.

❷ We want to be able to compare any two statements to see if they're equal. The other syntax classes inherit an implementation of #== from Struct, but DoNothing has to define its own.

A statement that does nothing might seem pointless, but it's convenient to have a special statement that represents a program whose execution has completed successfully. We'll arrange for other statements to eventually reduce to «do-nothing» once they've finished doing their work.

The simplest example of a statement that actually does something useful is an *assignment* like «x = x + 1», but before we can implement assignment, we need to decide what its reduction rules should be.

An assignment statement consists of a variable name (x), an equals symbol, and an expression («x + 1»). If the expression within the assignment is reducible, we can just reduce it according to the expression reduction rules and end up with a new assignment statement containing the reduced expression. For example, reducing «x = x + 1» in an environment where the variable x has the value «2» should leave us with the statement «x = 2 + 1», and reducing it again should produce «x = 3».

But then what? If the expression is already a value like «3», then we should just perform the assignment, which means updating the environment to associate that value with the appropriate variable name. So reducing a statement needs to produce not just a new, reduced statement but also a new environment, which will sometimes be different from the environment in which the reduction was performed.

 Our implementation will update the environment by using Hash#merge to create a new hash without modifying the old one:

```
>> old_environment = { y: Number.new(5) }
=> {:y=>«5»}
>> new_environment = old_environment.merge({ x: Number.new(3) })
=> {:y=>«5», :x=>«3»}
>> old_environment
=> {:y=>«5»}
```

We could choose to destructively modify the current environment instead of making a new one, but avoiding destructive updates forces us to make the consequences of #reduce completely explicit. If #reduce wants to change the current environment, it has to communicate that by returning an updated environment to its caller; conversely, if it doesn't return an environment, we can be sure it hasn't made any changes.

This constraint helps to highlight the difference between expressions and statements. For expressions, we pass an environment into #reduce and get a reduced expression back; no new environment is returned, so reducing an expression obviously doesn't change the environment. For statements, we'll call #reduce with the current environment and get a new environment back, which tells us that reducing a statement can have an effect on the environment. (In other words, the structure of SIMPLE's small-step semantics shows that its expressions are *pure* and its statements are *impure*.)

So reducing «x = 3» in an empty environment should produce the new environment { x: Number.new(3) }, but we also expect the statement to be reduced somehow; otherwise, our abstract machine will keep assigning «3» to x forever. That's what «do-nothing» is for: a completed assignment reduces to «do-nothing», indicating that reduction of the statement has finished and that whatever's in the new environment may be considered its result.

To summarize, the reduction rules for assignment are:

• If the assignment's expression can be reduced, then reduce it, resulting in a reduced assignment statement and an unchanged environment.

- If the assignment's expression can't be reduced, then update the environment to associate that expression with the assignment's variable, resulting in a «do-nothing» statement and a new environment.

This gives us enough information to implement an **Assign** class. The only difficulty is that **Assign#reduce** needs to return both a statement and an environment—Ruby methods can only return a single object—but we can pretend to return two objects by putting them into a two-element array and returning that.

```ruby
class Assign < Struct.new(:name, :expression)
  def to_s
    "#{name} = #{expression}"
  end

  def inspect
    "«#{self}»"
  end

  def reducible?
    true
  end

  def reduce(environment)
    if expression.reducible?
      [Assign.new(name, expression.reduce(environment)), environment]
    else
      [DoNothing.new, environment.merge({ name => expression })]
    end
  end
end
```

 As promised, the reduction rules for **Assign** ensure that an expression only gets added to the environment if it's irreducible (i.e., a value).

As with expressions, we can manually evaluate an assignment statement by repeatedly reducing it until it can't be reduced any more:

```ruby
>> statement = Assign.new(:x, Add.new(Variable.new(:x), Number.new(1)))
=> «x = x + 1»
>> environment = { x: Number.new(2) }
=> {:x=>«2»}
>> statement.reducible?
=> true
>> statement, environment = statement.reduce(environment)
=> [«x = 2 + 1», {:x=>«2»}]
>> statement, environment = statement.reduce(environment)
=> [«x = 3», {:x=>«2»}]
>> statement, environment = statement.reduce(environment)
=> [«do-nothing», {:x=>«3»}]
>> statement.reducible?
=> false
```

This process is even more laborious than manually reducing expressions, so let's re-implement our virtual machine to handle statements, showing the current statement and environment at each reduction step:

```
Object.send(:remove_const, :Machine)

class Machine < Struct.new(:statement, :environment)
  def step
    self.statement, self.environment = statement.reduce(environment)
  end

  def run
    while statement.reducible?
      puts "#{statement}, #{environment}"
      step
    end

    puts "#{statement}, #{environment}"
  end
end
```

Now the machine can do the work for us again:

```
>> Machine.new(
     Assign.new(:x, Add.new(Variable.new(:x), Number.new(1))),
     { x: Number.new(2) }
   ).run
x = x + 1, {:x=>«2»}
x = 2 + 1, {:x=>«2»}
x = 3, {:x=>«2»}
do-nothing, {:x=>«3»}
=> nil
```

We can see that the machine is still performing expression reduction steps («x + 1» to «2 + 1» to «3»), but they now happen inside a statement instead of at the top level of the syntax tree.

Now that we know how statement reduction works, we can extend it to support other kinds of statements. Let's begin with conditional statements like «if (x) { y = 1 } else { y = 2 }», which contain an expression called the *condition* («x»), and two statements that we'll call the *consequence* («y = 1») and the *alternative* («y = 2»).[7] The reduction rules for conditionals are straightforward:

- If the condition can be reduced, then reduce it, resulting in a reduced conditional statement and an unchanged environment.

- If the condition is the expression «true», reduce to the consequence statement and an unchanged environment.

---

7. This conditional is not the same as Ruby's if. In Ruby, if is an expression that returns a value, but in SIMPLE, it's a statement for choosing which of two other statements to evaluate, and its only result is the effect it has on the current environment.

- If the condition is the expression «false», reduce to the alternative statement and an unchanged environment.

In this case, none of the rules changes the environment—the reduction of the condition expression in the first rule will only produce a new expression, not a new environment.

Here are the rules translated into an If class:

```ruby
class If < Struct.new(:condition, :consequence, :alternative)
  def to_s
    "if (#{condition}) { #{consequence} } else { #{alternative} }"
  end

  def inspect
    "«#{self}»"
  end

  def reducible?
    true
  end

  def reduce(environment)
    if condition.reducible?
      [If.new(condition.reduce(environment), consequence, alternative), environment]
    else
      case condition
      when Boolean.new(true)
        [consequence, environment]
      when Boolean.new(false)
        [alternative, environment]
      end
    end
  end
end
```

And here's how the reduction steps look:

```ruby
>> Machine.new(
     If.new(
       Variable.new(:x),
       Assign.new(:y, Number.new(1)),
       Assign.new(:y, Number.new(2))
     ),
     { x: Boolean.new(true) }
   ).run
if (x) { y = 1 } else { y = 2 }, {:x=>«true»}
if (true) { y = 1 } else { y = 2 }, {:x=>«true»}
y = 1, {:x=>«true»}
do-nothing, {:x=>«true», :y=>«1»}
=> nil
```

That all works as expected, but it would be nice if we could support conditional statements with no «else» clause, like «if (x) { y = 1 }». Fortunately, we can already do that by writing statements like «if (x) { y = 1 } else { do-nothing }», which behave as though the «else» clause wasn't there:

```
>> Machine.new(
     If.new(Variable.new(:x), Assign.new(:y, Number.new(1)), DoNothing.new),
     { x: Boolean.new(false) }
   ).run
if (x) { y = 1 } else { do-nothing }, {:x=>«false»}
if (false) { y = 1 } else { do-nothing }, {:x=>«false»}
do-nothing, {:x=>«false»}
=> nil
```

Now that we've implemented assignment and conditional statements as well as expressions, we have the building blocks for programs that can do real work by performing calculations and making decisions. The main restriction is that we can't yet connect these blocks together: we have no way to assign values to more than one variable, or to perform more than one conditional operation, which drastically limits the usefulness of our language.

We can fix this by defining another kind of statement, the *sequence*, which connects two statements like «x = 1 + 1» and «y = x + 3» to make one larger statement like «x = 1 + 1; y = x + 3». Once we have sequence statements, we can use them repeatedly to build even larger statements; for example, the sequence «x = 1 + 1; y = x + 3» and the assignment «z = y + 5» can be combined to make the sequence «x = 1 + 1; y = x + 3; z = y + 5».[8]

The reduction rules for sequences are slightly subtle:

- If the first statement is a «do-nothing» statement, reduce to the second statement and the original environment.

- If the first statement is not «do-nothing», then reduce it, resulting in a new sequence (the reduced first statement followed by the second statement) and a reduced environment.

Seeing the code may make these rules clearer:

```
class Sequence < Struct.new(:first, :second)
  def to_s
    "#{first}; #{second}"
  end

  def inspect
    "«#{self}»"
  end

  def reducible?
    true
  end

  def reduce(environment)
    case first
```

---

8. For our purposes, it doesn't matter whether this statement has been constructed as «(x = 1 + 1; y = x + 3); z = y + 5» or «x = 1 + 1; (y = x + 3; z = y + 5)». This choice would affect the exact order of the reduction steps when we ran it, but the final result would be the same either way.

```
    when DoNothing.new
      [second, environment]
    else
      reduced_first, reduced_environment = first.reduce(environment)
      [Sequence.new(reduced_first, second), reduced_environment]
    end
  end
end
```

The overall effect of these rules is that, when we repeatedly reduce a sequence, it keeps reducing its first statement until it turns into «do-nothing», then reduces to its second statement. We can see this happening when we run a sequence in the virtual machine:

```
>> Machine.new(
    Sequence.new(
      Assign.new(:x, Add.new(Number.new(1), Number.new(1))),
      Assign.new(:y, Add.new(Variable.new(:x), Number.new(3)))
    ),
    {}
  ).run
x = 1 + 1; y = x + 3, {}
x = 2; y = x + 3, {}
do-nothing; y = x + 3, {:x=>«2»}
y = x + 3, {:x=>«2»}
y = 2 + 3, {:x=>«2»}
y = 5, {:x=>«2»}
do-nothing, {:x=>«2», :y=>«5»}
=> nil
```

The only really major thing still missing from SIMPLE is some kind of unrestricted looping construct, so to finish off, let's introduce a «while» statement so that programs can perform repeated calculations an arbitrary number of times.[9] A statement like «while (x < 5) { x = x * 3 }» contains an expression called the *condition* («x < 5») and a statement called the *body* («x = x * 3»).

Writing the correct reduction rules for a «while» statement is slightly tricky. We could try treating it like an «if» statement: reduce the condition if possible; otherwise, reduce to either the body or «do-nothing», depending on whether the condition is «true» or «false», respectively. But once the abstract machine has completely reduced the body, what next? The condition has been reduced to a value and thrown away, and the body has been reduced to «do-nothing», so how do we perform another iteration of the loop? Each reduction step can only communicate with future steps by producing a new statement and environment, and this approach doesn't give us anywhere to "remember" the original condition and body for use on the next iteration.

The small-step solution[10] is to use the sequence statement to *unroll* one level of the «while», reducing it to an «if» that performs a single iteration of the loop and then repeats the original «while». This means we only need one reduction rule:

---

9. We can already hardcode a fixed number of repetitions by using sequence statements, but that doesn't allow us to control the repetition behavior at runtime.

- Reduce «while (*condition*) { *body* }» to «if (*condition*) { *body*; while (*condition*) { *body* } } else { do-nothing }» and an unchanged environment.

And this rule is easy to implement in Ruby:

```ruby
class While < Struct.new(:condition, :body)
  def to_s
    "while (#{condition}) { #{body} }"
  end

  def inspect
    "«#{self}»"
  end

  def reducible?
    true
  end

  def reduce(environment)
    [If.new(condition, Sequence.new(body, self), DoNothing.new), environment]
  end
end
```

This gives the virtual machine the opportunity to evaluate the condition and body as many times as necessary:

```
>> Machine.new(
     While.new(
       LessThan.new(Variable.new(:x), Number.new(5)),
       Assign.new(:x, Multiply.new(Variable.new(:x), Number.new(3)))
     ),
     { x: Number.new(1) }
   ).run
while (x < 5) { x = x * 3 }, {:x=>«1»}
if (x < 5) { x = x * 3; while (x < 5) { x = x * 3 } } else { do-nothing }, {:x=>«1»}
if (1 < 5) { x = x * 3; while (x < 5) { x = x * 3 } } else { do-nothing }, {:x=>«1»}
if (true) { x = x * 3; while (x < 5) { x = x * 3 } } else { do-nothing }, {:x=>«1»}
x = x * 3; while (x < 5) { x = x * 3 }, {:x=>«1»}
x = 1 * 3; while (x < 5) { x = x * 3 }, {:x=>«1»}
x = 3; while (x < 5) { x = x * 3 }, {:x=>«1»}
do-nothing; while (x < 5) { x = x * 3 }, {:x=>«3»}
while (x < 5) { x = x * 3 }, {:x=>«3»}
if (x < 5) { x = x * 3; while (x < 5) { x = x * 3 } } else { do-nothing }, {:x=>«3»}
if (3 < 5) { x = x * 3; while (x < 5) { x = x * 3 } } else { do-nothing }, {:x=>«3»}
if (true) { x = x * 3; while (x < 5) { x = x * 3 } } else { do-nothing }, {:x=>«3»}
x = x * 3; while (x < 5) { x = x * 3 }, {:x=>«3»}
x = 3 * 3; while (x < 5) { x = x * 3 }, {:x=>«3»}
x = 9; while (x < 5) { x = x * 3 }, {:x=>«3»}
do-nothing; while (x < 5) { x = x * 3 }, {:x=>«9»}
while (x < 5) { x = x * 3 }, {:x=>«9»}
if (x < 5) { x = x * 3; while (x < 5) { x = x * 3 } } else { do-nothing }, {:x=>«9»}
```

10. There's a temptation to build the iterative behavior of «while» directly into its reduction rule instead of finding a way to get the abstract machine to handle it, but that's not how small-step semantics works. See "Big-Step Semantics" on page 42 for a style of semantics that lets the rules do the work.

```
if (9 < 5) { x = x * 3; while (x < 5) { x = x * 3 } } else { do-nothing }, {:x=>«9»}
if (false) { x = x * 3; while (x < 5) { x = x * 3 } } else { do-nothing }, {:x=>«9»}
do-nothing, {:x=>«9»}
=> nil
```

Perhaps this reduction rule seems like a bit of a dodge—it's almost as though we're perpetually postponing reduction of the «while» until later, without ever actually getting there—but on the other hand, it does a good job of explaining what we really mean by a «while» statement: check the condition, evaluate the body, then start again. It's curious that reducing «while» turns it into a syntactically larger program involving conditional and sequence statements instead of directly reducing its condition or body, and one reason why it's useful to have a technical framework for specifying the formal semantics of a language is to help us see how different parts of the language relate to each other like this.

Correctness

We've completely ignored what will happen when a syntactically valid but otherwise incorrect program is executed according to the semantics we've given. The statement «x = true; x = x + 1» is a valid piece of SIMPLE syntax—we can certainly construct an abstract syntax tree to represent it—but it'll blow up when we try to repeatedly reduce it, because the abstract machine will end up trying to add «1» to «true»:

```
>> Machine.new(
     Sequence.new(
       Assign.new(:x, Boolean.new(true)),
       Assign.new(:x, Add.new(Variable.new(:x), Number.new(1)))
     ),
     {}
   ).run
x = true; x = x + 1, {}
do-nothing; x = x + 1, {:x=>«true»}
x = x + 1, {:x=>«true»}
x = true + 1, {:x=>«true»}
NoMethodError: undefined method `+' for true:TrueClass
```

One way to handle this is to be more restrictive about when expressions can be reduced, which introduces the possibility that evaluation will get *stuck* rather than always trying to reduce to a value (and potentially blowing up in the process). We could have implemented Add#reducible? to only return true when both arguments to «+» are either reducible or an instance of Number, in which case the expression «true + 1» would get stuck and never turn into a value.

Ultimately, we need a more powerful tool than syntax, something that can "see the future" and prevent us from trying to execute any program that has the potential to blow up or get stuck. This chapter is about *dynamic semantics*—what a program does when it's executed—but that's not the only kind of meaning that a program can have; in Chapter 9, we'll investigate *static semantics* to see how we can decide whether a syntactically valid program has a useful meaning according to the language's dynamic semantics.

Applications

The programming language we've specified is very basic, but in writing down all the reduction rules, we've still had to make some design decisions and express them unambiguously. For example, unlike Ruby, SIMPLE is a language that makes a distinction between expressions, which return a value, and statements, which don't; like Ruby, SIMPLE evaluates expressions in a left-to-right order; and like Ruby, SIMPLE's environments associate variables only with fully reduced values, not with larger expressions that still have some unfinished computation to perform.[11] We could change any of these decisions by giving a different small-step semantics which would describe a new language with the same syntax but different runtime behavior. If we added more elaborate features to the language—data structures, procedure calls, exceptions, an object system—we'd need to make many more design decisions and express them unambiguously in the semantic definition.

The detailed, execution-oriented style of small-step semantics lends itself well to the task of unambiguously specifying real-world programming languages. For example, the latest R6RS standard for the Scheme programming language uses small-step semantics (*http://www.r6rs.org/final/html/r6rs/r6rs-Z-H-15.html*) to describe its execution, and provides a reference implementation of those semantics (*http://www.r6rs.org/refimpl/*) written in PLT Redex (*http://redex.racket-lang.org/*), "a domain-specific language designed for specifying and debugging operational semantics." The OCaml programming language, which is built as a series of layers on top of a simpler language called Core ML, also has a small-step semantic definition (*http://caml.inria.fr/pub/docs/u3-ocaml/ocaml-ml.html#htoc5*) of the base language's runtime behavior.

See "Semantics" on page 199 for another example of using small-step operational semantics to specify the meaning of expressions in an even simpler programming language called the lambda calculus.

Big-Step Semantics

We've now seen what small-step operational semantics looks like: we design an abstract machine that maintains some execution state, then define reduction rules that specify how each kind of program construct can make incremental progress toward being fully evaluated. In particular, small-step semantics has a mostly *iterative* flavor, requiring the abstract machine to repeatedly perform reduction steps (the Ruby `while` loop in `Machine#run`) that are themselves constructed to produce as output the same kind of

---

11. Ruby's procs permit complex expressions to be assigned to variables in some sense, but a proc is still a value: it can't perform any more evaluation by itself, but can be reduced as part of a larger expression involving other values.

information that they require as input, making them suitable for this kind of repeated application.[12]

The small-step approach has the advantage of slicing up the complex business of executing an entire program into smaller pieces that are easier to explain and analyze, but it does feel a bit indirect: instead of explaining how a whole program construct works, we just show how it can be reduced slightly. Why can't we explain a statement more directly, by telling a complete story about how its execution works? Well, we can, and that's the basis of *big-step semantics*.

The idea of big-step semantics is to specify how to get from an expression or statement straight to its result. This necessarily involves thinking about program execution as a *recursive* rather than an iterative process: big-step semantics says that, to evaluate a large expression, we evaluate all of its smaller subexpressions and then combine their results to get our final answer.

In many ways, this feels more natural than the small-step approach, but it does lack some of its fine-grained attention to detail. For example, our small-step semantics is explicit about the order in which operations are supposed to happen, because at every point, it identifies what the next step of reduction should be, but big-step semantics is often written in a looser style that just says which subcomputations to perform without necessarily specifying what order to perform them in.[13] Small-step semantics also gives us an easy way to observe the intermediate stages of a computation, whereas big-step semantics just returns a result and doesn't produce any direct evidence of how it was computed.

To understand this trade-off, let's revisit some common language constructs and see how to implement their big-step semantics in Ruby. Our small-step semantics required a `Machine` class to keep track of state and perform repeated reductions, but we won't need that here; big-step rules describe how to compute the result of an entire program by walking over its abstract syntax tree in a single attempt, so there's no state or repetition to deal with. We'll just define an `#evaluate` method on our expression and statement classes and call it directly.

Expressions

With small-step semantics we had to distinguish reducible expressions like «1 + 2» from irreducible expressions like «3» so that the reduction rules could tell when a subexpression was ready to be used as part of some larger computation, but in big-step semantics every expression can be evaluated. The only distinction, if we wanted to

---

12. Reducing an expression and an environment gives us a new expression, and we may reuse the old environment next time; reducing a statement and an environment gives us a new statement and a new environment.

13. Our Ruby implementation of big-step semantics won't be ambiguous in this way, because Ruby itself already makes these ordering decisions, but when a big-step semantics is specified mathematically, it can avoid spelling out the exact evaluation strategy.

make one, is that some expressions immediately evaluate to themselves, while others perform some computation and evaluate to a different expression.

The goal of big-step semantics is to model the same runtime behavior as the small-step semantics, which means we expect the big-step rules for each kind of program construct to agree with what repeated application of the small-step rules would eventually produce. (This is exactly the sort of thing that can be formally proved when an operational semantics is written mathematically.) The small-step rules for values like Number and Boolean say that we can't reduce them at all, so their big-step rules are very simple: values immediately evaluate to themselves.

```ruby
class Number
  def evaluate(environment)
    self
  end
end

class Boolean
  def evaluate(environment)
    self
  end
end
```

Variable expressions are unique in that their small-step semantics allow them to be reduced exactly once before they turn into a value, so their big-step rule is the same as their small-step one: look up the variable name in the environment and return its value.

```ruby
class Variable
  def evaluate(environment)
    environment[name]
  end
end
```

The binary expressions Add, Multiply, and LessThan are slightly more interesting, requiring recursive evaluation of their left and right subexpressions before combining both values with the appropriate Ruby operator:

```ruby
class Add
  def evaluate(environment)
    Number.new(left.evaluate(environment).value + right.evaluate(environment).value)
  end
end

class Multiply
  def evaluate(environment)
    Number.new(left.evaluate(environment).value * right.evaluate(environment).value)
  end
end

class LessThan
  def evaluate(environment)
    Boolean.new(left.evaluate(environment).value < right.evaluate(environment).value)
  end
end
```

To check that these big-step expression semantics are correct, here they are in action on the Ruby console:

```
>> Number.new(23).evaluate({})
=> «23»
>> Variable.new(:x).evaluate({ x: Number.new(23) })
=> «23»
>> LessThan.new(
     Add.new(Variable.new(:x), Number.new(2)),
     Variable.new(:y)
   ).evaluate({ x: Number.new(2), y: Number.new(5) })
=> «true»
```

Statements

This style of semantics shines when we come to specify the behavior of statements. Expressions reduce to other expressions under small-step semantics, but statements reduce to «do-nothing» and leave a modified environment behind. We can think of big-step statement evaluation as a process that always turns a statement and an initial environment into a final environment, avoiding the small-step complication of also having to deal with the intermediate statement generated by #reduce. Big-step evaluation of an assignment statement, for example, should fully evaluate its expression and return an updated environment containing the resulting value:

```
class Assign
  def evaluate(environment)
    environment.merge({ name => expression.evaluate(environment) })
  end
end
```

Similarly, DoNothing#evaluate will clearly return the unmodified environment, and If#evaluate has a pretty straightforward job on its hands: evaluate the condition, then return the environment that results from evaluating either the consequence or the alternative.

```
class DoNothing
  def evaluate(environment)
    environment
  end
end

class If
  def evaluate(environment)
    case condition.evaluate(environment)
    when Boolean.new(true)
      consequence.evaluate(environment)
    when Boolean.new(false)
      alternative.evaluate(environment)
    end
  end
end
```

The two interesting cases are sequence statements and «while» loops. For sequences, we just need to evaluate both statements, but the initial environment needs to be "threaded through" these two evaluations, so that the result of evaluating the first statement becomes the environment in which the second statement is evaluated. This can be written in Ruby by using the first evaluation's result as the argument to the second:

```
class Sequence
  def evaluate(environment)
    second.evaluate(first.evaluate(environment))
  end
end
```

This threading of the environment is vital to allow earlier statements to prepare variables for later ones:

```
>> statement =
     Sequence.new(
       Assign.new(:x, Add.new(Number.new(1), Number.new(1))),
       Assign.new(:y, Add.new(Variable.new(:x), Number.new(3)))
     )
=> «x = 1 + 1; y = x + 3»
>> statement.evaluate({})
=> {:x=>«2», :y=>«5»}
```

For «while» statements, we need to think through the stages of completely evaluating a loop:

- Evaluate the condition to get either «true» or «false».
- If the condition evaluates to «true», evaluate the body to get a new environment, then repeat the loop within that new environment (i.e., evaluate the whole «while» statement again) and return the resulting environment.
- If the condition evaluates to «false», return the environment unchanged.

This is a recursive explanation of how a «while» statement should behave. As with sequence statements, it's important that the updated environment generated by the loop body is used for the next iteration; otherwise, the condition will never stop being «true», and the loop will never get a chance to terminate.[14]

Once we know how big-step «while» semantics should behave, we can implement While#evaluate:

```
class While
  def evaluate(environment)
    case condition.evaluate(environment)
    when Boolean.new(true)
      evaluate(body.evaluate(environment)) ❶
    when Boolean.new(false)
```

---

14. Of course, there's nothing to prevent SIMPLE programmers from writing a «while» statement whose condition never becomes «false» anyway, but if that's what they ask for then that's what they're going to get.

```
          environment
        end
      end
    end
```

❶ This is where the looping happens: `body.evaluate(environment)` evaluates the loop body to get a new environment, then we pass that environment *back into the current method* to kick off the next iteration. This means we might stack up many nested invocations of `While#evaluate` until the condition eventually becomes «false» and the final environment is returned.

> As with any recursive code, there's a risk that the Ruby call stack will overflow if the nested invocations become too deep. Some Ruby implementations have experimental support for *tail call optimization*, a technique that reduces the risk of overflow by reusing the same stack frame when possible. In the official Ruby implementation (MRI) we can enable tail call optimization with:
>
> ```
> RubyVM::InstructionSequence.compile_option = {
>   tailcall_optimization: true,
>   trace_instruction: false
> }
> ```

To confirm that this works properly, we can try evaluating the same «while» statement we used to check the small-step semantics:

```
>> statement =
     While.new(
       LessThan.new(Variable.new(:x), Number.new(5)),
       Assign.new(:x, Multiply.new(Variable.new(:x), Number.new(3)))
     )
=> «while (x < 5) { x = x * 3 }»
>> statement.evaluate({ x: Number.new(1) })
=> {:x=>«9»}
```

This is the same result that the small-step semantics gave, so it looks like `While#evalu ate` does the right thing.

Applications

Our earlier implementation of small-step semantics makes only moderate use of the Ruby call stack: when we call `#reduce` on a large program, that might cause a handful of nested `#reduce` calls as the message travels down the abstract syntax tree until it reaches the piece of code that is ready to reduce.[15] But the virtual machine does the work of tracking the overall progress of the computation by maintaining the current

---

15. There is an alternative style of operational semantics, called *reduction semantics*, which explicitly separates these "what do we reduce next?" and "how do we reduce it?" phases by introducing so-called *reduction contexts*. These contexts are just patterns that concisely describe the places in a program where reduction can happen, meaning we only need to write reduction rules that perform real computation, thereby eliminating some of the boilerplate from the semantic definitions of larger languages.

program and environment as it repeatedly performs small reductions; in particular, the depth of the call stack is limited by the depth of the program's syntax tree, since the nested calls are only being used to traverse the tree looking for what to reduce next, not to perform the reduction itself.

By contrast, this big-step implementation makes much greater use of the stack, relying entirely on it to remember where we are in the overall computation, to perform smaller computations as part of performing larger ones, and to keep track of how much evaluation is left to do. What looks like a single call to `#evaluate` actually turns into a series of recursive calls, each one evaluating a subprogram deeper within the syntax tree.

This difference highlights the purpose of each approach. Small-step semantics assumes a simple abstract machine that can perform small operations, and therefore includes explicit detail about how to produce useful intermediate results; big-step semantics places the burden of assembling the whole computation on the machine or person executing it, requiring her to keep track of many intermediate subgoals as she turns the entire program into a final result in a single operation. Depending on what we wish to do with a language's operational semantics—perhaps build an efficient implementation, prove some properties of programs, or devise some optimizing transformations —one approach or the other might be more appropriate.

The most influential use of big-step semantics for specifying real programming languages is Chapter 6 of the original definition of the Standard ML programming language (*http://www.lfcs.inf.ed.ac.uk/reports/87/ECS-LFCS-87-36/*), which explains all of the runtime behavior of ML in big-step style. Following this example, OCaml's core language has a big-step semantics (*http://caml.inria.fr/pub/docs/u3-ocaml/ocaml-ml .html#htoc7*) to complement its more detailed small-step definition.

Big-step operational semantics is also used by the W3C: the XQuery 1.0 and XPath 2.0 specification (*http://www.w3.org/TR/xquery-semantics/*) uses mathematical inference rules to describe how its languages should be evaluated, and the XQuery and XPath Full Text 3.0 spec (*http://www.w3.org/TR/xpath-full-text-30/*) includes a big-step semantics written in XQuery.

It probably hasn't escaped your attention that, by writing down SIMPLE's small- and big-step semantics in Ruby instead of mathematics, we have implemented two different Ruby *interpreters* for it. And this is what operational semantics really is: explaining the meaning of a language by describing an interpreter. Normally, that description would be written in simple mathematical notation, which makes everything very clear and unambiguous as long as we can understand it, but comes at the price of being quite abstract and distanced from the reality of computers. Using Ruby has the disadvantage of introducing the extra complexity of a real-world programming language (classes, objects, method calls...) into what's supposed to be a simplifying explanation, but if we already understand Ruby, then it's probably easier to see what's going on, and being able to execute the description as an interpreter is a nice bonus.

Denotational Semantics

So far, we've looked at the meaning of programming languages from an operational perspective, explaining what a program means by showing what will happen when it's executed. Another approach, *denotational semantics*, is concerned instead with translating programs from their native language into some other representation.

This style of semantics doesn't directly address the question of executing a program at all. Instead, it concerns itself with leveraging the established meaning of another language—one that is lower-level, more formal, or at least better understood than the language being described—in order to explain a new one.

Denotational semantics is necessarily a more abstract approach than operational, because it just replaces one language with another instead of turning a language into real behavior. For example, if we needed to explain the meaning of the English verb "walk" to a person with whom we had no spoken language in common, we could communicate it operationally by actually walking back and forth. On the other hand, if we needed to explain "walk" to a French speaker, we could do so denotationally just by telling them the French verb "*marcher*"—an undeniably higher level form of communication, no messy exercise required.

Unsurprisingly, denotational semantics is conventionally used to turn programs into mathematical objects so they can be studied and manipulated with mathematical tools, but we can get some of the flavor of this approach by looking at how to denote SIMPLE programs in some other way.

Let's try giving a denotational semantics for SIMPLE by translating it into Ruby.[16] In practice, this means turning an abstract syntax tree into a string of Ruby code that somehow captures the intended meaning of that syntax.

But what is the "intended meaning"? What should Ruby denotations of our expressions and statements look like? We've already seen operationally that an expression takes an environment and turns it into a value; one way to express this in Ruby is with a proc that takes some argument representing an environment argument and returns some Ruby object representing a value. For simple constant expressions like «5» and «false», we won't be using the environment at all, so we only need to worry about how their eventual result can be represented as a Ruby object. Fortunately, Ruby already has objects specifically designed to represent these values: we can use the Ruby value 5 as the result of the SIMPLE expression «5», and likewise, the Ruby value false as the result of «false».

---

16. This means we'll be writing Ruby code that generates Ruby code, but the choice of the same language as both the denotation language and the implementation metalanguage is only to keep things simple. We could just as easily write Ruby that generates strings containing JavaScript, for example.

Expressions

We can use this idea to write implementations of a #to_ruby method for the Number and Boolean classes:

```ruby
class Number
  def to_ruby
    "-> e { #{value.inspect} }"
  end
end

class Boolean
  def to_ruby
    "-> e { #{value.inspect} }"
  end
end
```

Here is how they behave on the console:

```
>> Number.new(5).to_ruby
=> "-> e { 5 }"
>> Boolean.new(false).to_ruby
=> "-> e { false }"
```

Each of these methods produces a string that happens to contain Ruby code, and because Ruby is a language whose meaning we already understand, we can see that both of these strings are programs that build procs. Each proc takes an environment argument called e, completely ignores it, and returns a Ruby value.

Because these denotations are strings of Ruby source code, we can check their behavior in IRB by using Kernel#eval to turn them into real, callable Proc objects:[17]

```
>> proc = eval(Number.new(5).to_ruby)
=> #<Proc (lambda)>
>> proc.call({})
=> 5
>> proc = eval(Boolean.new(false).to_ruby)
=> #<Proc (lambda)>
>> proc.call({})
=> false
```

 At this stage, it's tempting to avoid procs entirely and use simpler implementations of #to_ruby that just turn Number.new(5) into the string '5' instead of '-> e { 5 }' and so on, but part of the point of building a denotational semantics is to capture the essence of constructs from the source language, and in this case, we're capturing the idea that expressions *in general* require an environment, even though these specific expressions don't make use of it.

---

17. We can only do this because Ruby is doing double duty as both the implementation and denotation languages. If our denotations were JavaScript source code, we'd have to try them out in a JavaScript console.

To denote expressions that do use the environment, we need to decide how environments are going to be represented in Ruby. We've already seen environments in our operational semantics, and since they were implemented in Ruby, we can just reuse our earlier idea of representing an environment as a hash. The details will need to change, though, so beware the subtle difference: in our operational semantics, the environment lived inside the virtual machine and associated variable names with SIMPLE abstract syntax trees like Number.new(5), but in our denotational semantics, the environment exists in the language we're translating our programs into, so it needs to make sense in that world instead of the "outside world" of a virtual machine.

In particular, this means that our denotational environments should associate variable names with native Ruby values like 5 rather than with objects representing SIMPLE syntax. We can think of an operational environment like { x: Number.new(5) } as having a denotation of '{ x: 5 }' in the language we're translating into, and we just need to keep our heads straight because both the implementation metalanguage and the denotation language happen to be Ruby.

Now we know that the environment will be a hash, we can implement Variable#to_ruby:

```
class Variable
  def to_ruby
    "-> e { e[#{name.inspect}] }"
  end
end
```

This translates a variable expression into the source code of a Ruby proc that looks up the appropriate value in the environment hash:

```
>> expression = Variable.new(:x)
=> «x»
>> expression.to_ruby
=> "-> e { e[:x] }"
>> proc = eval(expression.to_ruby)
=> #<Proc (lambda)>
>> proc.call({ x: 7 })
=> 7
```

An important aspect of denotational semantics is that it's *compositional*: the denotation of a program is constructed from the denotations of its parts. We can see this compositionality in practice when we move onto denoting larger expressions like Add, Multiply, and LessThan:

```
class Add
  def to_ruby
    "-> e { (#{left.to_ruby}).call(e) + (#{right.to_ruby}).call(e) }"
  end
end

class Multiply
  def to_ruby
    "-> e { (#{left.to_ruby}).call(e) * (#{right.to_ruby}).call(e) }"
```

```
    end
  end

  class LessThan
    def to_ruby
      "-> e { (#{left.to_ruby}).call(e) < (#{right.to_ruby}).call(e) }"
    end
  end
```

Here we're using string concatenation to compose the denotation of an expression out of the denotations of its subexpressions. We know that each subexpression will be denoted by a proc's Ruby source, so we can use them as part of a larger piece of Ruby source that calls those procs with the supplied environment and does some computation with their return values. Here's what the resulting denotations look like:

```
>> Add.new(Variable.new(:x), Number.new(1)).to_ruby
=> "-> e { (-> e { e[:x] }).call(e) + (-> e { 1 }).call(e) }"
>> LessThan.new(Add.new(Variable.new(:x), Number.new(1)), Number.new(3)).to_ruby
=> "-> e { (-> e { (-> e { e[:x] }).call(e) + (-> e { 1 }).call(e) }).call(e) < ↵
(-> e { 3 }).call(e) }"
```

These denotations are now complicated enough that it's difficult to see whether they do the right thing. Let's try them out to make sure:

```
>> environment = { x: 3 }
=> {:x=>3}
>> proc = eval(Add.new(Variable.new(:x), Number.new(1)).to_ruby)
=> #<Proc (lambda)>
>> proc.call(environment)
=> 4
>> proc = eval(
     LessThan.new(Add.new(Variable.new(:x), Number.new(1)), Number.new(3)).to_ruby
   )
=> #<Proc (lambda)>
>> proc.call(environment)
=> false
```

Statements

We can specify the denotational semantics of statements in a similar way, although remember from the operational semantics that evaluating a statement produces a new environment rather than a value. This means that Assign#to_ruby needs to produce code for a proc whose result is an updated environment hash:

```
  class Assign
    def to_ruby
      "-> e { e.merge({ #{name.inspect} => (#{expression.to_ruby}).call(e) }) }"
    end
  end
```

Again, we can check this on the console:

```
>> statement = Assign.new(:y, Add.new(Variable.new(:x), Number.new(1)))
=> «y = x + 1»
```

```
>> statement.to_ruby
=> "-> e { e.merge({ :y => (-> e { (-> e { e[:x] }).call(e) + (-> e { 1 }).call(e) })↵
.call(e) }) }"
>> proc = eval(statement.to_ruby)
=> #<Proc (lambda)>
>> proc.call({ x: 3 })
=> {:x=>3, :y=>4}
```

As always, the semantics of DoNothing is very simple:

```
class DoNothing
  def to_ruby
    '-> e { e }'
  end
end
```

For conditional statements, we can translate SIMPLE's «if (…) { … } else { … }» into a Ruby if … then … else … end, making sure that the environment gets to all the places where it's needed:

```
class If
  def to_ruby
    "-> e { if (#{condition.to_ruby}).call(e)" +
    " then (#{consequence.to_ruby}).call(e)" +
    " else (#{alternative.to_ruby}).call(e)" +
    " end }"
  end
end
```

As in big-step operational semantics, we need to be careful about specifying the sequence statement: the result of evaluating the first statement is used as the environment for evaluating the second.

```
class Sequence
  def to_ruby
    "-> e { (#{second.to_ruby}).call((#{first.to_ruby}).call(e)) }"
  end
end
```

And lastly, as with conditionals, we can translate «while» statements into procs that use Ruby while to repeatedly execute the body before returning the final environment:

```
class While
  def to_ruby
    "-> e {" +
    " while (#{condition.to_ruby}).call(e); e = (#{body.to_ruby}).call(e); end;" +
    " e" +
    " }"
  end
end
```

Even a simple «while» can have quite a verbose denotation, so it's worth getting the Ruby interpreter to check that its meaning is correct:

```
>> statement =
     While.new(
       LessThan.new(Variable.new(:x), Number.new(5)),
```

```
      Assign.new(:x, Multiply.new(Variable.new(:x), Number.new(3)))
    )
=> «while (x < 5) { x = x * 3 }»
>> statement.to_ruby
=> "-> e { while (-> e { (-> e { e[:x] }).call(e) < (-> e { 5 }).call(e) }).call(e); ↵
e = (-> e { e.merge({ :x => (-> e { (-> e { e[:x] }).call(e) * (-> e { 3 }).call(e) ↵
}).call(e) }) }).call(e); end; e }"
>> proc = eval(statement.to_ruby)
=> #<Proc (lambda)>
>> proc.call({ x: 1 })
=> {:x=>9}
```

Comparing Semantic Styles

«while» is a good example of the difference between small-step, big-step, and denotational semantics.

The small-step operational semantics of «while» is written as a reduction rule for an abstract machine. The overall looping behavior isn't part of the rule's action—reduction just turns a «while» statement into an «if» statement—but it emerges as a consequence of the future reductions performed by the machine. To understand what «while» does, we need to look at all of the small-step rules and work out how they interact over the course of a SIMPLE program's execution.

«while»'s big-step operational semantics is written as an evaluation rule that shows how to compute the final environment directly. The rule contains a recursive call to itself, so there's an explicit indication that «while» will cause a loop during evaluation, but it's not quite the kind of loop that a SIMPLE programmer would recognize. Big-step rules are written in a recursive style, describing the complete evaluation of an expression or statement in terms of the evaluation of other pieces of syntax, so this rule tells us that the result of evaluating a «while» statement may depend upon the result of evaluating the same statement in a different environment, but it requires a leap of intuition to connect this idea with the iterative behavior that «while» is supposed to exhibit. Fortunately the leap isn't too large: a bit of mathematical reasoning can show that the two kinds of loop are equivalent in principle, and when the metalanguage supports tail call optimization, they're also equivalent in practice.

The denotational semantics of «while» shows how to rewrite it in Ruby, namely by using Ruby's while keyword. This is a much more direct translation: Ruby has native support for iterative loops, and the denotation rule shows that «while» can be implemented with that feature. There's no leap required to understand how the two kinds of loop relate to each other, so if we understand how Ruby while loops work, we understand SIMPLE «while» loops too. Of course, this means we've just converted the problem of understanding SIMPLE into the problem of understanding the denotation language, which is a serious disadvantage when that language is as large and ill-specified as Ruby, but it becomes an advantage when we have a small mathematical language for writing denotations.

Applications

Having done all this work, what does this denotational semantics achieve? Its main purpose is to show how to translate SIMPLE into Ruby, using the latter as a tool to explain what various language constructs mean. This happens to give us a way to execute SIMPLE programs—because we've written the rules of the denotational semantics in executable Ruby, and because the rules' output is itself executable Ruby—but that's incidental, since we could have given the rules in plain English and used some mathematical language for the denotations. The important part is that we've taken an arbitrary language of our own devising and converted it into a language that someone or something else can understand.

To give this translation some explanatory power, it's helpful to bring parts of the language's meaning to the surface instead of allowing them to remain implicit. For example, this semantics makes the environment explicit by representing it as a tangible Ruby object—a hash that's passed in and out of procs—instead of denoting variables as real Ruby variables and relying on Ruby's own subtle scoping rules to specify how variable access works. In this respect the semantics is doing more than just offloading all the explanatory effort onto Ruby; it uses Ruby as a simple foundation, but does some extra work on top to show exactly how environments are used and changed by different program constructs.

We saw earlier that operational semantics is about explaining a language's meaning by designing an interpreter for it. By contrast, the language-to-language translation of denotational semantics is like a *compiler*: in this case, our implementations of #to_ruby effectively compile SIMPLE into Ruby. None of these styles of semantics necessarily says anything about how to *efficiently* implement an interpreter or compiler for a language, but they do provide an official baseline against which the correctness of any efficient implementation can be judged.

These denotational definitions also show up in the wild. Older versions of the Scheme standard use denotational semantics (*http://www.schemers.org/Documents/Standards/R5RS/HTML/r5rs-Z-H-10.html#%25_sec_7.2*) to specify the core language, unlike the current standard's small-step operational semantics, and the development of the XSLT document-transformation language was guided by Philip Wadler's denotational definitions of XSLT patterns (*http://homepages.inf.ed.ac.uk/wadler/topics/xml.html#xsl-semantics*) and XPath expressions (*http://homepages.inf.ed.ac.uk/wadler/topics/xml.html#xpath-semantics*).

See "Semantics" on page 83 for a practical example of using denotational semantics to specify the meaning of regular expressions.

Formal Semantics in Practice

This chapter has shown several different ways of approaching the problem of giving computer programs a meaning. In each case, we've avoided the mathematical details and tried to get a flavor of their intent by using Ruby, but formal semantics is usually done with mathematical tools.

Formality

Our tour of formal semantics hasn't been especially formal. We haven't paid any serious attention to mathematical notation, and using Ruby as a metalanguage has meant we've focused more on different ways of executing programs than on ways of understanding them. Proper denotational semantics is concerned with getting to the heart of programs' meanings by turning them into well-defined mathematical objects, with none of the evasiveness of representing a SIMPLE «while» loop with a Ruby while loop.

The branch of mathematics called *domain theory* was developed specifically to provide definitions and objects that are useful for denotational semantics, allowing a model of computation based on fixed points of monotonic functions on partially ordered sets. Programs can be understood by "compiling" them into mathematical functions, and the techniques of domain theory can be used to prove interesting properties of these functions.

On the other hand, while we only vaguely sketched denotational semantics in Ruby, our approach to operational semantics is closer in spirit to its formal presentation: our definitions of #reduce and #evaluate methods are really just Ruby translations of mathematical inference rules.

Finding Meaning

An important application of formal semantics is to give an unambiguous specification of the meaning of a programming language, rather than relying on more informal approaches like natural-language specification documents and "specification by implementation." A formal specification has other uses too, such as proving properties of the language in general and of specific programs in particular, proving equivalences between programs in the language, and investigating ways of safely transforming programs to make them more efficient without changing their behavior.

For example, since an operational semantics corresponds quite closely to the implementation of an interpreter, computer scientists can treat a suitable interpreter as an operational semantics for a language, and then prove its correctness with respect to a denotational semantics for that language—this means proving that there is a sensible connection between the meanings given by the interpreter and those given by the denotational semantics.

Denotational semantics has the advantage of being more abstract than operational semantics, by ignoring the detail of how a program executes and concentrating instead on how to convert it into a different representation. For example, this makes it possible to compare two programs written in different languages, if a denotational semantics exists to translate both languages into some shared representation.

This degree of abstraction can make denotational semantics seem circuitous. If the problem is how to explain the meaning of a programming language, how does translating one language into another get us any closer to a solution? A denotation is only as good as its meaning; in particular, a denotational semantics only gets us closer to being able to actually execute a program if the denotation language has some *operational* meaning, a semantics of its own that shows how it may be executed instead of how to translate it into yet another language.

Formal denotational semantics uses abstract mathematical objects, usually functions, to denote programming language constructs like expressions and statements, and because mathematical convention dictates how to do things like evaluate functions, this gives a direct way of thinking about the denotation in an operational sense. We've taken the less formal approach of thinking of a denotational semantics as a compiler from one language into another, and in reality, this is how most programming languages ultimately get executed: a Java program will get compiled into bytecode by `javac`, the bytecode will get just-in-time compiled into x86 instructions by the Java virtual machine, then a CPU will decode each x86 instruction into RISC-like microinstructions for execution on a core…where does it end? Is it compilers, or virtual machines, all the way down?

Of course programs do eventually execute, because the tower of semantics finally bottoms out at an *actual* machine: electrons in semiconductors, obeying the laws of physics.[18] A computer is a device for maintaining this precarious structure, many complex layers of interpretation balanced on top of one another, allowing human-scale ideas like multitouch gestures and `while` loops to be gradually translated down into the physical universe of silicon and electricity.

Alternatives

The semantic styles seen in this chapter go by many different names. Small-step semantics is also known as *structural operational semantics* and *transition semantics*; big-step semantics is more often called *natural semantics* or *relational semantics*; and denotational semantics is also called *fixed-point semantics* or *mathematical semantics*.

Other styles of formal semantics are available. One alternative is *axiomatic semantics*, which describes the meaning of a statement by making assertions about the state of the abstract machine before and after that statement executes: if one assertion (the *precondition*) is initially true before the statement is executed, then the other assertion (the *postcondition*) will be true afterward. Axiomatic semantics is useful for verifying the correctness of programs: as statements are plugged together to make larger programs,

---

18. Or, in the case of a mechanical computer like the Analytical Engine designed by Charles Babbage in 1837, cogs and paper obeying the laws of physics.

their corresponding assertions can be plugged together to make larger assertions, with the goal of showing that an overall assertion about a program matches up with its intended specification.

Although the details are different, axiomatic semantics is the style that best characterizes the RubySpec project (*http://www.rubyspec.org/*), an "executable specification for the Ruby programming language" that uses RSpec-style assertions to describe the behavior of Ruby's built-in language constructs, as well as its core and standard libraries. For example, here's a fragment of RubySpec's description of the **Array#<<** method:

```ruby
describe "Array#<<" do
  it "correctly resizes the Array" do
    a = []
    a.size.should == 0
    a << :foo
    a.size.should == 1
    a << :bar << :baz
    a.size.should == 3

    a = [1, 2, 3]
    a.shift
    a.shift
    a.shift
    a << :foo
    a.should == [:foo]
  end
end
```

Implementing Parsers

In this chapter, we've been building the abstract syntax trees of SIMPLE programs manually—writing longhand Ruby expressions like `Assign.new(:x, Add.new(Vari able.new(:x), Number.new(1)))`—rather than beginning with raw SIMPLE source code like `'x = x + 1'` and using a parser to automatically turn it into a syntax tree.

Implementing a SIMPLE parser entirely from scratch would involve a lot of detail and take us on a long diversion from our discussion of formal semantics. Hacking on toy programming languages is fun, though, and thanks to the existence of parsing tools and libraries it's not especially difficult to construct a parser by relying on other people's work, so here's a brief outline of how to do it.

One of the best parsing tools available for Ruby is Treetop (*http://treetop.rubyforge.org/*), a domain-specific language for describing syntax in a way that allows a parser to be automatically generated. A Treetop description of a language's syntax is written as a *parsing expression grammar* (PEG), a collection of simple, regular-expression-like rules that are easy to write and to understand. Best of all, these rules can be annotated with method definitions so that the Ruby objects generated by the parsing process can be given their own behavior. This ability to define both a syntactic structure and a collection of Ruby code that operates on that structure makes Treetop ideal for sketching out the syntax of a language and giving it an executable semantics.

To give us a taste of how this works, here's a cut-down version of the Treetop grammar for SIMPLE, containing only the rules needed to parse the string `'while (x < 5) { x = x * 3 }'`:

```
grammar Simple
  rule statement
    while / assign
  end

  rule while
    'while (' condition:expression ') { ' body:statement ' }' {
      def to_ast
        While.new(condition.to_ast, body.to_ast)
      end
    }
  end

  rule assign
    name:[a-z]+ ' = ' expression {
      def to_ast
        Assign.new(name.text_value.to_sym, expression.to_ast)
      end
    }
  end

  rule expression
    less_than
  end

  rule less_than
    left:multiply ' < ' right:less_than {
      def to_ast
        LessThan.new(left.to_ast, right.to_ast)
      end
    }
    /
    multiply
  end

  rule multiply
    left:term ' * ' right:multiply {
      def to_ast
        Multiply.new(left.to_ast, right.to_ast)
      end
    }
    /
    term
  end

  rule term
    number / variable
  end
```

```
    rule number
      [0-9]+ {
        def to_ast
          Number.new(text_value.to_i)
        end
      }
    end

    rule variable
      [a-z]+ {
        def to_ast
          Variable.new(text_value.to_sym)
        end
      }
    end
  end
```

This language looks a little like Ruby, but the similarity is only superficial; grammars are written in the special Treetop language. The `rule` keyword introduces a new rule for parsing a particular kind of syntax, and the expressions inside each rule describe the structure of the strings it will recognize. Rules can recursively call other rules—the `while` rule calls the `expression` and `statement` rules, for instance—and parsing begins at the first rule, which is `statement` in this grammar.

The order in which the expression-syntax rules call each other reflects the precedence of SIMPLE's operators. The `expression` rule calls `less_than`, which then immediately calls `multiply` to give it a chance to match the * operator somewhere in the string before `less_than` gets a chance to match the lower-precedence < operator. This makes sure that `'1 * 2 < 3'` is parsed as «(1 * 2) < 3» and not «1 * (2 < 3)».

> To keep things simple, this grammar makes no attempt to constrain what kinds of expression can appear inside other expressions, which means the parser will accept some programs that are obviously wrong.
>
> For example, we have two rules for binary expressions—`less_than` and `multiply`—but the only reason for having separate rules is to enforce operator precedence, so each rule only requires that a higher precedence rule matches its left operand and a same-or-higher-precedence one matches its right. This creates the situation where a string like `'1 < 2 < 3'` will be parsed successfully, even though the semantics of SIMPLE won't be able to give the resulting expression a meaning.
>
> Some of these problems can be resolved by tweaking the grammar, but there will always be other incorrect cases that the parser can't spot. We'll separate the two concerns by keeping the parser as liberal as possible and using a different technique to detect invalid programs in Chapter 9.

Most of the rules in the grammar are annotated with Ruby code inside curly brackets. In each case, this code defines a method called #to_ast, which will be available on the corresponding syntax objects built by Treetop when it parses a SIMPLE program.

If we save this grammar into a file called *simple.treetop*, we can load it with Treetop to generate a `SimpleParser` class. This parser allows us to turn a string of SIMPLE source code into a representation built out of Treetop's `SyntaxNode` objects:

```
>> require 'treetop'
=> true
>> Treetop.load('simple')
=> SimpleParser
>> parse_tree = SimpleParser.new.parse('while (x < 5) { x = x * 3 }')
=> SyntaxNode+While1+While0 offset=0, "...5) { x = x * 3 }" (to_ast,condition,body):
    SyntaxNode offset=0, "while ("
    SyntaxNode+LessThan1+LessThan0 offset=7, "x < 5" (to_ast,left,right):
      SyntaxNode+Variable0 offset=7, "x" (to_ast):
        SyntaxNode offset=7, "x"
      SyntaxNode offset=8, " < "
      SyntaxNode+Number0 offset=11, "5" (to_ast):
        SyntaxNode offset=11, "5"
    SyntaxNode offset=12, ") { "
    SyntaxNode+Assign1+Assign0 offset=16, "x = x * 3" (to_ast,name,expression):
      SyntaxNode offset=16, "x":
        SyntaxNode offset=16, "x"
      SyntaxNode offset=17, " = "
      SyntaxNode+Multiply1+Multiply0 offset=20, "x * 3" (to_ast,left,right):
        SyntaxNode+Variable0 offset=20, "x" (to_ast):
          SyntaxNode offset=20, "x"
        SyntaxNode offset=21, " * "
        SyntaxNode+Number0 offset=24, "3" (to_ast):
          SyntaxNode offset=24, "3"
    SyntaxNode offset=25, " }"
```

This `SyntaxNode` structure is a *concrete syntax tree*: it's designed specifically for manipulation by the Treetop parser and contains a lot of extraneous information about how its nodes are related to the raw source code that produced them. Here's what the Treetop documentation (*http://treetop.rubyforge.org/using_in_ruby.html*) has to say about it:

> Please don't try to walk down the syntax tree yourself, and please don't use the tree as your own convenient data structure. It contains many more nodes than your application needs, often even more than one for every character of input.

> Instead, add methods to the root rule that return the information you require in a sensible form. Each rule can call its sub-rules, and this method of walking the syntax tree is much preferable to attempting to walk it from the outside.

And that's what we've done. Rather than manipulate this messy tree directly, we've used annotations in the grammar to define a `#to_ast` method on each of its nodes. If we call that method on the root node, it'll build an abstract syntax tree made from SIMPLE syntax objects:

```
>> statement = parse_tree.to_ast
=> «while (x < 5) { x = x * 3 }»
```

So we've automatically converted source code to an abstract syntax tree, and now we can use that tree to explore the meaning of the program in the usual ways:

```
>> statement.evaluate({ x: Number.new(1) })
=> {:x=>«9»}
>> statement.to_ruby
=> "-> e { while (-> e { (-> e { e[:x] }).call(e) < (-> e { 5 }).call(e) }).call(e); ↵
e = (-> e { e.merge({ :x => (-> e { (-> e { e[:x] }).call(e) * (-> e { 3 }).call(e) ↵
}).call(e) }) }).call(e); end; e }"
```

Another drawback of this parser, and of Treetop in general, is that it generates a *right-associative* concrete syntax tree. This means that the string '1 * 2 * 3 * 4' is parsed as if it had been written '1 * (2 * (3 * 4))':

```
>> expression = SimpleParser.new.parse('1 * 2 * 3 * 4', root: :expression).to_ast
=> «1 * 2 * 3 * 4»
>> expression.left
=> «1»
>> expression.right
=> «2 * 3 * 4»
```

But multiplication is conventionally *left-associative*: when we write '1 * 2 * 3 * 4' we actually mean '((1 * 2) * 3) * 4', with the numbers grouped together starting at the lefthand end of the expression, not the right. That doesn't matter much for multiplication—both ways produce the same result when evaluated—but for operations like subtraction and division, it creates a problem, because «((1 - 2) - 3) - 4» does *not* evaluate to the same value as «1 - (2 - (3 - 4))».

To fix this, we'd have to make the rules and #to_ast implementations more complicated. See "Parsing" on page 204 for a Treetop grammar that builds a left-associative AST.

It's convenient to be able to parse SIMPLE programs like this, but Treetop is doing all the hard work for us, so we haven't learned much about how a parser actually works. In "Parsing with Pushdown Automata" on page 125, we'll see how to implement a parser directly.

## CHAPTER 3

The Simplest Computers

In the space of a few short years, we've become surrounded by computers. They used to be safely hidden away in military research centers and university laboratories, but now they're everywhere: on our desks, in our pockets, under the hoods of our cars, implanted inside our bodies. As programmers, we work with sophisticated computing devices every day, but how well do we understand the way they work?

The power of modern computers comes with a lot of complexity. It's difficult to understand every detail of a computer's many subsystems, and more difficult still to understand how those subsystems interact to create the system as a whole. This complexity makes it impractical to reason directly about the capabilities and behavior of real computers, so it's useful to have simplified models of computers that share interesting features with real machines but that can still be understood in their entirety.

In this chapter, we'll strip back the idea of a computing machine to its barest essentials, see what it can be used for, and explore the limits of what such a simple computer can do.

Deterministic Finite Automata

Real computers typically have large amounts of volatile memory (RAM) and nonvolatile storage (hard drive or SSD), many input/output devices, and several processor cores capable of executing multiple instructions simultaneously. A *finite state machine*, also known as a *finite automaton*, is a drastically simplified model of a computer that throws out all of these features in exchange for being easy to understand, easy to reason about, and easy to implement in hardware or software.

States, Rules, and Input

A finite automaton has no permanent storage and virtually no RAM. It's a little machine with a handful of possible *states* and the ability to keep track of which one of those states it's currently in—think of it as a computer with enough RAM to store a single value. Similarly, finite automata don't have a keyboard, mouse, or network interface for receiving input, just a single external stream of input characters that they can read one at a time.

Instead of a general-purpose CPU for executing arbitrary programs, each finite automaton has a hardcoded collection of *rules* that determine how it should move from one state to another in response to input. The automaton starts in one particular state and reads individual characters from its input stream, following a rule each time it reads a character.

Here's a way of visualizing the structure of one particular finite automaton:

The two circles represent the automaton's two states, 1 and 2, and the arrow coming from nowhere shows that the automaton always starts in state 1, its *start state*. The arrows between states represent the rules of the machine, which are:

- When in state 1 and the character a is read, move into state 2.
- When in state 2 and the character a is read, move into state 1.

This is enough information for us to investigate how the machine processes a stream of inputs:

- The machine starts in state 1.
- The machine only has rules for reading the character a from its input stream, so that's the only thing that can happen. When it reads an a, it moves from state 1 into state 2.
- When the machine reads another a, it moves back into state 1.

Once it gets back to state 1, it'll start repeating itself, so that's the extent of this particular machine's behavior. Information about the current state is assumed to be internal to the automaton—it operates as a "black box" that doesn't reveal its inner workings—so the boringness of this behavior is compounded by the uselessness of it not causing any kind of observable output. Nobody in the outside world can see that anything is happening while the machine is bouncing between states 1 and 2, so in this case, we might as well have a single state and not bother with any internal structure at all.

Output

To address this problem, finite automata also have a rudimentary way of producing output. This is nothing as sophisticated as the output capabilities of real computers; we just mark some of the states as being special, and say that the machine's single-bit

```
    rule_for(state, character).follow
  end

  def rule_for(state, character)
    rules.detect { |rule| rule.applies_to?(state, character) }
  end
end
```

This code establishes a simple API for rules: each rule has an #applies_to? method, which returns true or false to indicate whether that rule applies in a particular situation, and a #follow method that returns information about how the machine should change when a rule is followed.[1] DFARulebook#next_state uses these methods to locate the correct rule and discover what the next state of the DFA should be.

 By using Enumerable#detect, the implementation of DFARulebook#next_state assumes that there will always be exactly one rule that applies to the given state and character. If there's more than one applicable rule, only the first will have any effect and the others will be ignored; if there are none, the #detect call will return nil and the simulation will crash when it tries to call nil.follow.

This is why the class is called DFARulebook rather than just FARulebook: it only works properly if the determinism constraints are respected.

A rulebook lets us wrap up many rules into a single object and ask it questions about which state comes next:

```
>> rulebook = DFARulebook.new([
     FARule.new(1, 'a', 2), FARule.new(1, 'b', 1),
     FARule.new(2, 'a', 2), FARule.new(2, 'b', 3),
     FARule.new(3, 'a', 3), FARule.new(3, 'b', 3)
   ])
=> #<struct DFARulebook …>
>> rulebook.next_state(1, 'a')
=> 2
>> rulebook.next_state(1, 'b')
=> 1
>> rulebook.next_state(2, 'b')
=> 3
```

---

1. This design is general enough to accommodate different kinds of machines and rules, so we'll be able to reuse it later in the book when things get more complicated.

We had a choice here about how to represent the states of our automaton as Ruby values. All that matters is the ability to tell the states apart: our implementation of DFARulebook#next_state needs to be able to compare two states to decide whether they're the same, but otherwise, it doesn't care whether those objects are numbers, symbols, strings, hashes, or faceless instances of the Object class.

In this case, it's clearest to use plain old Ruby numbers—they match up nicely with the numbered states on the diagrams—so we'll do that for now.

Once we have a rulebook, we can use it to build a DFA object that keeps track of its current state and can report whether it's currently in an accept state or not:

```ruby
class DFA < Struct.new(:current_state, :accept_states, :rulebook)
  def accepting?
    accept_states.include?(current_state)
  end
end
```

```
>> DFA.new(1, [1, 3], rulebook).accepting?
=> true
>> DFA.new(1, [3], rulebook).accepting?
=> false
```

We can now write a method to read a character of input, consult the rulebook, and change state accordingly:

```ruby
class DFA
  def read_character(character)
    self.current_state = rulebook.next_state(current_state, character)
  end
end
```

This lets us feed characters to the DFA and watch its output change:

```
>> dfa = DFA.new(1, [3], rulebook); dfa.accepting?
=> false
>> dfa.read_character('b'); dfa.accepting?
=> false
>> 3.times do dfa.read_character('a') end; dfa.accepting?
=> false
>> dfa.read_character('b'); dfa.accepting?
=> true
```

Feeding the DFA one character at a time is a little unwieldy, so let's add a convenience method for reading an entire string of input:

```ruby
class DFA
  def read_string(string)
    string.chars.each do |character|
      read_character(character)
    end
  end
end
```

Now we can provide the DFA a whole string of input instead of having to pass its characters individually:

```
>> dfa = DFA.new(1, [3], rulebook); dfa.accepting?
=> false
>> dfa.read_string('baaab'); dfa.accepting?
=> true
```

Once a DFA object has been fed some input, it's probably not in its start state anymore, so we can't reliably reuse it to check a completely new sequence of inputs. That means we have to recreate it from scratch—using the same start state, accept states, and rulebook as before—every time we want to see whether it will accept a new string. We can avoid doing this manually by wrapping up its constructor's arguments in an object that represents the *design* of a particular DFA and relying on that object to automatically build one-off instances of that DFA whenever we want to check for acceptance of a string:

```
class DFADesign < Struct.new(:start_state, :accept_states, :rulebook)
  def to_dfa
    DFA.new(start_state, accept_states, rulebook)
  end

  def accepts?(string)
    to_dfa.tap { |dfa| dfa.read_string(string) }.accepting?
  end
end
```

 The #tap method evaluates a block and then returns the object it was called on.

DFADesign#accepts? uses the DFADesign#to_dfa method to create a new instance of DFA and then calls #read_string? to put it into an accepting or rejecting state:

```
>> dfa_design = DFADesign.new(1, [3], rulebook)
=> #<struct DFADesign …>
>> dfa_design.accepts?('a')
=> false
>> dfa_design.accepts?('baa')
=> false
>> dfa_design.accepts?('baba')
=> true
```

Nondeterministic Finite Automata

DFAs are simple to understand and to implement, but that's because they're very similar to machines we're already familiar with. Having stripped away all the complexity of a real computer, we now have the opportunity to experiment with less conventional ideas that take us further away from the machines we're used to, without having to deal with the incidental difficulties of making those ideas work in a real system.

One way to explore is by chipping away at our existing assumptions and constraints. For one thing, the determinism constraints seem restrictive: maybe we don't care about every possible input character at every state, so why can't we just leave out rules for characters we don't care about and assume that the machine can go into a generic failure state when something unexpected happens? More exotically, what would it mean to allow the machine to have contradictory rules, so that more than one execution path is possible? Our setup also assumes that each state change must happen in response to a character being read from the input stream, but what would happen if the machine could change state without having to read anything?

In this section, we'll investigate these ideas and see what new possibilities are opened up by tweaking a finite automaton's capabilities.

Nondeterminism

Suppose we wanted a finite automaton that would accept any string of as and bs as long as the third character was b. It's easy enough to come up with a suitable DFA design:

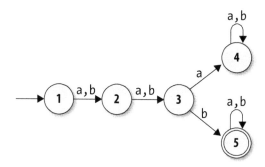

What if we wanted a machine that would accept strings where the *third-from-last* character is b? How would that work? It seems more difficult: the DFA above is guaranteed to be in state 3 when it reads the third character, but a machine can't know in advance *when* it's reading the third-from-last character, because it doesn't know how long the string is until it's finished reading it. It might not be immediately clear whether such a DFA is even possible.

However, if we relax the determinism constraints and allow the rulebook to contain multiple rules (or no rules at all) for a given state and input, we can design a machine that does the job:

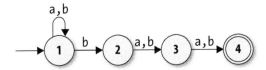

This state machine, a *nondeterministic finite automaton* (NFA), no longer has exactly one execution path for each sequence of inputs. When it's in state 1 and reads b as input, it's possible for it to follow a rule that keeps it in state 1, but it's also possible for it to follow a different rule that takes it into state 2 instead. Conversely, once it gets into state 4, it has no rules to follow and therefore no way to read any more input. A DFA's next state is always completely determined by its current state and its input, but an NFA sometimes has more than one possibility for which state to move into next, and sometimes none at all.

A DFA accepts a string if reading the characters and blindly following the rules causes the machine to end up in an accept state, so what does it mean for an NFA to accept or reject a string? The natural answer is that a string is accepted if there's *some* way for the NFA to end up in an accept state by following some of its rules—that is, if finishing in an accept state is *possible*, even if it's not inevitable.

For example, this NFA accepts the string 'baa', because, starting at state 1, the rules say there is a way for the machine to read a b and move into state 2, then read an a and move into state 3, and finally read another a and finish in state 4, which is an accept state. It also accepts the string 'bbbbb', because it's possible for the NFA to initially follow a different rule and stay in state 1 while reading the first two bs, and only use the rule for moving into state 2 when reading the third b, which then lets it read the rest of the string and finish in state 4 as before.

On the other hand, there's no way for it to read 'abb' and end up in state 4—depending on which rules it follows, it can only end up in state 1, 2, or 3—so 'abb' is not accepted by this NFA. Neither is 'bbabb', which can only ever get as far as state 3; if it goes straight into state 2 when reading the first b, it will end up in state 4 too early, with two characters still left to read but no more rules to follow.

The collection of strings that are accepted by a particular machine is called a *language*: we say that the machine *recognizes* that language. Not all possible languages have a DFA or NFA that can recognize them (see Chapter 4 for more information), but those languages that can be recognized by finite automata are called *regular languages*.

Relaxing the determinism constraints has produced an imaginary machine that is very different from the real, deterministic computers we're familiar with. An NFA deals in possibilities rather than certainties; we talk about its behavior in terms of what *can* happen rather than what *will* happen. This seems powerful, but how can such a machine work in the real world? At first glance it looks like a real implementation of an NFA would need some kind of foresight in order to know which of several possibilities to choose while it reads input: to stand a chance of accepting a string, our example NFA must stay in state 1 until it reads the third-from-last character, but it has no way of knowing how many more characters it will receive. How can we simulate an exciting machine like this in boring, deterministic Ruby?

The key to simulating an NFA on a deterministic computer is to find a way to explore *all possible executions* of the machine. This brute-force approach eliminates the spooky foresight that would be required to simulate only one possible execution by somehow making all the right decisions along the way. When an NFA reads a character, there are only ever a finite number of possibilities for what it can do next, so we can simulate the nondeterminism by somehow trying all of them and seeing whether any of them ultimately allows it to reach an accept state.

We could do this by recursively trying all possibilities: each time the simulated NFA reads a character and there's more than one applicable rule, follow one of those rules and try reading the rest of the input; if that doesn't leave the machine in an accept state, then go back into the earlier state, rewind the input to its earlier position, and try again by following a different rule; repeat until some choice of rules leads to an accept state, or until all possible choices have been tried without success.

Another strategy is to simulate all possibilities in parallel by spawning new threads every time the machine has more than one rule it can follow next, effectively copying the simulated NFA so that each copy can try a different rule to see how it pans out. All those threads can be run at once, each reading from its own copy of the input string, and if any thread ends up with a machine that's read every character and stopped in an accept state, then we can say the string has been accepted.

Both of these implementations are feasible, but they're a bit complicated and inefficient. Our DFA simulation was simple and could read individual characters while constantly reporting back on whether the machine is in an accept state, so it would be nice to simulate an NFA in a way that gives us the same simplicity and transparency.

Fortunately, there's an easy way to simulate an NFA without needing to rewind our progress, spawn threads, or know all the input characters in advance. In fact, just as we simulated a single DFA by keeping track of its current state, we can simulate a single NFA by keeping track of all its *possible* current states. This is simpler and more efficient than simulating multiple NFAs that go off in different directions, and it turns out to achieve the same thing in the end. If we did simulate many separate machines, then all we'd care about is what state each of them was in, but any machines in the same state are completely indistinguishable,[2] so we don't lose anything by collapsing all those

---

2. A finite automaton has no record of its own history and no storage aside from its current state, so two identical machines in the same state are interchangeable for any purpose.

possibilities down into a single machine and asking "which states *could* it be in by now?" instead.

For example, let's walk through what happens to our example NFA as it reads the string 'bab':

- Before the NFA has read any input, it's definitely in state 1, its start state.
- It reads the first character, b. From state 1, there's one b rule that lets the NFA stay in state 1 and another b rule that takes it to state 2, so we know it can be in either state 1 or 2 afterward. Neither of those is an accept state, which tells us there's no possible way for the NFA to reach an accept state by reading the string 'b'.
- It reads the second character, a. If it's in state 1 then there's only one a rule it can follow, which will keep it in state 1; if it's in state 2, it'll have to follow the a rule that leads to state 3. It must end up in state 1 or 3, and again, these aren't accept states, so there's no way the string 'ba' can be accepted by this machine.
- It reads the third character, b. If it's in state 1 then, as before it can stay in state 1 or go to state 2; if it's in state 3, then it must go to state 4.
- Now we know that it's possible for the NFA to be in state 1, state 2, or state 4 after reading the whole input string. State 4 *is* an accept state, and our simulation shows that there must be *some* way for the machine to reach state 4 by reading that string, so the NFA *does* accept 'bab'.

This simulation strategy is easy to turn into code. First we need a rulebook suitable for storing an NFA's rules. A DFA rulebook always returns a single state when we ask it where the DFA should go next after reading a particular character while in a specific state, but an NFA rulebook needs to answer a different question: when an NFA is possibly in one of several states, and it reads a particular character, what states can it possibly be in next? The implementation looks like this:

```
require 'set'

class NFARulebook < Struct.new(:rules)
  def next_states(states, character)
    states.flat_map { |state| follow_rules_for(state, character) }.to_set
  end

  def follow_rules_for(state, character)
    rules_for(state, character).map(&:follow)
  end

  def rules_for(state, character)
    rules.select { |rule| rule.applies_to?(state, character) }
  end
end
```

We're using the Set class, from Ruby's standard library, to store the collection of possible states returned by #next_states. We could have used an Array, but Set has three useful features:

1. It automatically eliminates duplicate elements. Set[1, 2, 2, 3, 3, 3] is equal to Set[1, 2, 3].

2. It ignores the order of elements. Set[3, 2, 1] is equal to Set[1, 2, 3].

3. It provides standard set operations like intersection (#&), union (#+), and subset testing (#subset?).

The first feature is useful because it doesn't make sense to say "the NFA is in state 3 or state 3," and returning a Set makes sure we never include any duplicates. The other two features will be useful later.

We can create a nondeterministic rulebook and ask it questions:

```
>> rulebook = NFARulebook.new([
     FARule.new(1, 'a', 1), FARule.new(1, 'b', 1), FARule.new(1, 'b', 2),
     FARule.new(2, 'a', 3), FARule.new(2, 'b', 3),
     FARule.new(3, 'a', 4), FARule.new(3, 'b', 4)
   ])
=> #<struct NFARulebook rules=[…]>
>> rulebook.next_states(Set[1], 'b')
=> #<Set: {1, 2}>
>> rulebook.next_states(Set[1, 2], 'a')
=> #<Set: {1, 3}>
>> rulebook.next_states(Set[1, 3], 'b')
=> #<Set: {1, 2, 4}>
```

The next step is to implement an NFA class to represent the simulated machine:

```
class NFA < Struct.new(:current_states, :accept_states, :rulebook)
  def accepting?
    (current_states & accept_states).any?
  end
end
```

NFA#accepting? works by checking whether there are any states in the intersection between current_states and accept_states—that is, whether any of the possible current states is also one of the accept states.

This NFA class is very similar to our DFA class from earlier. The difference is that it has a set of possible current_states instead of a single definite current_state, so it'll say it's in an accept state if any of its current_states is an accept state:

```
>> NFA.new(Set[1], [4], rulebook).accepting?
=> false
>> NFA.new(Set[1, 2, 4], [4], rulebook).accepting?
=> true
```

As with the DFA class, we can implement a #read_character method for reading a single character of input, and a #read_string method for reading several in sequence:

```ruby
class NFA
  def read_character(character)
    self.current_states = rulebook.next_states(current_states, character)
  end

  def read_string(string)
    string.chars.each do |character|
      read_character(character)
    end
  end
end
```

These methods really are almost identical to their DFA counterparts; we're just saying current_states and next_states in #read_character instead of current_state and next_state.

That's the hard work over with. Now we're able to start a simulated NFA, pass characters in, and ask whether the input so far has been accepted:

```ruby
>> nfa = NFA.new(Set[1], [4], rulebook); nfa.accepting?
=> false
>> nfa.read_character('b'); nfa.accepting?
=> false
>> nfa.read_character('a'); nfa.accepting?
=> false
>> nfa.read_character('b'); nfa.accepting?
=> true
>> nfa = NFA.new(Set[1], [4], rulebook)
=> #<struct NFA current_states=#<Set: {1}>, accept_states=[4], rulebook=…>
>> nfa.accepting?
=> false
>> nfa.read_string('bbbbb'); nfa.accepting?
=> true
```

As we saw with the DFA class, it's convenient to use an NFADesign object to automatically manufacture new NFA instances on demand rather than creating them manually:

```ruby
class NFADesign < Struct.new(:start_state, :accept_states, :rulebook)
  def accepts?(string)
    to_nfa.tap { |nfa| nfa.read_string(string) }.accepting?
  end

  def to_nfa
    NFA.new(Set[start_state], accept_states, rulebook)
  end
end
```

This makes it easier to check different strings against the same NFA:

```ruby
>> nfa_design = NFADesign.new(1, [4], rulebook)
=> #<struct NFADesign start_state=1, accept_states=[4], rulebook=…>
>> nfa_design.accepts?('bab')
=> true
```

```
>> nfa_design.accepts?('bbbbb')
=> true
>> nfa_design.accepts?('bbabb')
=> false
```

And that's it: we've successfully built a simple implementation of an unusual nonde-terministic machine by simulating all of its possible executions. Nondeterminism is a convenient tool for designing more sophisticated finite automata, so it's fortunate that NFAs are usable in practice rather than just a theoretical curiosity.

Free Moves

We've seen how relaxing the determinism constraints gives us new ways of designing machines without sacrificing our ability to implement them. What else can we safely relax to give ourselves more design freedom?

It's easy to design a DFA that accepts strings of as whose length is a multiple of two ('aa', 'aaaa'...):

But how can we design a machine that accepts strings whose length is a multiple of *two or three*? We know that nondeterminism gives a machine more than one execution path to follow, so perhaps we can design an NFA that has one "multiple of two" path and one "multiple of three" path. A naïve attempt might look like this:

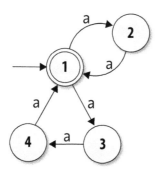

The idea here is for the NFA to move between states 1 and 2 to accept strings like 'aa' and 'aaaa', and between states 1, 3, and 4 to accept strings like 'aaa' and 'aaaaaaaaa'. That works fine, but the problem is that the machine also accepts the string 'aaaaa', because it can move from state 1 to state 2 and back to 1 when reading the first two characters, and then move through states 3, 4, and back to 1 when reading the next three, ending up in an accept state even though the string's length is not a multiple of two or three.[3]

Again it may not be immediately obvious whether an NFA can do this job at all, but we can address the problem by introducing another machine feature called *free moves*. These are rules that the machine may spontaneously follow without reading any input, and they help here because they give the NFA an initial choice between two separate groups of states:

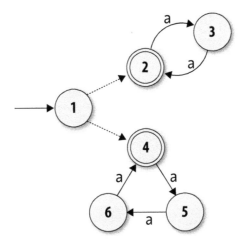

The free moves are shown by the dotted unlabeled arrows from state 1 to states 2 and 4. This machine can still accept the string 'aaaa' by spontaneously moving into state 2, and then moving between states 2 and 3 as it reads the input, and likewise for 'aaaaaaaaa' if it begins with a free move into state 4. Now, though, there is no way for it to accept the string 'aaaaa': in any possible execution, it must begin by committing to a free move into either state 2 or state 4, and once it's gone one way, there's no route back again. Once it's in state 2, it can only accept a string whose length is a multiple of 2, and likewise once it's in state 4, it can only accept a string whose length is a multiple of 3.

How do we support free moves in our Ruby NFA simulation? Well, this new choice between staying in state 1, spontaneously moving into state 2, or spontaneously moving into state 4 is not really any stranger than the nondeterminism we already have, and our implementation can handle it in a similar way. We already have the idea of a simulated machine having many possible states at once, so we just need to broaden those possible states to include any that are reachable by performing one or more free moves. In this case, the machine starting in state 1 really means that it can be in state 1, 2, or 4 before it's read any input.

First we need a way to represent free moves in Ruby. The easiest way is to use normal FARule instances with a nil where a character should be. Our existing implementation

---

3. This NFA actually accepts any string of a characters except for the single-character string 'a'.

of NFARulebook will treat nil like any other character, so we can ask "from state 1, what states can we get to by performing one free move?" (instead of "...by reading one a character?"):

```
>> rulebook = NFARulebook.new([
     FARule.new(1, nil, 2), FARule.new(1, nil, 4),
     FARule.new(2, 'a', 3),
     FARule.new(3, 'a', 2),
     FARule.new(4, 'a', 5),
     FARule.new(5, 'a', 6),
     FARule.new(6, 'a', 4)
   ])
=> #<struct NFARulebook rules=[…]>
>> rulebook.next_states(Set[1], nil)
=> #<Set: {2, 4}>
```

Next we need some helper code for finding all the states that can be reached by following free moves from a particular set of states. This code will have to follow free moves repeatedly, because an NFA can spontaneously change states as many times as it likes as long as there are free moves leading from its current state. A method on the NFARu lebook class is a convenient place to put it:

```
class NFARulebook
  def follow_free_moves(states)
    more_states = next_states(states, nil)

    if more_states.subset?(states)
      states
    else
      follow_free_moves(states + more_states)
    end
  end
end
```

NFARulebook#follow_free_moves works by recursively looking for more and more states that can be reached from a given set of states by following free moves. When it can't find any more—that is, when every state found by next_states(states, nil) is already in states—it returns all the states it's found.[4]

This code correctly identifies the possible states of our NFA before it's read any input:

```
>> rulebook.follow_free_moves(Set[1])
=> #<Set: {1, 2, 4}>
```

Now we can bake this free move support into NFA by overriding the existing implementation of NFA#current_states (as provided by Struct). Our new implementation will hook into NFARulebook#follow_free_moves and ensure that the possible current states of the automaton always include any states that are reachable via free moves:

---

4. Technically speaking, this process computes a *fixed point* of the "add more states by following free moves" function.

```
class NFA
  def current_states
    rulebook.follow_free_moves(super)
  end
end
```

Since all other NFA methods access the set of possible current states by calling the #current_states method, this transparently provides support for free moves without having to change the rest of NFA's code.

That's it. Now our simulation supports free moves, and we can see which strings are accepted by our NFA:

```
>> nfa_design = NFADesign.new(1, [2, 4], rulebook)
=> #<struct NFADesign …>
>> nfa_design.accepts?('aa')
=> true
>> nfa_design.accepts?('aaa')
=> true
>> nfa_design.accepts?('aaaaa')
=> false
>> nfa_design.accepts?('aaaaaa')
=> true
```

So free moves are pretty straightforward to implement, and they give us extra design freedom on top of what nondeterminism already provides.

 Some of the terminology in this chapter is unconventional. The characters read by finite automata are usually called *symbols*, the rules for moving between states are called *transitions*, and the collection of rules making up a machine is called a *transition function* (or sometimes *transition relation* for NFAs) rather than a rulebook. Because the mathematical symbol for the empty string is the Greek letter ε (epsilon), an NFA with free moves is known as an NFA-ε, and free moves themselves are usually called *ε-transitions*.

Regular Expressions

We've seen that nondeterminism and free moves make finite automata more expressive without interfering with our ability to simulate them. In this section, we'll look at an important practical application of these features: regular expression matching.

Regular expressions provide a language for writing textual *patterns* against which strings may be matched. Some example regular expressions are:

- hello, which only matches the string 'hello'
- hello|goodbye, which matches the strings 'hello' and 'goodbye'
- (hello)*, which matches the strings 'hello', 'hellohello', 'hellohellohello', and so on, as well as the empty string

In this chapter, we'll always think of a regular expression as matching an *entire* string. Real-world implementations of regular expressions typically use them for matching *parts* of strings, with extra syntax needed if we want to specify that an entire string should be matched.

For example, our regular expression hello|goodbye would be written in Ruby as /\A(hello|goodbye)\z/ to make sure that any match is anchored to the beginning (\A) and end (\z) of the string.

Given a regular expression and a string, how do we write a program to decide whether the string matches that expression? Most programming languages, Ruby included, already have regular expression support built in, but how does that support work? How would we implement regular expressions in Ruby if the language didn't already have them?

It turns out that finite automata are perfectly suited to this job. As we'll see, it's possible to convert any regular expression into an equivalent NFA—every string matched by the regular expression is accepted by the NFA, and vice versa—and then match a string by feeding it to a simulation of that NFA to see whether it gets accepted. In the language of Chapter 2, we can think of this as providing a sort of denotational semantics for regular expressions: we may not know how to execute a regular expression directly, but we can show how to denote it as an NFA, and because we have an operational semantics for NFAs ("change state by reading characters and following rules"), we can execute the denotation to achieve the same result.

Syntax

Let's be precise about what we mean by "regular expression." To get us off the ground, here are two kinds of extremely simple regular expression that are not built out of anything simpler:

- An empty regular expression. This matches the empty string and nothing else.
- A regular expression containing a single, literal character. For example, a and b are regular expressions that match only the strings 'a' and 'b' respectively.

Once we have these simple kinds of pattern, there are three ways we can combine them to build more complex expressions:

- Concatenate two patterns. We can concatenate the regular expressions a and b to get the regular expression ab, which only matches the string 'ab'.
- Choose between two patterns, written by joining them with the | operator. We can join the regular expressions a or b to get the regular expression a|b, which matches the strings 'a' and 'b'.
- Repeat a pattern zero or more times, written by suffixing it with the * operator. We can suffix the regular expression a to get a*, which matches the strings 'a', 'aa', 'aaa', and so on, as well as the empty string '' (i.e., zero repetitions).

Real-world regular expression engines, like the one built into Ruby, support more features than this. In the interests of simplicity, we won't try to implement these extra features, many of which are technically redundant and only provided as a convenience.

For example, omitting the repetition operators ? and + doesn't make an important difference, because their effects—"repeat one or zero times" and "repeat one or more times," respectively—are easy enough to achieve with the features we already have: the regular expression ab? can be rewritten as ab|a, and the pattern ab+ matches the same strings as abb*. The same is true of other convenience features like counted repetition (e.g., a{2,5}) and character classes (e.g., [abc]).

More advanced features like capture groups, backreferences and lookahead/lookbehind assertions are outside of the scope of this chapter.

To implement this syntax in Ruby, we can define a class for each kind of regular expression and use instances of those classes to represent the abstract syntax tree of any regular expression, just as we did for SIMPLE expressions in Chapter 2:

```ruby
module Pattern
  def bracket(outer_precedence)
    if precedence < outer_precedence
      '(' + to_s + ')'
    else
      to_s
    end
  end

  def inspect
    "/#{self}/"
  end
end

class Empty
  include Pattern

  def to_s
    ''
  end

  def precedence
    3
  end
end

class Literal < Struct.new(:character)
  include Pattern

  def to_s
    character
  end
```

```ruby
    def precedence
      3
    end
  end

  class Concatenate < Struct.new(:first, :second)
    include Pattern

    def to_s
      [first, second].map { |pattern| pattern.bracket(precedence) }.join
    end

    def precedence
      1
    end
  end

  class Choose < Struct.new(:first, :second)
    include Pattern

    def to_s
      [first, second].map { |pattern| pattern.bracket(precedence) }.join('|')
    end

    def precedence
      0
    end
  end

  class Repeat < Struct.new(:pattern)
    include Pattern

    def to_s
      pattern.bracket(precedence) + '*'
    end

    def precedence
      2
    end
  end
```

In the same way that multiplication binds its arguments more tightly than addition in arithmetic expressions (1 + 2 × 3 equals 7, not 9), the convention for the concrete syntax of regular expressions is for the * operator to bind more tightly than concatenation, which in turn binds more tightly than the | operator. For example, in the regular expression abc* it's understood that the * applies only to the c ('abc', 'abcc', 'abccc'...), and to make it apply to all of abc ('abc', 'abcabc'...), we'd need to add brackets and write (abc)* instead.

The syntax classes' implementations of #to_s, along with the Pat tern#bracket method, deal with automatically inserting these brackets when necessary so that we can view a simple string representation of an abstract syntax tree without losing information about its structure.

These classes let us manually build trees to represent regular expressions:

```
>> pattern =
    Repeat.new(
      Choose.new(
        Concatenate.new(Literal.new('a'), Literal.new('b')),
        Literal.new('a')
      )
    )
=> /(ab|a)*/
```

Of course, in a real implementation, we'd use a parser to build these trees instead of constructing them by hand; see "Parsing" on page 92 for instructions on how to do this.

Semantics

Now that we have a way of representing the syntax of a regular expression as a tree of Ruby objects, how can we convert that syntax into an NFA?

We need to decide how instances of each syntax class should be turned into NFAs. The easiest class to convert is Empty, which we should always turn into the one-state NFA that only accepts the empty string:

Similarly, we should turn any literal, single-character pattern into the NFA that only accepts the single-character string containing that character. Here's the NFA for the pattern a:

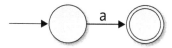

It's easy enough to implement #to_nfa_design methods for Empty and Literal to generate these NFAs:

```ruby
class Empty
  def to_nfa_design
    start_state = Object.new
    accept_states = [start_state]
    rulebook = NFARulebook.new([])

    NFADesign.new(start_state, accept_states, rulebook)
  end
end

class Literal
  def to_nfa_design
    start_state = Object.new
    accept_state = Object.new
    rule = FARule.new(start_state, character, accept_state)
    rulebook = NFARulebook.new([rule])

    NFADesign.new(start_state, [accept_state], rulebook)
  end
end
```

 As mentioned in "Simulation" on page 66, the states of an automaton must be implemented as Ruby objects that can be distinguished from each other. Here, instead of using numbers (i.e., Fixnum instances) as states, we're using freshly created instances of Object.

This is so that each NFA gets its own unique states, which gives us the ability to combine small machines into larger ones without accidentally merging any of their states. If two distinct NFAs both used the Ruby Fixnum object 1 as a state, for example, they couldn't be connected together while keeping those two states separate. We'll want to be able to do that as part of implementing more complex regular expressions.

Similarly, we won't label states on the diagrams any more, so that we don't have to relabel them when we start connecting diagrams together.

We can check that the NFAs generated from Empty and Literal regular expressions accept the strings we want them to:

```
>> nfa_design = Empty.new.to_nfa_design
=> #<struct NFADesign …>
>> nfa_design.accepts?('')
=> true
>> nfa_design.accepts?('a')
=> false
>> nfa_design = Literal.new('a').to_nfa_design
=> #<struct NFADesign …>
>> nfa_design.accepts?('')
=> false
>> nfa_design.accepts?('a')
=> true
>> nfa_design.accepts?('b')
=> false
```

There's an opportunity here to wrap #to_nfa_design in a #matches? method to give patterns a nicer interface:

```
module Pattern
  def matches?(string)
    to_nfa_design.accepts?(string)
  end
end
```

This lets us match patterns directly against strings:

```
>> Empty.new.matches?('a')
=> false
>> Literal.new('a').matches?('a')
=> true
```

Now that we know how to turn simple Empty and Literal regular expressions into NFAs, we need a similar setup for Concatenate, Choose, and Repeat.

Let's begin with Concatenate: if we have two regular expressions that we already know how to turn into NFAs, how can we build an NFA to represent the concatenation of those regular expressions? For example, given that we can turn the single-character regular expressions a and b into NFAs, how do we turn ab into one?

In the ab case, we can connect the two NFAs in sequence, joining them together with a free move, and keeping the second NFA's accept state:

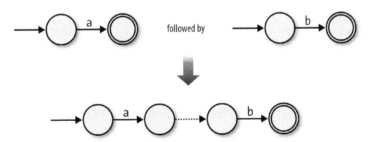

This technique works in other cases too. Any two NFAs can be concatenated by turning every accept state from the first NFA into a nonaccept state and connecting it to the start state of the second NFA with a free move. Once the concatenated machine has read a sequence of inputs that would have put the first NFA into an accept state, it can spontaneously move into a state corresponding to the start state of the second NFA, and then reach an accept state by reading a sequence of inputs that the second NFA would have accepted.

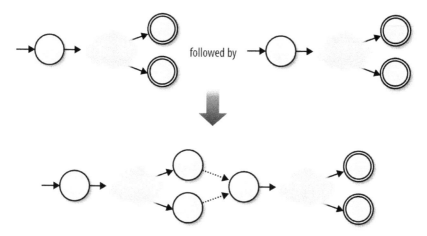

So, the raw ingredients for the combined machine are:

- The start state of the first NFA
- The accept states of the second NFA
- All the rules from both NFAs
- Some extra free moves to connect each of the first NFA's old accept states to the second NFA's old start state

We can turn this idea into an implementation of Concatenate#to_nfa_design:

```
class Concatenate
  def to_nfa_design
    first_nfa_design = first.to_nfa_design
    second_nfa_design = second.to_nfa_design

    start_state = first_nfa_design.start_state
    accept_states = second_nfa_design.accept_states
    rules = first_nfa_design.rulebook.rules + second_nfa_design.rulebook.rules
    extra_rules = first_nfa_design.accept_states.map { |state|
      FARule.new(state, nil, second_nfa_design.start_state)
    }
    rulebook = NFARulebook.new(rules + extra_rules)

    NFADesign.new(start_state, accept_states, rulebook)
```

```
    end
  end
```

This code first converts the first and second regular expressions into NFADesigns, then combines their states and rules in the appropriate way to make a new NFADesign. It works as expected for the simple ab case:

```
>> pattern = Concatenate.new(Literal.new('a'), Literal.new('b'))
=> /ab/
>> pattern.matches?('a')
=> false
>> pattern.matches?('ab')
=> true
>> pattern.matches?('abc')
=> false
```

This conversion process is recursive—Concatenate#to_nfa_design calls #to_nfa_design on other objects—so it also works for more deeply nested cases like the regular expression abc, which contains two concatenations (a concatenated with b concatenated with c):

```
>> pattern =
    Concatenate.new(
      Literal.new('a'),
      Concatenate.new(Literal.new('b'), Literal.new('c'))
    )
=> /abc/
>> pattern.matches?('a')
=> false
>> pattern.matches?('ab')
=> false
>> pattern.matches?('abc')
=> true
```

 This is another example of a denotational semantics being *compositional*: the NFA denotation of a compound regular expression is composed from the denotations of its parts.

We can use a similar strategy to convert a Choose expression into an NFA. In the simplest case, the NFAs for the regular expressions a and b can be combined to build an NFA for the regular expression a|b by adding a new start state and using free moves to connect it to the previous start states of the two original machines:

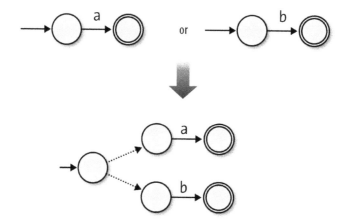

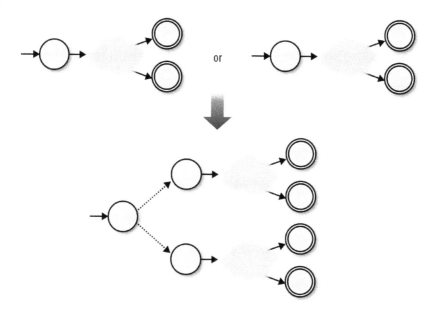

Before the a|b NFA has read any input, it can use a free move to go into either of the original machines' start states, from which point it can read either 'a' or 'b' to reach an accept state. Again, it's just as easy to glue together any two machines by adding a new start state and two free moves:

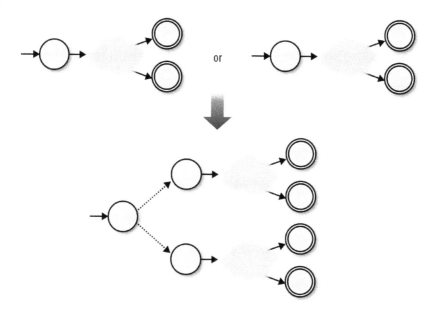

In this case, the ingredients for the combined machine are:

- A new start state
- All the accept states from both NFAs
- All the rules from both NFAs

- Two extra free moves to connect the new start state to each of the NFA's old start states

Again, this is easy to implement as Choose#to_nfa_design:

```
class Choose
  def to_nfa_design
    first_nfa_design = first.to_nfa_design
    second_nfa_design = second.to_nfa_design

    start_state = Object.new
    accept_states = first_nfa_design.accept_states + second_nfa_design.accept_states
    rules = first_nfa_design.rulebook.rules + second_nfa_design.rulebook.rules
    extra_rules = [first_nfa_design, second_nfa_design].map { |nfa_design|
      FARule.new(start_state, nil, nfa_design.start_state)
    }
    rulebook = NFARulebook.new(rules + extra_rules)

    NFADesign.new(start_state, accept_states, rulebook)
  end
end
```

The implementation works nicely:

```
>> pattern = Choose.new(Literal.new('a'), Literal.new('b'))
=> /a|b/
>> pattern.matches?('a')
=> true
>> pattern.matches?('b')
=> true
>> pattern.matches?('c')
=> false
```

And finally, repetition: how can we turn an NFA that matches a string exactly once into an NFA that matches the same string zero or more times? We can build an NFA for a* by starting with the NFA for a and making two additions:

- Add a free move from its accept state to its start state, so it can match more than one 'a'.
- Add a new accepting start state with a free move to the old start state, so it can match the empty string.

Here's how that looks:

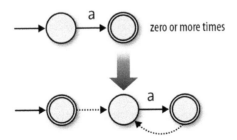

The free move from the old accept state to the old start state allows the machine to match several times instead of just once ('aa', 'aaa', etc.), and the new start state allows it to match the empty string without affecting what other strings it can accept.[5] We can do the same for any NFA as long as we connect each old accept state to the old start state with a free move:

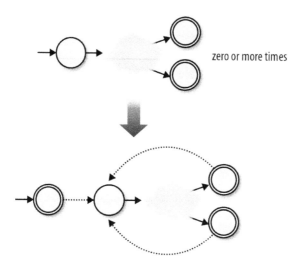

zero or more times

This time we need:

- A new start state, which is also an accept state
- All the accept states from the old NFA
- All the rules from the old NFA
- Some extra free moves to connect each of the old NFA's accept states to its old start state
- Another extra free move to connect the new start state to the old start state

Let's turn that into code:

```
class Repeat
  def to_nfa_design
    pattern_nfa_design = pattern.to_nfa_design

    start_state = Object.new
    accept_states = pattern_nfa_design.accept_states + [start_state]
    rules = pattern_nfa_design.rulebook.rules
    extra_rules =
      pattern_nfa_design.accept_states.map { |accept_state|
```

---

5. In this simple case, we could get away with just turning the original start state into an accept state instead of adding a new one, but in more complex cases (e.g., (a*b)*), that technique can produce a machine that accepts other undesirable strings in addition to the empty string.

```
          FARule.new(accept_state, nil, pattern_nfa_design.start_state)
        } +
        [FARule.new(start_state, nil, pattern_nfa_design.start_state)]
      rulebook = NFARulebook.new(rules + extra_rules)

      NFADesign.new(start_state, accept_states, rulebook)
    end
  end
```

And check that it works:

```
>> pattern = Repeat.new(Literal.new('a'))
=> /a*/
>> pattern.matches?('')
=> true
>> pattern.matches?('a')
=> true
>> pattern.matches?('aaaa')
=> true
>> pattern.matches?('b')
=> false
```

Now that we have #to_nfa_design implementations for each class of regular expression syntax, we can build up complex patterns and use them to match strings:

```
>> pattern =
    Repeat.new(
      Concatenate.new(
        Literal.new('a'),
        Choose.new(Empty.new, Literal.new('b'))
      )
    )
=> /(a(|b))*/
>> pattern.matches?('')
=> true
>> pattern.matches?('a')
=> true
>> pattern.matches?('ab')
=> true
>> pattern.matches?('aba')
=> true
>> pattern.matches?('abab')
=> true
>> pattern.matches?('abaab')
=> true
>> pattern.matches?('abba')
=> false
```

This is a nice result. We began with a syntax for patterns and have now given a semantics for that syntax by showing how to convert any pattern into an NFA, a kind of abstract machine that we already know how to execute. In conjunction with a parser, this gives us a practical way of reading a regular expression and deciding whether it matches a particular string. Free moves are useful for this conversion because they provide an unobtrusive way to glue together smaller machines into larger ones without affecting the behavior of any of the components.

The majority of real-world implementations of regular expressions, like the Onigmo library used by Ruby, don't work by literally compiling patterns into finite automata and simulating their execution. Although it's a fast and efficient way of matching regular expressions against strings, this approach makes it harder to support more advanced features like capture groups and lookahead/lookbehind assertions. Consequently most libraries use some kind of *backtracking algorithm* that deals with regular expressions more directly instead of converting them into finite automata.

Russ Cox's RE2 library (*http://code.google.com/p/re2/*) is a production-quality C++ regular expression implementation that *does* compile patterns into automata,[6] while Pat Shaughnessy has written a detailed blog post (*http://patshaughnessy.net/2012/4/3/exploring-rubys-regular-expression-algorithm*) exploring how Ruby's regular expression algorithm works.

Parsing

We've almost built a complete (albeit basic) regular expression implementation. The only missing piece is a parser for pattern syntax: it would be much more convenient if we could just write (a(|b))* instead of building the abstract syntax tree manually with Repeat.new(Concatenate.new(Literal.new('a'), Choose.new(Empty.new, Literal.new ('b')))). We saw in "Implementing Parsers" on page 58 that it's not difficult to use Treetop to generate a parser that can automatically transform raw syntax into an AST, so let's do that here to finish off our implementation.

Here's a Treetop grammar for simple regular expressions:

```
grammar Pattern
  rule choose
    first:concatenate_or_empty '|' rest:choose {
      def to_ast
        Choose.new(first.to_ast, rest.to_ast)
      end
    }
    /
    concatenate_or_empty
  end

  rule concatenate_or_empty
    concatenate / empty
  end

  rule concatenate
    first:repeat rest:concatenate {
      def to_ast
```

6. RE2's tagline is "an efficient, principled regular expression library," which is difficult to argue with.

```
        Concatenate.new(first.to_ast, rest.to_ast)
      end
    }
    /
    repeat
  end

  rule empty
    '' {
      def to_ast
        Empty.new
      end
    }
  end

  rule repeat
    brackets '*' {
      def to_ast
        Repeat.new(brackets.to_ast)
      end
    }
    /
    brackets
  end

  rule brackets
    '(' choose ')' {
      def to_ast
        choose.to_ast
      end
    }
    /
    literal
  end

  rule literal
    [a-z] {
      def to_ast
        Literal.new(text_value)
      end
    }
  end
end
```

 Again, the order of rules reflects the precedence of each operator: the | operator binds loosest, so the choose rule goes first, with the higher precedence operator rules appearing farther down the grammar.

Now we have all the pieces we need to parse a regular expression, turn it into an abstract syntax tree, and use it to match strings:

```
>> require 'treetop'
=> true
>> Treetop.load('pattern')
=> PatternParser
>> parse_tree = PatternParser.new.parse('(a(|b))*')
=> SyntaxNode+Repeat1+Repeat0 offset=0, "(a(|b))*" (to_ast,brackets):
     SyntaxNode+Brackets1+Brackets0 offset=0, "(a(|b))" (to_ast,choose):
       SyntaxNode offset=0, "("
       SyntaxNode+Concatenate1+Concatenate0 offset=1, "a(|b)" (to_ast,first,rest):
         SyntaxNode+Literal0 offset=1, "a" (to_ast)
         SyntaxNode+Brackets1+Brackets0 offset=2, "(|b)" (to_ast,choose):
           SyntaxNode offset=2, "("
           SyntaxNode+Choose1+Choose0 offset=3, "|b" (to_ast,first,rest):
             SyntaxNode+Empty0 offset=3, "" (to_ast)
             SyntaxNode offset=3, "|"
             SyntaxNode+Literal0 offset=4, "b" (to_ast)
           SyntaxNode offset=5, ")"
       SyntaxNode offset=6, ")"
     SyntaxNode offset=7, "*"
>> pattern = parse_tree.to_ast
=> /(a(|b))*/
>> pattern.matches?('abaab')
=> true
>> pattern.matches?('abba')
=> false
```

Equivalence

This chapter has described the idea of a deterministic state machine and added more features to it: first nondeterminism, which makes it possible to design machines that can follow many possible execution paths instead of a single path, and then free moves, which allow nondeterministic machines to change state without reading any input.

Nondeterminism and free moves make it easier to design finite state machines to perform specific jobs—we've already seen that they're very useful for translating regular expressions into state machines—but do they let us do anything that we can't do with a standard DFA?

Well, it turns out that it's possible to convert any nondeterministic finite automaton into a deterministic one that accepts exactly the same strings. This might be surprising given the extra constraints of a DFA, but it makes sense when we think about the way we simulated the execution of both kinds of machine.

Imagine we have a particular DFA whose behavior we want to simulate. The simulation of this hypothetical DFA reading a particular sequence of characters might go something like this:

- Before the machine has read any input, it's in state 1.

- The machine reads the character 'a', and now it's in state 2.
- The machine reads the character 'b', and now it's in state 3.
- There is no more input, and state 3 is an accept state, so the string 'ab' has been accepted.

There is something slightly subtle going on here: the simulation, which in our case is a Ruby program running on a real computer, is recreating the behavior of the DFA, which is an abstract machine that can't run at all because it doesn't exist. Every time the imaginary DFA changes state, so does the simulation that we are running—that's what makes it a simulation.

It's hard to see this separation, because both the DFA and the simulation are deterministic and their states match up exactly: when the DFA is in state 2, the simulation is in a state that means "the DFA is in state 2." In our Ruby simulation, this *simulation state* is effectively the value of the DFA instance's current_state attribute.

Despite the extra overhead of dealing with nondeterminism and free moves, the simulation of a hypothetical NFA reading some characters doesn't look hugely different:

- Before the machine has read any input, it's possible for it to be in either state 1 or state 3.[7]
- The machine reads the character c, and now it's possible for it to be in one of states 1, 3, or 4.
- The machine reads the character d, and now it's possible for it to be in either state 2 or state 5.
- There is no more input, and state 5 is an accept state, so the string 'cd' has been accepted.

This time it's easier to see that the state of the simulation is not the same thing as the state of the NFA. In fact, at every point of this simulation we are never certain which state the NFA is in, but the simulation itself is still deterministic because it has states that accommodate that uncertainty. When it's *possible* for the NFA to be in one of states 1, 3 or 4, we are *certain* that the simulation is in the single state that means "the NFA is in state 1, 3, or 4."

The only real difference between these two examples is that the DFA simulation moves from one current state to another, whereas the NFA simulation moves from one current *set of possible states* to another. Although an NFA's rulebook can be nondeterministic, the decision about which possible states follow from the current ones for a given input is always completely deterministic.

This determinism means that we can always construct a DFA whose job is to simulate a particular NFA. The DFA will have a state to represent each set of possible states of

---

7. Although an NFA only has one start state, free moves can make other states possible before any input has been read.

the NFA, and the rules between these DFA states will correspond to the ways in which a deterministic simulation of the NFA can move between its sets of possible states. The resulting DFA will be able to completely simulate the behavior of the NFA, and as long as we choose the right accept states for the DFA—as per our Ruby implementation, these will be any states that correspond to the NFA *possibly* being in an accept state—it'll accept the same strings too.

Let's try doing the conversion for a specific NFA. Take this one:

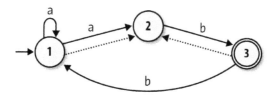

It's possible for this NFA to be in state 1 or state 2 before it has read any input (state 1 is the start state, and state 2 is reachable via a free move), so the simulation will begin in a state we can call "1 or 2." From this starting point the simulation will end up in different states depending on whether it reads a or b:

- If it reads an a, the simulation will remain in state "1 or 2": when the NFA's in state 1 it can read an a and either follow the rule that keeps it in state 1 or the rule that takes it into state 2, while from state 2, it has no way of reading an a at all.

- If it reads a b, it's possible for the NFA to end up in state 2 or state 3—from state 1, it can't read a b, but from state 2, it can move into state 3 and potentially take a free move back into state 2—so we'll say the simulation moves into a state called "2 or 3" when the input is b.

By thinking through the behavior of a simulation of the NFA, we've begun to construct a state machine for that simulation:

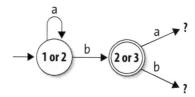

 "2 or 3" is an accept state for the simulation, because state 3 is an accept state for the NFA.

We can continue this process of discovering new states of the simulation until there are no more to discover, which must happen eventually because there are only a limited number of possible combinations of the original NFA's states.[8] By repeating the discovery process for our example NFA, we find that there are only four distinct combinations of states that its simulation can encounter by starting at "1 or 2" and reading sequences of as and bs:

If the NFA is in state(s)...	and reads the character...	it can end up in state(s)...
1 or 2	a	1 or 2
	b	2 or 3
2 or 3	a	none
	b	1, 2, or 3
None	a	none
	b	none
1, 2, or 3	a	1 or 2
	b	1, 2, or 3

This table completely describes a DFA, pictured below, that accepts the same strings as the original NFA:

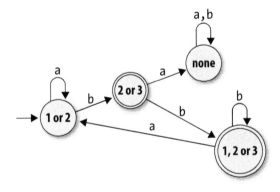

 This DFA only has one more state than the NFA we started with, and for some NFAs, this process can produce a DFA with *fewer* states than the original machine. In the worst case, though, an NFA with n states may require a DFA with 2^n states, because there are a total of 2^n possible combinations of n states—think of representing each combination as a different n-bit number, where the nth bit indicates whether state n is included in that combination—and the simulation might need to be able to visit all of them instead of just a few.

8. The worst-case scenario for a simulation of a three-state NFA is "1," "2," "3," "1 or 2," "1 or 3," "2 or 3," "1, 2, or 3" and "none."

Let's try implementing this NFA-to-DFA conversion in Ruby. Our strategy is to introduce a new class, NFASimulation, for collecting information about the simulation of an NFA and then assembling that information into a DFA. An instance of NFASimulation can be created for a specific NFADesign and will ultimately provide a #to_dfa_design method for converting it to an equivalent DFADesign.

We already have an NFA class that can simulate an NFA, so NFASimulation can work by creating and driving instances of NFA to find out how they respond to all possible inputs. Before starting on NFASimulation, let's go back to NFADesign and add an optional "current states" parameter to NFADesign#to_nfa so that we can build an NFA instance with any set of current states, not just the NFADesign's start state:

```
class NFADesign
  def to_nfa(current_states = Set[start_state])
    NFA.new(current_states, accept_states, rulebook)
  end
end
```

Previously, the simulation of an NFA could only begin in its start state, but this new parameter gives us a way of jumping in at any other point:

```
>> rulebook = NFARulebook.new([
     FARule.new(1, 'a', 1), FARule.new(1, 'a', 2), FARule.new(1, nil, 2),
     FARule.new(2, 'b', 3),
     FARule.new(3, 'b', 1), FARule.new(3, nil, 2)
   ])
=> #<struct NFARulebook rules=[…]>
>> nfa_design = NFADesign.new(1, [3], rulebook)
=> #<struct NFADesign start_state=1, accept_states=[3], rulebook=…>
>> nfa_design.to_nfa.current_states
=> #<Set: {1, 2}>
>> nfa_design.to_nfa(Set[2]).current_states
=> #<Set: {2}>
>> nfa_design.to_nfa(Set[3]).current_states
=> #<Set: {3, 2}>
```

 The NFA class automatically takes account of free moves—we can see that when our NFA is started in state 3, it's already possible for it to be in state 2 or 3 before it has read any input—so we won't need to do anything special in NFASimulation to support them.

Now we can create an NFA in any set of possible states, feed it a character, and see what states it might end up in, which is a crucial step for converting an NFA into a DFA. When our NFA is in state 2 or 3 and reads a b, what states can it be in afterward?

```
>> nfa = nfa_design.to_nfa(Set[2, 3])
=> #<struct NFA current_states=#<Set: {2, 3}>, accept_states=[3], rulebook=…>
>> nfa.read_character('b'); nfa.current_states
=> #<Set: {3, 1, 2}>
```

The answer: state 1, 2, or 3, as we already discovered during the manual conversion process. (Remember that the order of elements in a Set doesn't matter.)

Let's use this idea by creating the NFASimulation class and giving it a method to calculate how the state of the simulation will change in response to a particular input. We're thinking of the state of the simulation as being the current set of possible states for the NFA (e.g., "1, 2, or 3"), so we can write a #next_state method that takes a simulation state and a character, feeds that character to an NFA corresponding to that state, and gets a new state back out by inspecting the NFA afterward:

```
class NFASimulation < Struct.new(:nfa_design)
  def next_state(state, character)
    nfa_design.to_nfa(state).tap { |nfa|
      nfa.read_character(character)
    }.current_states
  end
end
```

 It's easy to get confused between the two kinds of state we're talking about here. A single simulation state (the state parameter of NFASimulation#next_state) is a set of many NFA states, which is why we can provide it as NFADesign#to_nfa's current_states argument.

This gives us a convenient way to explore the different states of the simulation:

```
>> simulation = NFASimulation.new(nfa_design)
=> #<struct NFASimulation nfa_design=…>
>> simulation.next_state(Set[1, 2], 'a')
=> #<Set: {1, 2}>
>> simulation.next_state(Set[1, 2], 'b')
=> #<Set: {3, 2}>
>> simulation.next_state(Set[3, 2], 'b')
=> #<Set: {1, 3, 2}>
>> simulation.next_state(Set[1, 3, 2], 'b')
=> #<Set: {1, 3, 2}>
>> simulation.next_state(Set[1, 3, 2], 'a')
=> #<Set: {1, 2}>
```

Now we need a way to systematically explore the simulation states and record our discoveries as the states and rules of a DFA. We intend to use each simulation state directly as a DFA state, so the first step is to implement NFASimulation#rules_for, which builds all the rules leading from a particular simulation state by using #next_state to discover the destination of each rule. "All the rules" means a rule for each possible input character, so we also define an NFARulebook#alphabet helper method to tell us what characters the original NFA can read:

```
class NFARulebook
  def alphabet
    rules.map(&:character).compact.uniq
  end
end
```

```
class NFASimulation
  def rules_for(state)
    nfa_design.rulebook.alphabet.map { |character|
      FARule.new(state, character, next_state(state, character))
    }
  end
end
```

As intended, this lets us see how different inputs will take the simulation between different states:

```
>> rulebook.alphabet
=> ["a", "b"]
>> simulation.rules_for(Set[1, 2])
=> [
     #<FARule #<Set: {1, 2}> --a--> #<Set: {1, 2}>>,
     #<FARule #<Set: {1, 2}> --b--> #<Set: {3, 2}>>
   ]
>> simulation.rules_for(Set[3, 2])
=> [
     #<FARule #<Set: {3, 2}> --a--> #<Set: {}>>,
     #<FARule #<Set: {3, 2}> --b--> #<Set: {1, 3, 2}>>
   ]
```

The #rules_for method gives us a way of exploring outward from a known simulation state and discovering new ones, and by doing this repeatedly, we can find all possible simulation states. We can do this with an NFASimulation#discover_states_and_rules method, which recursively finds more states in a similar way to NFARulebook#fol low_free_moves:

```
class NFASimulation
  def discover_states_and_rules(states)
    rules = states.flat_map { |state| rules_for(state) }
    more_states = rules.map(&:follow).to_set

    if more_states.subset?(states)
      [states, rules]
    else
      discover_states_and_rules(states + more_states)
    end
  end
end
```

 #discover_states_and_rules doesn't care about the underlying structure of a simulation state, only that it can be used as an argument to
#rules_for, but as programmers, we have another opportunity for con-
fusion. The states and more_states variables are sets of simulation
states, but we know that each simulation state is itself a set of NFA states,
so states and more_states are actually *sets of sets* of NFA states.

Initially, we only know about a single state of the simulation: the set of possible states of our NFA when we put it into its start state. #discover_states_and_rules explores outward from this starting point, eventually finding all four states and eight rules of the simulation:

```
>> start_state = nfa_design.to_nfa.current_states
=> #<Set: {1, 2}>
>> simulation.discover_states_and_rules(Set[start_state])
=> [
    #<Set: {
      #<Set: {1, 2}>,
      #<Set: {3, 2}>,
      #<Set: {}>,
      #<Set: {1, 3, 2}>
    }>,
    [
      #<FARule #<Set: {1, 2}> --a--> #<Set: {1, 2}>>,
      #<FARule #<Set: {1, 2}> --b--> #<Set: {3, 2}>>,
      #<FARule #<Set: {3, 2}> --a--> #<Set: {}>>,
      #<FARule #<Set: {3, 2}> --b--> #<Set: {1, 3, 2}>>,
      #<FARule #<Set: {}> --a--> #<Set: {}>>,
      #<FARule #<Set: {}> --b--> #<Set: {}>>,
      #<FARule #<Set: {1, 3, 2}> --a--> #<Set: {1, 2}>>,
      #<FARule #<Set: {1, 3, 2}> --b--> #<Set: {1, 3, 2}>>
    ]
  ]
```

The final thing we need to know for each simulation state is whether it should be treated as an accept state, but that's easy to check by asking the NFA at that point in the simulation:

```
>> nfa_design.to_nfa(Set[1, 2]).accepting?
=> false
>> nfa_design.to_nfa(Set[2, 3]).accepting?
=> true
```

Now that we have all the pieces of the simulation DFA, we just need an NFASimula tion#to_dfa_design method to wrap them up neatly as an instance of DFADesign:

```
class NFASimulation
  def to_dfa_design
    start_state   = nfa_design.to_nfa.current_states
    states, rules = discover_states_and_rules(Set[start_state])
    accept_states = states.select { |state| nfa_design.to_nfa(state).accepting? }

    DFADesign.new(start_state, accept_states, DFARulebook.new(rules))
  end
end
```

And that's it. We can build an NFASimulation instance with any NFA and turn it into a DFA that accepts the same strings:

```
>> dfa_design = simulation.to_dfa_design
=> #<struct DFADesign …>
>> dfa_design.accepts?('aaa')
=> false
>> dfa_design.accepts?('aab')
=> true
```

```
>> dfa_design.accepts?('bbbabb')
=> true
```

Excellent!

At the beginning of this section, we asked whether the extra features of NFAs let us do anything that we can't do with a DFA. It's clear now that the answer is no, because if any NFA can be turned into a DFA that does the same job, NFAs can't possibly have any extra power. Nondeterminism and free moves are just a convenient repackaging of what a DFA can already do, like syntactic sugar in a programming language, rather than new capabilities that take us beyond what's possible within the constraints of determinism.

It's theoretically interesting that adding more features to a simple machine didn't make it fundamentally any more capable, but it's also useful in practice, because a DFA is easier to simulate than an NFA: there's only a single current state to keep track of, and a DFA is simple enough to implement directly in hardware, or as machine code that uses program locations as states and conditional branch instructions as rules. This means that a regular expression implementation can convert a pattern into first an NFA and then a DFA, resulting in a very simple machine that can be simulated quickly and efficiently.

DFA Minimization

Some DFAs have the property of being *minimal*, which means there's no way to design a DFA with fewer states that will accept the same strings. The NFA-to-DFA conversion process can sometimes produce nonminimal DFAs that contain redundant states, but there's an elegant way to eliminate this redundancy, known as *Brzozowski's algorithm*:

1. Begin with your nonminimal DFA.
2. Reverse all of the rules. Visually, this means that every arrow in the machine's diagram stays in the same place but points backward; in code terms, every `FARule.new(state, character, next_state)` is replaced with `FARule.new(next_state, character, state)`. Reversing the rules usually breaks the determinism constraints, so now you have an NFA.
3. Exchange the roles of start and accept states: the start state becomes an accept state, and each of the accept states becomes a start state. (You can't directly convert all the accept states into start states because an NFA can only have one start state, but you can get the same effect by creating a new start state and connecting it to each of the old accept states with a free move.)
4. Convert this reversed NFA to a DFA in the usual way.

Surprisingly, the resulting DFA is guaranteed to be minimal and contain no redundant states. The unhappy downside is that it will only accept *reversed* versions of the original DFA's strings: if our original DFA accepted the strings 'ab', 'aab', 'aaab', and so on, the minimized DFA will accept strings of the form 'ba', 'baa', and 'baaa'. The trick is to fix this by simply performing the whole procedure a second time, beginning with the reversed DFA and ending up with a double-reversed DFA, which is again guaranteed to be minimal but this time accepts the same strings as the machine we started with.

It's nice to have an automatic way of eliminating redundancy in a design, but interestingly, a minimized DFA is also *canonical*: any two DFAs that accept exactly the same strings will minimize to the same design, so we can check whether two DFAs are equivalent by minimizing them and comparing the resulting machine designs to see if they have the same structure.[9] This in turn gives us an elegant way of checking whether two regular expressions are equivalent: if we convert two patterns that match the same strings (e.g., ab(ab)* and a(ba)*b) into NFAs, convert those NFAs into DFAs, then minimize both DFAs with Brzozowski's algorithm, we'll end up with two identical-looking machines.

9. Solving this *graph isomorphism problem* requires a clever algorithm in itself, but informally, it's easy enough to look at two machine diagrams and decide whether they're "the same."

## CHAPTER 4

Just Add Power

In Chapter 3, we investigated finite automata, imaginary machines that strip away the complexity of a real computer and reduce it to its simplest possible form. We explored the behavior of those machines in detail and saw what they're useful for; we also discovered that, despite having an exotic method of execution, nondeterministic finite automata have no more power than their more conventional deterministic counterparts.

The fact that we can't make a finite automaton more capable by adding fancy features like nondeterminism and free moves suggests that we're stuck on a plateau, a level of computational power that's shared by all these simple machines, and that we can't break away from that plateau without making more drastic changes to the way the machines work. So how much power do all these machines really have? Well, not much. They're limited to a very specific application—accepting or rejecting sequences of characters—and even within that small scope, it's still easy to come up with languages that no machine can recognize.

For example, think about designing a finite state machine capable of reading a string of opening and closing brackets and accepting that string only if the brackets are *balanced*—that is, if each closing bracket can be paired up with an opening bracket from earlier in the string.[1]

The general strategy for solving this problem is to read characters one at a time while keeping track of a number that represents the current *nesting level*: reading an opening bracket increases the nesting level, and reading a closing bracket decreases it. Whenever the nesting level is zero, we know that the brackets we've read so far are balanced—because the nesting level has gone up and come down by exactly the same amount—and if we try to decrease the nesting level below zero, then we know we've seen too

---

1. This isn't quite the same as accepting strings that merely contain equal numbers of opening and closing brackets. The strings '()' and ')(' each contain a single opening and closing bracket, but only '()' is balanced.

many closing brackets (e.g., '())') and that the string must be unbalanced, no matter what its remaining characters are.

We can make a respectable start at designing an NFA for this job. Here's one with four states:

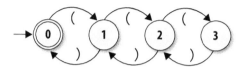

Each state corresponds to a particular nesting level, and reading an opening or closing bracket moves the machine into a state for a higher or lower level respectively, with "no nesting" being the accept state. Since we've already implemented everything we need to simulate this NFA in Ruby, let's fire it up:

```
>> rulebook = NFARulebook.new([
     FARule.new(0, '(', 1), FARule.new(1, ')', 0),
     FARule.new(1, '(', 2), FARule.new(2, ')', 1),
     FARule.new(2, '(', 3), FARule.new(3, ')', 2)
   ])
=> #<struct NFARulebook rules=[…]>
>> nfa_design = NFADesign.new(0, [0], rulebook)
=> #<struct NFADesign start_state=0, accept_states=[0], rulebook=…>
```

Our NFA design works fine on certain inputs. It can tell that '(()' and '())' aren't balanced and that '(())' is, and it even has no problem spotting more elaborate balanced strings like '(()(()()))':

```
>> nfa_design.accepts?('(()')
=> false
>> nfa_design.accepts?('())')
=> false
>> nfa_design.accepts?('(())')
=> true
>> nfa_design.accepts?('(()(()()))')
=> true
```

But the design has a serious flaw: it'll fail as soon as the brackets become nested more than three levels deep. It doesn't have enough states to keep track of the nesting in a string like '(((()))', so it rejects that string even though the brackets are clearly balanced:

```
>> nfa_design.accepts?('(((())))')
=> false
```

We can fix this temporarily by adding more states. An NFA with five states can recognize '(((())))' and any other balanced string with fewer than five levels of nesting, and an NFA with ten, a hundred, or a thousand states can recognize any balanced string whose nesting level stays within that machine's hard limit. But how can we design an NFA that can recognize *any* balanced string, to an arbitrary level of nesting? It turns out that we can't: a finite automaton must always have a finite number of states, so for any given machine, there's always a finite limit to how many levels of nesting it can support, and we can always break it by asking about a string whose brackets nest one level deeper than it can handle.

The underlying problem is that a finite automaton has only limited storage in the form of its fixed collection of states, which means it has no way to keep track of an *arbitrary* amount of information. In the case of the balanced brackets problem, an NFA can easily count up to some maximum number baked into its design, but it can't keep counting indefinitely to accommodate inputs of any possible size.[2] This doesn't matter for jobs that are inherently fixed in size, like matching the literal string 'abc', or ones where there's no need to keep track of the amount of repetition, like matching the regular expression ab*c, but it does make finite automata unable to handle tasks where an unpredictable amount of information needs to be stored up during the computation and reused later.

Regular Expressions and Nested Strings

We've seen that finite automata are intimately related to regular expressions. "Semantics" on page 83 showed how to turn any regular expression into an NFA, and in fact, there's another algorithm for converting any NFA back into a regular expression again.[3] This tells us that regular expressions are equivalent to NFAs and have the same limitations, so it can't be possible to use a regular expression to recognize balanced strings of brackets, or any other language whose definition involves pairs of things that nest to an arbitrary depth.

Perhaps the best-known example of this weakness is the fact that regular expressions can't distinguish between valid and invalid HTML (*http://stackoverflow.com/a/1732454*). Many HTML elements require opening and closing tags to appear in pairs, and those pairs can themselves enclose other elements, so finite automata don't have enough power to read a string of HTML while keeping track of which unclosed tags have been seen and how deeply they're nested.

In practice, though, real-world "regular expression" libraries often go beyond what regular expressions are technically capable of. Ruby's Regexp objects have many features that aren't part of the formal definition of regular expressions, and those bonus features provide enough extra power to allow more languages to be recognized.

One of Regexp's enhancements is the ability to label a subexpression with the (?<*name*>) syntax and then "call" that subexpression elsewhere with \g<*name*>. Being able to refer to its own subexpressions allows a Regexp to call itself recursively, which makes it possible to match nested pairs to an arbitrary depth.

---

2. This doesn't mean that an input string can ever actually be infinite, just that we can make it as finitely large as we like.

3. Briefly, this algorithm works by converting an NFA into a *generalized nondeterministic finite automaton* (GNFA), a finite state machine where each rule is labeled with a regular expression instead of a single character, and then repeatedly merging the states and rules of the GNFA until there are only two states and one rule left. The regular expression that labels that final rule always matches the same strings as the original NFA.

For example, subexpression calls let us write a `Regexp` that actually does match balanced strings of brackets, even though NFAs (and therefore, technically, regular expressions) can't do it. Here's what that `Regexp` looks like:

```
balanced =
  /
    \A              # match beginning of string
    (?<brackets>    # begin subexpression called "brackets"
      \(            # match a literal opening bracket
      \g<brackets>* # match "brackets" subexpression zero or more times
      \)            # match a literal closing bracket
    )               # end subexpression
    *               # repeat the whole pattern zero or more times
    \z              # match end of string
  /x
```

The `(?<brackets>…)` subexpression matches a single pair of opening and closing brackets, but inside that pair, it can match any number of recursive occurrences of itself, so the whole pattern can correctly identify brackets nested to any depth:

```
>> ['(()', '())', '(())', '(()(()())', '((((((((((())))))))))'].grep(balanced)
=> ["(())", "(()(()())", "((((((((((())))))))))"]
```

This only works because Ruby's regular expression engine uses a *call stack* to keep track of the recursive invocations of `(?<brackets>…)`, something that DFAs and NFAs can't do. In the next section, we'll see how to extend finite automata to give them exactly this sort of power.

And yes, you could use the same idea to write a `Regexp` that matches properly nested HTML tags, but it's guaranteed not to be a good use of your time.

It's clear that there are limitations to these machines' capabilities. If nondeterminism isn't enough to make a finite automaton more capable, what else can we do to give it more power? The current problems stem from the machines' limited storage, so let's add some extra storage and see what happens.

Deterministic Pushdown Automata

We can solve the storage problem by extending a finite state machine with some dedicated scratch space where data can be kept during computation. This space gives the machine a sort of *external memory* in addition to the limited internal memory provided by its state—and as we'll discover, having an external memory makes all the difference to a machine's computational power.

Storage

A simple way to add storage to a finite automaton is to give it access to a *stack*, a last-in first-out data structure that characters can be pushed onto and then popped off again. A stack is a simple and restrictive data structure—only the top character is accessible at any one time, we have to discard the top character to find out what's underneath it, and once we've pushed a sequence of characters onto the stack, we can only pop them off in reverse order—but it does neatly deal with the problem of limited storage. There's no built-in limit to the size of a stack, so in principle, it can grow to hold as much data as necessary.[4]

A finite state machine with a built-in stack is called a *pushdown automaton* (PDA), and when that machine's rules are deterministic, we call it a *deterministic pushdown automaton* (DPDA). Having access to a stack opens up new possibilities; for example, it's easy to design a DPDA that recognizes balanced strings of brackets. Here's how it works:

- Give the machine two states, 1 and 2, with state 1 being the accept state.
- Start the machine in state 1 with an empty stack.
- When in state 1 and an opening bracket is read, push some character—let's use b for "bracket"—onto the stack and move into state 2.
- When in state 2 and an opening bracket is read, push the character b onto the stack.
- When in state 2 and a closing bracket is read, pop the character b off the stack.
- When in state 2 and the stack is empty, move back into state 1.

This DPDA uses the size of the stack to count how many unclosed opening brackets it's seen so far. When the stack's empty it means that every opening bracket has been closed, so the string must be balanced. Watch how the stack grows and shrinks as the machine reads the string '(()((()()))':

State	Accepting?	Stack contents	Remaining input	Action
1	yes		(()((()()))	read (, push b, go to state 2
2	no	b	()((()()))	read (, push b
2	no	bb	)((()()))	read), pop b
2	no	b	((()()))	read (, push b
2	no	bb	(()()))	read (, push b
2	no	bbb	)()))	read), pop b
2	no	bb	()))	read (, push b
2	no	bbb	)))	read), pop b
2	no	bb	))	read), pop b
2	no	b	)	read), pop b
2	no			go to state 1
1	yes		—	

---

4. Of course, any real-world implementation of a stack is always going to be limited by the size of a computer's RAM, or the free space on its hard drive, or the number of atoms in the universe, but for the purposes of our thought experiment, we'll assume that none of those constraints exist.

Rules

The idea behind the balanced-brackets DPDA is straightforward, but there are some fiddly technical details to work out before we can actually build it. First of all, we have to decide exactly how pushdown automata rules should work. There are several design issues here:

- Does every rule have to modify the stack, or read input, or change state, or all three?
- Should there be two different kinds of rule for pushing and popping?
- Do we need a special kind of rule for changing state when the stack is empty?
- Is it okay to change state without reading from the input, like a free move in an NFA?
- If a DPDA can change state spontaneously like that, what does "deterministic" mean?

We can answer all of these questions by choosing a single rule style that is flexible enough to support everything we need. We'll break down a PDA rule into five parts:

- The current state of the machine
- The character that must be read from the input (optional)
- The next state of the machine
- The character that must be popped off the stack
- The *sequence* of characters to push onto the stack after the top character has been popped off

The first three parts are familiar from DFA and NFA rules. If a rule doesn't want the machine to change state, it can make the next state the same as the current one; if it doesn't want to read any input (i.e., a free move), it can omit the input character, as long as that doesn't make the machine nondeterministic (see "Determinism" on page 111).

The other two parts—a character to pop and a sequence of characters to push—are specific to PDAs. The assumption is that a PDA will *always* pop the top character off the stack, and then push some other characters onto the stack, every time it follows a rule. Each rule declares which character it wants to pop, and the rule will only apply when that character is on the top of the stack; if the rule wants that character to stay on the stack instead of getting popped, it can include it in the sequence of characters that get pushed back on afterward.

This five-part rule format doesn't give us a way to write rules that apply when the stack is empty, but we can work around that by choosing a special character to mark the bottom of the stack—the dollar sign, $, is a popular choice—and then checking for that character whenever we want to detect the empty stack. When using this convention, it's important that the stack never becomes truly empty, because no rule can apply when there's nothing on the top of the stack. The machine should start with the special bottom symbol already on the stack, and any rule that pops that symbol must push it back on again afterward.

It's easy enough to rewrite the balanced-bracket DPDA's rules in this format:

- When in state 1 and an opening bracket is read, pop the character $, push the characters b$, and move into state 2.
- When in state 2 and an opening bracket is read, pop the character b, push the characters bb, and stay in state 2.
- When in state 2 and a closing bracket is read, pop the character b, push no characters, and stay in state 2.
- When in state 2 (without reading any character), pop the character $, push the character $, and move into state 1.

We can show these rules on a diagram of the machine. A DPDA diagram looks a lot like an NFA diagram, except that each arrow needs to be labelled with the characters that are popped and pushed by that rule as well as the character that it reads from the input. If we use the notation a;b/cd to label a rule that reads a from the input, pops b from the stack, and then pushes cd onto the stack, the machine looks like this:

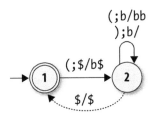

Determinism

The next hurdle is to define exactly what it means for a PDA to be deterministic. For DFAs, we had the "no contradictions" constraint: there should be no states where the machine's next move is ambiguous because of conflicting rules. The same idea applies to DPDAs, so for example, we can only have one rule that applies when the machine's in state 2, the next input character is an opening bracket, and there's a b on the top of the stack. It's even okay to write a free move rule that doesn't read any input, as long as there aren't any other rules for the same state and top-of-stack character, because that would create an ambiguity about whether or not a character should be read from the input.

DFAs also have a "no omissions" constraint—there should be a rule for every possible situation—but that idea becomes unwieldy for DPDAs because of the large number of possible combinations of state, input character, and top-of-stack character. It's conventional to just ignore this constraint and allow DPDAs to specify only the interesting rules that they need to get their job done, and assume that a DPDA will go into an implicit *stuck state* if it gets into a situation where none of its rules apply. This is what happens to our balanced-brackets DPDA when it reads a string like ')' or '())', because there's no rule for reading a closing bracket while in state 1.

Simulation

Now that we've dealt with the technical details, let's build a Ruby simulation of a deterministic pushdown automaton so we can interact with it. We already did most of the hard work when we simulated DFAs and NFAs, so this'll just take a bit of fine-tuning.

The most important thing we're missing is a stack. Here's one way of implementing a Stack class:

```ruby
class Stack < Struct.new(:contents)
  def push(character)
    Stack.new([character] + contents)
  end

  def pop
    Stack.new(contents.drop(1))
  end

  def top
    contents.first
  end

  def inspect
    "#<Stack (#{top})#{contents.drop(1).join}>"
  end
end
```

A Stack object stores its contents in an underlying array and exposes simple #push and #pop operations to push characters onto the stack and pop them off, plus a #top operation to read the character at the top of the stack:

```ruby
>> stack = Stack.new(['a', 'b', 'c', 'd', 'e'])
=> #<Stack (a)bcde>
>> stack.top
=> "a"
>> stack.pop.pop.top
=> "c"
>> stack.push('x').push('y').top
=> "y"
>> stack.push('x').push('y').pop.top
=> "x"
```

This is a *purely functional* stack. The #push and #pop methods are non-destructive: they each return a new Stack instance rather than modifying the existing one. Creating a new object every time makes this implementation less efficient than a conventional stack with destructive #push and #pop operations (and we could just use Array directly if we wanted that) but also makes it easier to work with, because we don't need to worry about the consequences of modifying a Stack that's being used in more than one place.

In Chapter 3, we saw that we can simulate a deterministic finite automaton by keeping track of just one piece of information—the DFA's current state—and then using the rulebook to update that information each time a character is read from the input. But there are *two* important things to know about a pushdown automaton at each step of its computation: what its current state is, and what the current contents of its stack are. If we use the word *configuration* to refer to this combination of a state and a stack, we can talk about a pushdown automaton moving from one configuration to another as it reads input characters, which is easier than always having to refer to the state and stack separately. Viewed this way, a DPDA just has a current configuration, and the rulebook tells us how to turn the current configuration into the next configuration each time we read a character.

Here's a PDAConfiguration class to hold the configuration of a PDA—a state and a stack —and a PDARule class to represent one rule in a PDA's rulebook:[5]

```
class PDAConfiguration < Struct.new(:state, :stack)
end

class PDARule < Struct.new(:state, :character, :next_state,
                           :pop_character, :push_characters)
  def applies_to?(configuration, character)
    self.state == configuration.state &&
      self.pop_character == configuration.stack.top &&
      self.character == character
  end
end
```

A rule only applies when the machine's state, topmost stack character, and next input character all have the values it expects:

```
>> rule = PDARule.new(1, '(', 2, '$', ['b', '$'])
=> #<struct PDARule
     state=1,
     character="(",
     next_state=2,
     pop_character="$",
     push_characters=["b", "$"]
   >
```

5. These class names begin with PDA, rather than DPDA, because their implementations don't make any assumptions about determinism, so they'd work just as well for simulating a nondeterministic PDA.

```
>> configuration = PDAConfiguration.new(1, Stack.new(['$']))
=> #<struct PDAConfiguration state=1, stack=#<Stack ($)>>
>> rule.applies_to?(configuration, '(')
=> true
```

For a finite automaton, following a rule just means changing from one state to another, but a PDA rule updates the stack contents as well as the state, so PDARule#follow needs to take the machine's current configuration as an argument and return the next one:

```
class PDARule
  def follow(configuration)
    PDAConfiguration.new(next_state, next_stack(configuration))
  end

  def next_stack(configuration)
    popped_stack = configuration.stack.pop

    push_characters.reverse.
      inject(popped_stack) { |stack, character| stack.push(character) }
  end
end
```

 If we push several characters onto a stack and then pop them off, they come out in the opposite order:

```
>> stack = Stack.new(['$']).push('x').push('y').push('z')
=> #<Stack (z)yx$>
>> stack.top
=> "z"
>> stack = stack.pop; stack.top
=> "y"
>> stack = stack.pop; stack.top
=> "x"
```

PDARule#next_stack anticipates this by reversing the push_characters array before pushing its characters onto the stack. For example, the last character in push_characters is the actually the *first* one to be pushed onto the stack, so it'll be the last to be popped off again. This is just a convenience so that we can read a rule's push_characters as the sequence of characters (in "popping order") that will be on top of the stack after the rule is applied, without having to worry about the mechanics of how they get on there.

So, if we have a PDARule that applies to a PDAConfiguration, we can follow it to find out what the next state and stack will be:

```
>> rule.follow(configuration)
=> #<struct PDAConfiguration state=2, stack=#<Stack (b)$>>
```

This gives us enough to implement a rulebook for DPDAs. The implementation is very similar to the DFARulebook from "Simulation" on page 66:

```
class DPDARulebook < Struct.new(:rules)
  def next_configuration(configuration, character)
```

```
    rule_for(configuration, character).follow(configuration)
  end

  def rule_for(configuration, character)
    rules.detect { |rule| rule.applies_to?(configuration, character) }
  end
end
```

Now we can assemble the rulebook for the balanced-brackets DPDA and try stepping through a few configurations and input characters by hand:

```
>> rulebook = DPDARulebook.new([
     PDARule.new(1, '(', 2, '$', ['b', '$']),
     PDARule.new(2, '(', 2, 'b', ['b', 'b']),
     PDARule.new(2, ')', 2, 'b', []),
     PDARule.new(2, nil, 1, '$', ['$'])
   ])
=> #<struct DPDARulebook rules=[…]>
>> configuration = rulebook.next_configuration(configuration, '(')
=> #<struct PDAConfiguration state=2, stack=#<Stack (b)$>>
>> configuration = rulebook.next_configuration(configuration, '(')
=> #<struct PDAConfiguration state=2, stack=#<Stack (b)b$>>
>> configuration = rulebook.next_configuration(configuration, ')')
=> #<struct PDAConfiguration state=2, stack=#<Stack (b)$>>
```

Instead of doing this job manually, let's use the rulebook to build a DPDA object that can keep track of the machine's current configuration as it reads characters from the input:

```
class DPDA < Struct.new(:current_configuration, :accept_states, :rulebook)
  def accepting?
    accept_states.include?(current_configuration.state)
  end

  def read_character(character)
    self.current_configuration =
      rulebook.next_configuration(current_configuration, character)
  end

  def read_string(string)
    string.chars.each do |character|
      read_character(character)
    end
  end
end
```

So we can create a DPDA, feed it input, and see whether it's accepted it:

```
>> dpda = DPDA.new(PDAConfiguration.new(1, Stack.new(['$'])), [1], rulebook)
=> #<struct DPDA …>
>> dpda.accepting?
=> true
>> dpda.read_string('(()'); dpda.accepting?
=> false
>> dpda.current_configuration
=> #<struct PDAConfiguration state=2, stack=#<Stack (b)$>>
```

Fine so far, but the rulebook we're using contains a free move, so the simulation needs to support free moves before it'll work properly. Let's add a DPDARulebook helper method for dealing with free moves, similar to the one in NFARulebook (see "Free Moves" on page 76):

```ruby
class DPDARulebook
  def applies_to?(configuration, character)
    !rule_for(configuration, character).nil?
  end

  def follow_free_moves(configuration)
    if applies_to?(configuration, nil)
      follow_free_moves(next_configuration(configuration, nil))
    else
      configuration
    end
  end
end
```

DPDARulebook#follow_free_moves will repeatedly follow any free moves that apply to the current configuration, stopping when there are none:

```
>> configuration = PDAConfiguration.new(2, Stack.new(['$']))
=> #<struct PDAConfiguration state=2, stack=#<Stack ($)>>
>> rulebook.follow_free_moves(configuration)
=> #<struct PDAConfiguration state=1, stack=#<Stack ($)>>
```

 For the first time in our experiments with state machines, this introduces the possibility of an infinite loop in the simulation. A loop can happen whenever there's a chain of free moves that begins and ends at the same state; the simplest example is when there's one free move that doesn't change the configuration at all:

```
>> DPDARulebook.new([PDARule.new(1, nil, 1, '$', ['$'])]).
     follow_free_moves(PDAConfiguration.new(1, Stack.new(['$'])))
SystemStackError: stack level too deep
```

These infinite loops aren't useful, so we'll just take care to avoid them in any pushdown automata we design.

We also need to wrap the default implementation of DPDA#current_configuration to take advantage of the rulebook's free move support:

```ruby
class DPDA
  def current_configuration
    rulebook.follow_free_moves(super)
  end
end
```

Now we have a simulation of a DPDA that we can start up, feed characters to, and check for acceptance:

```
>> dpda = DPDA.new(PDAConfiguration.new(1, Stack.new(['$'])), [1], rulebook)
=> #<struct DPDA ...>
>> dpda.read_string('(()('); dpda.accepting?
```

```
=> false
>> dpda.current_configuration
=> #<struct PDAConfiguration state=2, stack=#<Stack (b)b$>>
>> dpda.read_string(')()'); dpda.accepting?
=> true
>> dpda.current_configuration
=> #<struct PDAConfiguration state=1, stack=#<Stack ($)>>
```

If we wrap this simulation up in a DPDADesign as usual, we can easily check as many strings as we like:

```
class DPDADesign < Struct.new(:start_state, :bottom_character,
                               :accept_states, :rulebook)
  def accepts?(string)
    to_dpda.tap { |dpda| dpda.read_string(string) }.accepting?
  end

  def to_dpda
    start_stack = Stack.new([bottom_character])
    start_configuration = PDAConfiguration.new(start_state, start_stack)
    DPDA.new(start_configuration, accept_states, rulebook)
  end
end
```

As expected, our DPDA design can recognize complex strings of balanced brackets nested to arbitrary depth:

```
>> dpda_design = DPDADesign.new(1, '$', [1], rulebook)
=> #<struct DPDADesign …>
>> dpda_design.accepts?('(((((((((())))))))))')
=> true
>> dpda_design.accepts?('()(())((()))(()(()))')
=> true
>> dpda_design.accepts?('(()(()()()(()()))()')
=> false
```

There's one final detail to take care of. Our simulation works perfectly on inputs that leave the DPDA in a valid state, but it blows up when the machine gets stuck:

```
>> dpda_design.accepts?('())')
NoMethodError: undefined method `follow' for nil:NilClass
```

This happens because DPDARulebook#next_configuration assumes it will be able to find an applicable rule, so we shouldn't call it when none of the rules apply. We'll fix the problem by modifying DPDA#read_character to check for a usable rule and, if there isn't one, put the DPDA into a special stuck state that it can never move out of:

```
class PDAConfiguration
  STUCK_STATE = Object.new

  def stuck
    PDAConfiguration.new(STUCK_STATE, stack)
  end

  def stuck?
    state == STUCK_STATE
```

```
      end
   end

   class DPDA
     def next_configuration(character)
       if rulebook.applies_to?(current_configuration, character)
         rulebook.next_configuration(current_configuration, character)
       else
         current_configuration.stuck
       end
     end

     def stuck?
       current_configuration.stuck?
     end

     def read_character(character)
       self.current_configuration = next_configuration(character)
     end

     def read_string(string)
       string.chars.each do |character|
         read_character(character) unless stuck?
       end
     end
   end
end
```

Now the DPDA will gracefully become stuck instead of blowing up:

```
>> dpda = DPDA.new(PDAConfiguration.new(1, Stack.new(['$'])), [1], rulebook)
=> #<struct DPDA …>
>> dpda.read_string('())'); dpda.current_configuration
=> #<struct PDAConfiguration state=#<Object>, stack=#<Stack ($)>>
>> dpda.accepting?
=> false
>> dpda.stuck?
=> true
>> dpda_design.accepts?('())')
=> false
```

Nondeterministic Pushdown Automata

While the balanced-brackets machine does need the stack to do its job, it's really only using the stack as a counter, and its rules are only interested in the distinction between "the stack is empty" and "the stack isn't empty." More sophisticated DPDAs will push more than one kind of symbol onto the stack and make use of that information as they perform a computation. A simple example is a machine for recognizing strings that contain equal numbers of two characters, say a and b:

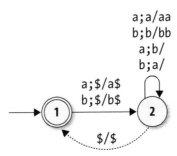

Our simulation shows that it does the job:

```
>> rulebook = DPDARulebook.new([
     PDARule.new(1, 'a', 2, '$', ['a', '$']),
     PDARule.new(1, 'b', 2, '$', ['b', '$']),
     PDARule.new(2, 'a', 2, 'a', ['a', 'a']),
     PDARule.new(2, 'b', 2, 'b', ['b', 'b']),
     PDARule.new(2, 'a', 2, 'b', []),
     PDARule.new(2, 'b', 2, 'a', []),
     PDARule.new(2, nil, 1, '$', ['$'])
   ])
=> #<struct DPDARulebook rules=[…]>
>> dpda_design = DPDADesign.new(1, '$', [1], rulebook)
=> #<struct DPDADesign …>
>> dpda_design.accepts?('ababab')
=> true
>> dpda_design.accepts?('bbbaaaab')
=> true
>> dpda_design.accepts?('baa')
=> false
```

This is similar to the balanced-brackets machine, except its behavior is controlled by which character is uppermost on the stack. An a on the top of the stack means that the machine's seen a surplus of as, so any extra as read from the input will accumulate on the stack, and each b read will pop an a off the stack to cancel it out; conversely, when there's a b on the stack, it's the bs that accumulate and the as that cancel them out.

Even this DPDA isn't taking full advantage of the stack, though. There's never any interesting history stored up beneath the top character, just a featureless pile of as or bs, so we can achieve the same result by pushing only one kind of character onto the stack (i.e., treating it as a simple counter again) and using two separate states to distinguish "counting surplus as" from "counting surplus bs":

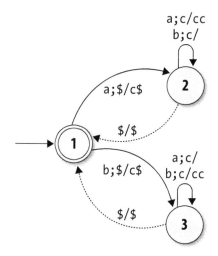

To really exploit the potential of the stack, we need a tougher problem that'll force us to store structured information. The classic example is recognizing palindromes: as we read the input string, character by character, we have to remember what we see; once we pass the halfway point, we check our memory to decide whether the characters we saw earlier are now appearing in reverse order. Here's a DPDA that can recognize palindromes made up of a and b characters, as long as they have an m character (for "middle") at the halfway point of the string:

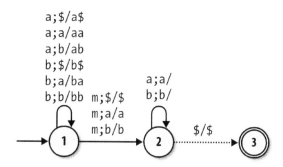

This machine starts in state 1, repeatedly reading as and bs from the input and pushing them onto the stack. When it reads an m, it moves into state 2, where it keeps reading input characters while trying to pop each one *off* the stack. If every character in the second half of the string matches the stack contents as they're popped off, the machine stays in state 2 and eventually hits the $ at the bottom of the stack, at which point it moves into state 3 and accepts the input string. If any of the characters it reads while in state 2 don't match what's on the top of the stack, there's no rule for it to follow, so it'll go into a stuck state and reject the string.

We can simulate this DPDA to check that it works:

```
>> rulebook = DPDARulebook.new([
     PDARule.new(1, 'a', 1, '$', ['a', '$']),
     PDARule.new(1, 'a', 1, 'a', ['a', 'a']),
     PDARule.new(1, 'a', 1, 'b', ['a', 'b']),
     PDARule.new(1, 'b', 1, '$', ['b', '$']),
     PDARule.new(1, 'b', 1, 'a', ['b', 'a']),
     PDARule.new(1, 'b', 1, 'b', ['b', 'b']),
     PDARule.new(1, 'm', 2, '$', ['$']),
     PDARule.new(1, 'm', 2, 'a', ['a']),
     PDARule.new(1, 'm', 2, 'b', ['b']),
     PDARule.new(2, 'a', 2, 'a', []),
     PDARule.new(2, 'b', 2, 'b', []),
     PDARule.new(2, nil, 3, '$', ['$'])
   ])
=> #<struct DPDARulebook rules=[…]>
>> dpda_design = DPDADesign.new(1, '$', [3], rulebook)
=> #<struct DPDADesign …>
>> dpda_design.accepts?('abmba')
=> true
>> dpda_design.accepts?('babbamabbab')
=> true
>> dpda_design.accepts?('abmb')
=> false
>> dpda_design.accepts?('baambaa')
=> false
```

That's great, but the m in the middle of the input string is a cop-out. Why can't we design a machine that just recognizes palindromes—aa, abba, babbaabbab, etc.—without having to put a marker halfway through?

The machine has to change from state 1 to state 2 as soon as it reaches the halfway point of the string, and without a marker, it has no way of knowing when to do that. As we've seen before with NFAs, these "how do I know when to…?" problems can be solved by relaxing the determinism constraints and allowing the machine the freedom to make that vital state change at any point, so that it's *possible* for it to accept a palindrome by following the right rule at the right time.

Unsurprisingly, a pushdown automaton without determinism constraints is called a *nondeterministic pushdown automaton*. Here's one for recognizing palindromes with an even number of letters:[6]

---

6. The "even number of letters" restriction keeps the machine simple: a palindrome of length 2n can be accepted by pushing n characters onto the stack and then popping n characters off. To recognize *any* palindrome requires a few more rules going from state 1 to state 2.

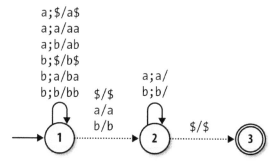

This is identical to the DPDA version except for the rules that lead from state 1 to state 2: in the DPDA, they read an m from the input, but here they're free moves. This gives the NPDA the opportunity to change state anywhere during the input string without needing a marker.

Simulation

A nondeterministic machine is more difficult to simulate than a deterministic one, but we've already done the hard work for NFAs in "Nondeterminism" on page 70, and we can reuse the same ideas for NPDAs. We need an NPDARulebook for holding a nondeterministic collection of PDARules, and its implementation is almost exactly the same as NFARulebook:

```ruby
require 'set'

class NPDARulebook < Struct.new(:rules)
  def next_configurations(configurations, character)
    configurations.flat_map { |config| follow_rules_for(config, character) }.to_set
  end

  def follow_rules_for(configuration, character)
    rules_for(configuration, character).map { |rule| rule.follow(configuration) }
  end

  def rules_for(configuration, character)
    rules.select { |rule| rule.applies_to?(configuration, character) }
  end
end
```

In "Nondeterminism" on page 70, we simulated an NFA by keeping track of a Set of possible states; here we're simulating an NPDA with a Set of possible *configurations*.

Our rulebook needs the usual support for free moves, again virtually identical to NFAR ulebook's implementation:

```ruby
class NPDARulebook
  def follow_free_moves(configurations)
    more_configurations = next_configurations(configurations, nil)
```

```
          if more_configurations.subset?(configurations)
            configurations
          else
            follow_free_moves(configurations + more_configurations)
          end
      end
  end
```

And we need an NPDA class to wrap up a rulebook alongside the Set of current config-urations:

```
class NPDA < Struct.new(:current_configurations, :accept_states, :rulebook)
  def accepting?
    current_configurations.any? { |config| accept_states.include?(config.state) }
  end

  def read_character(character)
    self.current_configurations =
      rulebook.next_configurations(current_configurations, character)
  end

  def read_string(string)
    string.chars.each do |character|
      read_character(character)
    end
  end

  def current_configurations
    rulebook.follow_free_moves(super)
  end
end
```

This lets us step through a simulation of all possible configurations of an NPDA as each character is read:

```
>> rulebook = NPDARulebook.new([
     PDARule.new(1, 'a', 1, '$', ['a', '$']),
     PDARule.new(1, 'a', 1, 'a', ['a', 'a']),
     PDARule.new(1, 'a', 1, 'b', ['a', 'b']),
     PDARule.new(1, 'b', 1, '$', ['b', '$']),
     PDARule.new(1, 'b', 1, 'a', ['b', 'a']),
     PDARule.new(1, 'b', 1, 'b', ['b', 'b']),
     PDARule.new(1, nil, 2, '$', ['$']),
     PDARule.new(1, nil, 2, 'a', ['a']),
     PDARule.new(1, nil, 2, 'b', ['b']),
     PDARule.new(2, 'a', 2, 'a', []),
     PDARule.new(2, 'b', 2, 'b', []),
     PDARule.new(2, nil, 3, '$', ['$'])
   ])
=> #<struct NPDARulebook rules=[…]>
>> configuration = PDAConfiguration.new(1, Stack.new(['$']))
=> #<struct PDAConfiguration state=1, stack=#<Stack ($)>>
>> npda = NPDA.new(Set[configuration], [3], rulebook)
=> #<struct NPDA …>
>> npda.accepting?
=> true
```

```
>> npda.current_configurations
=> #<Set: {
      #<struct PDAConfiguration state=1, stack=#<Stack ($)>>,
      #<struct PDAConfiguration state=2, stack=#<Stack ($)>>,
      #<struct PDAConfiguration state=3, stack=#<Stack ($)>>
   }>
>> npda.read_string('abb'); npda.accepting?
=> false
>> npda.current_configurations
=> #<Set: {
      #<struct PDAConfiguration state=1, stack=#<Stack (b)ba$>>,
      #<struct PDAConfiguration state=2, stack=#<Stack (a)$>>,
      #<struct PDAConfiguration state=2, stack=#<Stack (b)ba$>>
   }>
>> npda.read_character('a'); npda.accepting?
=> true
>> npda.current_configurations
=> #<Set: {
      #<struct PDAConfiguration state=1, stack=#<Stack (a)bba$>>,
      #<struct PDAConfiguration state=2, stack=#<Stack ($)>>,
      #<struct PDAConfiguration state=2, stack=#<Stack (a)bba$>>,
      #<struct PDAConfiguration state=3, stack=#<Stack ($)>>
   }>
```

And finally an NPDADesign class for testing strings directly:

```
class NPDADesign < Struct.new(:start_state, :bottom_character,
                              :accept_states, :rulebook)
  def accepts?(string)
    to_npda.tap { |npda| npda.read_string(string) }.accepting?
  end

  def to_npda
    start_stack = Stack.new([bottom_character])
    start_configuration = PDAConfiguration.new(start_state, start_stack)
    NPDA.new(Set[start_configuration], accept_states, rulebook)
  end
end
```

Now we can check that our NPDA actually does recognize palindromes:

```
>> npda_design = NPDADesign.new(1, '$', [3], rulebook)
=> #<struct NPDADesign …>
>> npda_design.accepts?('abba')
=> true
>> npda_design.accepts?('babbaabbab')
=> true
>> npda_design.accepts?('abb')
=> false
>> npda_design.accepts?('baabaa')
=> false
```

Looks good! Nondeterminism has apparently given us the power to recognize languages that deterministic machines can't handle.

Nonequivalence

But wait: we saw in "Equivalence" on page 94 that nondeterministic machines without a stack are exactly equivalent in power to deterministic ones. Our Ruby NFA simulation behaved like a DFA—moving between a finite number of "simulation states" as it read each character of the input string—which gave us a way to turn any NFA into a DFA that accepts the same strings. So has nondeterminism really given us any extra power, or does our Ruby NPDA simulation just behave like a DPDA? Is there an algorithm for converting any nondeterministic pushdown automaton into a deterministic one?

Well, no, it turns out that there isn't. The NFA-to-DFA trick only works because we can use a single DFA state to represent many possible NFA states. To simulate an NFA, we only need to keep track of what states it could currently be in, then pick a different set of possible states each time we read an input character, and a DFA can easily do that job if we give it the right rules.

But that trick doesn't work for PDAs: we can't usefully represent multiple NPDA configurations as a single DPDA configuration. The problem, unsurprisingly, is the stack. An NPDA simulation needs to know all the characters that could currently be on top of the stack, and it must be able to pop and push several of the simulated stacks simultaneously. There's no way to combine all the possible stacks into a single stack so that a DPDA can still see all the topmost characters and access every possible stack individually. We didn't have any difficulty writing a Ruby program to do all this, but a DPDA just isn't powerful enough to handle it.

So unfortunately, our NPDA simulation does *not* behave like a DPDA, and there isn't an NPDA-to-DPDA algorithm. The unmarked palindrome problem is an example of a job where an NPDA can do something that a DPDA can't, so nondeterministic pushdown automata really *do* have more power than deterministic ones.

Parsing with Pushdown Automata

"Regular Expressions" on page 79 showed how nondeterministic finite automata can be used to implement regular expression matching. Pushdown automata have an important practical application too: they can be used to parse programming languages.

We already saw in "Implementing Parsers" on page 58 how to use Treetop to build a parser for part of the SIMPLE language. Treetop parsers use a single *parsing expression grammar* to describe the complete syntax of the language being parsed, but that's a relatively modern idea. A more traditional approach is to break the parsing process apart into two separate stages:

Lexical analysis
> Read a raw string of characters and turn it into a sequence of *tokens*. Each token represents an individual building block of program syntax, like "variable name," "opening bracket," or "while keyword." A lexical analyzer uses a language-specific

set of rules called a *lexical grammar* to decide which sequences of characters should produce which tokens. This stage deals with messy character-level details like variable-naming rules, comments, and whitespace, leaving a clean sequence of tokens for the next stage to consume.

Syntactic analysis

Read a sequence of tokens and decide whether they represent a valid program according to the *syntactic grammar* of the language being parsed. If the program is valid, the syntactic analyzer may produce additional information about its structure (e.g., a parse tree).

Lexical Analysis

The lexical analysis stage is usually pretty straightforward. It can be done with regular expressions (and therefore by an NFA), because it involves simply matching a flat sequence of characters against some rules and deciding whether those characters look like a keyword, a variable name, an operator, or whatever else. Here's some quick-and-dirty Ruby code to chop up a SIMPLE program into tokens:

```ruby
class LexicalAnalyzer < Struct.new(:string)
  GRAMMAR = [
    { token: 'i', pattern: /if/        }, # if keyword
    { token: 'e', pattern: /else/      }, # else keyword
    { token: 'w', pattern: /while/     }, # while keyword
    { token: 'd', pattern: /do-nothing/ }, # do-nothing keyword
    { token: '(', pattern: /\(/        }, # opening bracket
    { token: ')', pattern: /\)/        }, # closing bracket
    { token: '{', pattern: /\{/        }, # opening curly bracket
    { token: '}', pattern: /\}/        }, # closing curly bracket
    { token: ';', pattern: /;/         }, # semicolon
    { token: '=', pattern: /=/         }, # equals sign
    { token: '+', pattern: /\+/        }, # addition sign
    { token: '*', pattern: /\*/        }, # multiplication sign
    { token: '<', pattern: /</         }, # less-than sign
    { token: 'n', pattern: /[0-9]+/    }, # number
    { token: 'b', pattern: /true|false/ }, # boolean
    { token: 'v', pattern: /[a-z]+/    }  # variable name
  ]

  def analyze
    [].tap do |tokens|
      while more_tokens?
        tokens.push(next_token)
      end
    end
  end

  def more_tokens?
    !string.empty?
  end

  def next_token
```

```
    rule, match = rule_matching(string)
    self.string = string_after(match)
    rule[:token]
  end

  def rule_matching(string)
    matches = GRAMMAR.map { |rule| match_at_beginning(rule[:pattern], string) }
    rules_with_matches = GRAMMAR.zip(matches).reject { |rule, match| match.nil? }
    rule_with_longest_match(rules_with_matches)
  end

  def match_at_beginning(pattern, string)
    /\A#{pattern}/.match(string)
  end

  def rule_with_longest_match(rules_with_matches)
    rules_with_matches.max_by { |rule, match| match.to_s.length }
  end

  def string_after(match)
    match.post_match.lstrip
  end
end
```

 This implementation uses single characters as tokens—w means "the while keyword," + means "the addition sign," and so on—because soon we're going to be feeding those tokens to a PDA, and our Ruby PDA simulations expect to read characters as input.

Single-character tokens are good enough for a basic demonstration where we don't need to retain the names of variables or the values of literals. In a real parser, however, we'd want to use a proper data structure to represent tokens so they could communicate more information than just "some unknown variable name" or "some unknown Boolean."

By creating a LexicalAnalyzer instance with a string of SIMPLE code and calling its #analyze method, we can get back an array of tokens showing how the code breaks down into keywords, operators, punctuation, and other pieces of syntax:

```
>> LexicalAnalyzer.new('y = x * 7').analyze
=> ["v", "=", "v", "*", "n"]
>> LexicalAnalyzer.new('while (x < 5) { x = x * 3 }').analyze
=> ["w", "(", "v", "<", "n", ")", "{", "v", "=", "v", "*", "n", "}"]
>> LexicalAnalyzer.new('if (x < 10) { y = true; x = 0 } else { do-nothing }').analyze
=> ["i", "(", "v", "<", "n", ")", "{", "v", "=", "b", ";", "v", "=", "n", "}", "e", ↵
"{", "d", "}"]
```

Choosing the rule with the longest match allows the lexical analyzer to handle variables whose names would otherwise cause them to be wrongly identified as keywords:

```
>> LexicalAnalyzer.new('x = false').analyze
=> ["v", "=", "b"]
>> LexicalAnalyzer.new('x = falsehood').analyze
=> ["v", "=", "v"]
```

There are other ways of dealing with this problem. One alternative would be to write more restrictive regular expressions in the rules: if the Boolean rule used the pattern /(true|false)(?![a-z])/, then it wouldn't match the string 'falsehood' in the first place.

Syntactic Analysis

Once we've done the easy work of turning a string into tokens, the harder problem is to decide whether those tokens represent a syntactically valid SIMPLE program. We can't use regular expressions or NFAs to do it—SIMPLE's syntax allows arbitrary nesting of brackets, and we already know that finite automata aren't powerful enough to recognize languages like that. It *is* possible to use a pushdown automaton to recognize valid sequences of tokens, though, so let's see how to construct one.

First we need a syntactic grammar that describes how tokens may be combined to form programs. Here's part of a grammar for SIMPLE, based on the structure of the Treetop grammar in "Implementing Parsers" on page 58:

```
<statement>  ::= <while> | <assign>
<while>      ::= 'w' '(' <expression> ')' '{' <statement> '}'
<assign>     ::= 'v' '=' <expression>
<expression> ::= <less-than>
<less-than>  ::= <multiply> '<' <less-than> | <multiply>
<multiply>   ::= <term> '*' <multiply> | <term>
<term>       ::= 'n' | 'v'
```

This is called a *context-free grammar* (CFG).[7] Each rule has a *symbol* on the lefthand side and one or more sequences of symbols and tokens on the right. For example, the rule `<statement> ::= <while> | <assign>` means that a SIMPLE statement is either a while loop or an assignment, and `<assign> ::= 'v' '=' <expression>` means that an assignment statement consists of a variable name followed by an equals sign and an expression.

The CFG is a static description of SIMPLE's structure, but we can also think of it as a set of rules for *generating* SIMPLE programs. Starting from the `<statement>` symbol, we can

---

7. The grammar is "context free" in the sense that its rules don't say anything about the context in which each piece of syntax may appear; an assignment statement *always* consists of a variable name, equals sign, and expression, regardless of what other tokens surround it. Not all imaginable languages can be described by this kind of grammar, but almost all programming languages can.

apply the grammar rules to recursively expand symbols until only tokens remain. Here's one of many ways to fully expand `<statement>` according to the rules:

```
<statement> → <assign>
            → 'v' '=' <expression>
            → 'v' '=' <less-than>
            → 'v' '=' <multiply>
            → 'v' '=' <term> '*' <multiply>
            → 'v' '=' 'v' '*' <multiply>
            → 'v' '=' 'v' '*' <term>
            → 'v' '=' 'v' '*' 'n'
```

This tells us that `'v' '=' 'v' '*' 'n'` represents a syntactically valid program, but we want the ability to go in the opposite direction: to *recognize* valid programs, not generate them. When we get a sequence of tokens out of the lexical analyzer, we'd like to know whether it's possible to expand the `<statement>` symbol into those tokens by applying the grammar rules in some order. Fortunately, there's a way to turn a context-free grammar into a nondeterministic pushdown automaton that can make exactly this decision.

The technique for converting a CFG into a PDA works like this:

1. Pick a character to represent each symbol from the grammar. In this case, we'll use the uppercase initial of each symbol—S for `<statement>`, W for `<while>`, and so on—to distinguish them from the lowercase characters we're using as tokens.

2. Use the PDA's stack to store characters that represent grammar symbols (S, W, A, E, …) and tokens (w, v, =, *, …). When the PDA starts, have it immediately push a symbol onto the stack to represent the structure it's trying to recognize. We want to recognize SIMPLE statements, so our PDA will begin by pushing S onto the stack:

```
>> start_rule = PDARule.new(1, nil, 2, '$', ['S', '$'])
=> #<struct PDARule …>
```

3. Translate the grammar rules into PDA rules that expand symbols on the top of the stack without reading any input. Each grammar rule describes how to expand a single symbol into a sequence of other symbols and tokens, and we can turn that description into a PDA rule that pops a particular symbol's character off the stack and pushes other characters on:

```
>> symbol_rules = [
    # <statement> ::= <while> | <assign>
    PDARule.new(2, nil, 2, 'S', ['W']),
    PDARule.new(2, nil, 2, 'S', ['A']),

    # <while> ::= 'w' '(' <expression> ')' '{' <statement> '}'
    PDARule.new(2, nil, 2, 'W', ['w', '(', 'E', ')', '{', 'S', '}']),

    # <assign> ::= 'v' '=' <expression>
    PDARule.new(2, nil, 2, 'A', ['v', '=', 'E']),

    # <expression> ::= <less-than>
    PDARule.new(2, nil, 2, 'E', ['L']),
```

```
# <less-than> ::= <multiply> '<' <less-than> | <multiply>
PDARule.new(2, nil, 2, 'L', ['M', '<', 'L']),
PDARule.new(2, nil, 2, 'L', ['M']),

# <multiply> ::= <term> '*' <multiply> | <term>
PDARule.new(2, nil, 2, 'M', ['T', '*', 'M']),
PDARule.new(2, nil, 2, 'M', ['T']),

# <term> ::= 'n' | 'v'
PDARule.new(2, nil, 2, 'T', ['n']),
PDARule.new(2, nil, 2, 'T', ['v'])
]
=> [#<struct PDARule …>, #<struct PDARule …>, …]
```

For example, the rule for assignment statements says that the <assign> symbol can be expanded to the tokens v and = followed by the <expression> symbol, so we have a corresponding PDA rule that spontaneously pops an A off the stack and pushes the characters v=E back on. The <statement> rule says that we can replace the <statement> symbol with a <while> or <assign> symbol; we've turned that into one PDA rule that pops an S from the stack and replaces it with a W, and another rule that pops an S and pushes an A.

4. Give every token character a PDA rule that reads that character from the input and pops it off the stack:

    ```
    >> token_rules = LexicalAnalyzer::GRAMMAR.map do |rule|
         PDARule.new(2, rule[:token], 2, rule[:token], [])
       end
    => [#<struct PDARule …>, #<struct PDARule …>, …]
    ```

    These token rules work in opposition to the symbol rules. The symbol rules tend to make the stack larger, sometimes pushing several characters to replace the one that's been popped; the token rules always make the stack smaller, consuming input as they go.

5. Finally, make a PDA rule that will allow the machine to enter an accept state if the stack becomes empty:

    ```
    >> stop_rule = PDARule.new(2, nil, 3, '$', ['$'])
    => #<struct PDARule …>
    ```

Now we can build a PDA with these rules and feed it a string of tokens to see whether it recognizes them. The rules generated by the SIMPLE grammar are nondeterministic—there's more than one applicable rule whenever the character S, L, M, or T is topmost on the stack—so it'll have to be an NPDA:

```
>> rulebook = NPDARulebook.new([start_rule, stop_rule] + symbol_rules + token_rules)
=> #<struct NPDARulebook rules=[…]>
>> npda_design = NPDADesign.new(1, '$', [3], rulebook)
=> #<struct NPDADesign …>
>> token_string = LexicalAnalyzer.new('while (x < 5) { x = x * 3 }').analyze.join
=> "w(v<n){v=v*n}"
>> npda_design.accepts?(token_string)
```

```
=> true
>> npda_design.accepts?(LexicalAnalyzer.new('while (x < 5 x = x * }').analyze.join)
=> false
```

To show exactly what's going on, here's one possible execution of the NPDA when it's fed the string 'w(v<n){v=v*n}':

State	Accepting?	Stack contents	Remaining input	Action
1	no	$	w(v<n){v=v*n}	push S, go to state 2
2	no	S$	w(v<n){v=v*n}	pop S, push W
2	no	W$	w(v<n){v=v*n}	pop W, push w(E){S}
2	no	w(E){S}$	w(v<n){v=v*n}	read w, pop w
2	no	(E){S}$	(v<n){v=v*n}	read (, pop (
2	no	E){S}$	v<n){v=v*n}	pop E, push L
2	no	L){S}$	v<n){v=v*n}	pop L, push M<L
2	no	M<L){S}$	v<n){v=v*n}	pop M, push T
2	no	T<L){S}$	v<n){v=v*n}	pop T, push v
2	no	v<L){S}$	v<n){v=v*n}	read v, pop v
2	no	<L){S}$	<n){v=v*n}	read <, pop <
2	no	L){S}$	n){v=v*n}	pop L, push M
2	no	M){S}$	n){v=v*n}	pop M, push T
2	no	T){S}$	n){v=v*n}	pop T, push n
2	no	n){S}$	n){v=v*n}	read n, pop n
2	no	){S}$	){v=v*n}	read), pop)
2	no	{S}$	{v=v*n}	read {, pop {
2	no	S}$	v=v*n}	pop S, push A
2	no	A}$	v=v*n}	pop A, push v=E
2	no	v=E}$	v=v*n}	read v, pop v
2	no	=E}$	=v*n}	read =, pop =
2	no	E}$	v*n}	pop E, push L
2	no	L}$	v*n}	pop L, push M
2	no	M}$	v*n}	pop M, push T*M
2	no	T*M}$	v*n}	pop T, push v
2	no	v*M}$	v*n}	read v, pop v
2	no	*M}$	*n}	read *, pop *
2	no	M}$	n}	pop M, push T
2	no	T}$	n}	pop T, push n
2	no	n}$	n}	read n, pop n

State	Accepting?	Stack contents	Remaining input	Action
2	no	}$	}	read }, pop }
2	no	$		go to state 3
3	yes	$		—

This execution trace shows us how the machine ping-pongs between symbol and token rules: the symbol rules repeatedly expand the symbol on the top of the stack until it gets replaced by a token, then the token rules consume the stack (and the input) until they hit a symbol. This back and forth eventually results in an empty stack as long as the input string can be generated by the grammar rules.[8]

How does the PDA know which rule to choose at each step of execution? Well, that's the power of nondeterminism: our NPDA simulation tries all possible rules, so as long as there's *some* way of getting to an empty stack, we'll find it.

Practicalities

This parsing procedure relies on nondeterminism, but in real applications, it's best to avoid nondeterminism, because a deterministic PDA is much faster and easier to simulate than a nondeterministic one. Fortunately, it's almost always possible to eliminate nondeterminism by using the input tokens themselves to make decisions about which symbol rule to apply at each stage—a technique called *lookahead*—but that makes the translation from CFG to PDA more complicated.

It's also not really good enough to only be able to *recognize* valid programs. As we saw in "Implementing Parsers" on page 58, the whole point of parsing a program is to turn it into a structured representation that we can then do something useful with. In practice, we can create this representation by instrumenting our PDA simulation to record the sequence of rules it follows to reach an accept state, which provides enough information to construct a parse tree. For example, the above execution trace shows us how the symbols on the stack get expanded to form the desired sequence of tokens, and that tells us the shape of the parse tree for the string 'w(v<n){v=v*n}':

---

8. This algorithm is called *LL parsing*. The first L stands for "left-to-right," because the input string is read in that direction, and the second L stands for "left derivation," because it's always the leftmost (i.e., uppermost) symbol on the stack that gets expanded.

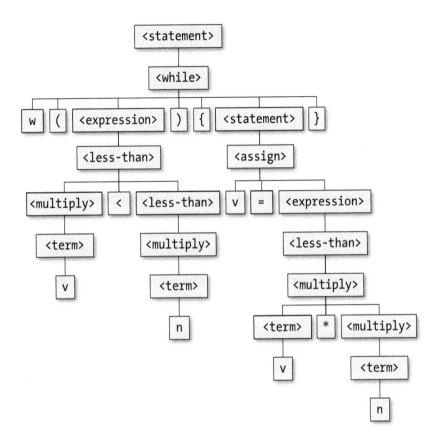

How Much Power?

In this chapter, we've encountered two new levels of computing power: DPDAs are more powerful than DFAs and NFAs, and NPDAs are more powerful again. Having access to a stack, it seems, gives pushdown automata a bit more power and sophistication than finite automata.

The main consequence of having a stack is the ability to recognize certain languages that finite automata aren't capable of recognizing, like palindromes and strings of balanced brackets. The unlimited storage provided by a stack lets a PDA remember arbitrary amounts of information during a computation and refer back to it later.

Unlike finite automata, a PDA can loop indefinitely without reading any input, which is curious even if it's not particularly useful. A DFA can only ever change state by consuming a character of input, and although an NFA can change state spontaneously by following a free move, it can only do that a finite number of times before it ends up back where it started. A PDA, on the other hand, can sit in a single state and keep pushing characters onto its stack forever, never once repeating the same configuration.

Pushdown automata can also control themselves to a limited extent. There's a feedback loop between the rules and the stack—the contents of the stack affect which rules the machine can follow, and following a rule will affect the stack contents—which allows a PDA to store away information on the stack that will influence its future execution. Finite automata rely upon a similar feedback loop between their rules and current state, but the feedback is less powerful because the current state is completely forgotten when it changes, whereas pushing characters onto a stack preserves the old contents for later use.

Okay, so PDAs are a bit more powerful, but what are their limitations? Even if we're only interested in the kinds of pattern-matching applications we've already seen, pushdown automata are still seriously limited by the way a stack works. There's no random access to stack contents below the topmost character, so if a machine wants to read a character that's buried halfway down the stack, it has to pop everything above it. Once characters have been popped, they're gone forever; we designed a PDA to recognize strings with equal numbers of as and bs, but we can't adapt it to recognize strings with equal numbers of *three* different types of character ('abc', 'aabbcc', 'aaabbbccc', ...) because the information about the number of as gets destroyed by the process of counting the bs.

Aside from the *number* of times that pushed characters can be used, the last-in-first-out nature of a stack causes a problem with the *order* in which information is stored and retrieved. PDAs can recognize palindromes, but they can't recognize doubled-up strings like 'abab' and 'baaabaaa', because once information has been pushed onto a stack, it can only be consumed in reverse order.

If we move away from the specific problem of recognizing strings and try to treat these machines as a model of general-purpose computers, we can see that DFAs, NFAs, and PDAs are still a long way from being properly useful. For starters, none of them has a decent output mechanism: they can communicate success by going into an accept state, but can't output even a single character (much less a whole string of characters) to indicate a more detailed result. This inability to send information back out into the world means that they can't implement even a simple algorithm like adding two numbers together. And like finite automata, an individual PDA has a fixed program; there isn't an obvious way to build a PDA that can somehow read a program from its input and run it.

All of these weaknesses mean that we need a better model of computation to really investigate what computers are capable of, and that's exactly what the next chapter is about.

## CHAPTER 5

The Ultimate Machine

In Chapter 3 and Chapter 4, we investigated the capabilities of simple models of computation. We've seen how to recognize strings of increasing complexity, how to match regular expressions, and how to parse programming languages, all using basic machines with very little complexity.

But we've also seen that these machines—finite automata and pushdown automata—come with serious limitations that undermine their usefulness as realistic models of computation. How much more powerful do our toy systems need to get before they're able to escape these limitations and do everything that a normal computer can do? How much more complexity is required to model the behavior of RAM, or a hard drive, or a proper output mechanism? What does it take to design a machine that can actually *run programs* instead of always executing a single hardcoded task?

In the 1930s, Alan Turing was working on essentially this problem. At that time, the word "computer" meant a person, usually a woman, whose job was to perform long calculations by repeating a series of laborious mathematical operations by hand. Turing was looking for a way to understand and characterize the operation of a human computer so that the same tasks could be performed entirely by machines. In this chapter, we'll look at Turing's revolutionary ideas about how to design the simplest possible "automatic machine" that captures the full power and complexity of manual computation.

Deterministic Turing Machines

In Chapter 4, we were able to increase the computational power of a finite automaton by giving it a stack to use as external memory. Compared to the finite internal memory provided by a machine's states, the real advantage of a stack is that it can grow dynamically to accommodate any amount of information, allowing a pushdown automaton to handle problems where an arbitrary amount of data needs to be stored.

However, this particular form of external memory imposes inconvenient limitations on how data can be used after it's been stored. By replacing the stack with a more flexible storage mechanism, we can remove those limitations and achieve another increase in power.

Storage

> Computing is normally done by writing certain symbols on paper. We may suppose this paper is divided into squares like a child's arithmetic book. In elementary arithmetic the two-dimensional character of the paper is sometimes used. But such a use is always avoidable, and I think that it will be agreed that the two-dimensional character of paper is no essential of computation. I assume then that the computation is carried out on one-dimensional paper, i.e. on a tape divided into squares.
>
> —Alan Turing, *On Computable Numbers, with an Application to the Entscheidungsproblem* (*http://dx.doi.org/10.1112/plms/s2-42.1.230*)

Turing's solution was to equip a machine with a blank tape of unlimited length—effectively a one-dimensional array that can grow at both ends as needed—and allow it to read and write characters anywhere on the tape. A single tape serves as both storage and input: it can be prefilled with a string of characters to be treated as input, and the machine can read those characters during execution and overwrite them if necessary.

A finite state machine with access to an infinitely long tape is called a *Turing machine* (TM). That name usually refers to a machine with deterministic rules, but we can also call it a *deterministic Turing machine* (DTM) to be completely unambiguous.

We already know that a pushdown automaton can only access a single fixed location in its external storage—the top of the stack—but that seems too restrictive for a Turing machine. The whole point of providing a tape is to allow arbitrary amounts of data to be stored anywhere on it and read off again in any order, so how do we design a machine that can interact with the entire length of its tape?

One option is make the tape addressable by random access, labeling each square with a unique numerical address like computer RAM, so that the machine can immediately read or write any location. But that's more complicated than strictly necessary, and requires working out details like how to assign addresses to all the squares of an infinite tape and how the machine should specify the address of the square it wants to access.

Instead, a conventional Turing machine uses a simpler arrangement: a *tape head* that points at a specific position on the tape and can only read or write the character at that position. The tape head can move left or right by a single square after each step of computation, which means that a Turing machine has to move its head laboriously back and forth over the tape in order to reach distant locations. The use of a slow-moving head doesn't affect the machine's ability to access any of the data on the tape, only the amount of time it takes to do it, so it's a worthwhile trade-off for the sake of keeping things simple.

Having access to a tape allows us to solve new kinds of problems beyond simply accepting or rejecting strings. For example, we can design a DTM for incrementing a binary number in-place on the tape. To do this, we need to know how to increment a single *digit* of a binary number, but fortunately, that's easy: if the digit is a zero, replace it with a one; if the digit is a one, replace it with a zero, then increment the digit immediately to its left ("carry the one") using the same technique. The Turing machine just has to use this procedure to increment the binary number's rightmost digit and then return the tape head to its starting position:

- Give the machine three states, 1, 2 and 3, with state 3 being the accept state.
- Start the machine in state 1 with the tape head positioned over the rightmost digit of a binary number.
- When in state 1 and a zero (or blank) is read, overwrite it with a one, move the head right, and go into state 2.
- When in state 1 and a one is read, overwrite it with a zero and move the head left.
- When in state 2 and a zero or one is read, move the head right.
- When in state 2 and a blank is read, move the head left and go into state 3.

This machine is in state 1 when it's trying to increment a digit, state 2 when it's moving back to its starting position, and state 3 when it has finished. Below is a trace of its execution when the initial tape contains the string '1011'; the character currently underneath the tape head is shown surrounded by brackets, and the underscores represent the blank squares on either side of the input string.

State	Accepting?	Tape contents	Action
1	no	_101(1)__	write 0, move left
1	no	__10(1)0_	write 0, move left
1	no	___1(0)00	write 1, move right, go to state 2
2	no	__11(0)0_	move right
2	no	_110(0)__	move right
2	no	1100(_)__	move left, go to state 3
3	yes	_110(0)__	—

Moving the tape head back to its initial position isn't strictly necessary —if we made state 2 an accept state, the machine would halt immediately once it had successfully replaced a zero with a one, and the tape would still contain the correct result—but it's a desirable feature, because it leaves the head in a position where the machine can be run again by simply changing its state back to 1. By running the machine several times, we can repeatedly increment the number stored on the tape. This functionality could be reused as part of a larger machine for, say, adding or multiplying two binary numbers.

Rules

> Let us imagine the operations performed by the computer to be split up into "simple operations" that are so elementary that it is not easy to imagine them further divided. [...] The operation actually performed is determined [...] by the state of mind of the computer and the observed symbols. In particular, they determine the state of mind of the computer after the operation is carried out.
>
> We may now construct a machine to do the work of this computer.
>
> —Alan Turing, *On Computable Numbers, with an Application to the Entscheidungsproblem*

There are several "simple operations" we might want a Turing machine to perform in each step of computation: read the character at the tape head's current position, write a new character at that position, move the head left or right, or change state. Instead of having different kinds of rule for all these actions, we can keep things simple by designing a single format of rule that is flexible enough for every situation, just as we did for pushdown automata.

This unified rule format has five parts:

- The current state of the machine
- The character that must appear at the tape head's current position
- The next state of the machine
- The character to write at the tape head's current position
- The direction (left or right) in which to move the head after writing to the tape

Here we're making the assumption that a Turing machine will change state and write a character to the tape every time it follows a rule. As usual for a state machine, we can always make the "next state" the same as the current one if we want a rule that doesn't actually change state; similarly, if we want a rule that doesn't change the tape contents, we can just use one that writes the same character that it reads.

 We're also assuming that the tape head always moves at every step. This makes it impossible to write a single rule that updates the state or the tape contents without moving the head, but we can get the same effect by writing one rule that makes the desired change and another rule that moves the head back to its original position afterward.

The Turing machine for incrementing a binary number has six rules when they're written in this style:

- When in state 1 and a zero is read, write a one, move right, and go into state 2.
- When in state 1 and a one is read, write a zero, move left, and stay in state 1.
- When in state 1 and a blank is read, write a one, move right, and go into state 2.

- When in state 2 and a zero is read, write a zero, move right, and stay in state 2.
- When in state 2 and a one is read, write a one, move right, and stay in state 2.
- When in state 2 and a blank is read, write a blank, move left, and go into state 3.

We can show this machine's states and rules on a diagram similar to the ones we've already been using for finite and pushdown automata:

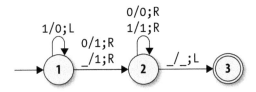

In fact, this is just like a DFA diagram except for the labels on the arrows. A label of the form a/b;L indicates a rule that reads character a from the tape, writes character b, and then moves the tape head one square to the left; a rule labelled a/b;R does almost the same, but moves the head to the right instead of the left.

Let's see how to use a Turing machine to solve a string-recognition problem that pushdown automata can't handle: identifying inputs that consist of one or more a characters followed by the same number of bs and cs (e.g., 'aaabbbccc'). The Turing machine that solves this problem has 6 states and 16 rules:

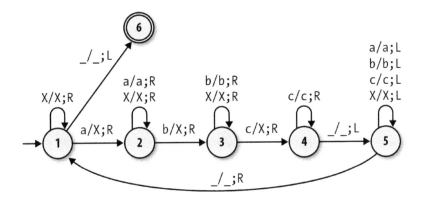

It works roughly like this:

1. Scan across the input string by repeatedly moving the tape head to the right until an a is found, then cross it out by replacing it with an X (state 1).
2. Scan right looking for a b, then cross it out (state 2).
3. Scan right looking for a c, then cross it out (state 3).
4. Scan right looking for the end of the input string (state 4), then scan left looking for the beginning (state 5).

5. Repeat these steps until all characters have been crossed out.

If the input string consists of one or more **a** characters followed by the same number of **b**s and **c**s, the machine will make repeated passes across the whole string, crossing out one of each character on every pass, and then enter an accept state when the entire string has been crossed out. Here's a trace of its execution when the input is `'aabbcc'`:

State	Accepting?	Tape contents	Action
1	no	_____(a)abbcc_	write X, move right, go to state 2
2	no	_____X(a)bbcc__	move right
2	no	____Xa(b)bcc___	write X, move right, go to state 3
3	no	___XaX(b)cc____	move right
3	no	__XaXb(c)c_____	write X, move right, go to state 4
4	no	_XaXbX(c)_____	move right
4	no	XaXbXc(_)_____	move left, go to state 5
5	no	_XaXbX(c)_____	move left
5	no	__XaXb(X)c_____	move left
5	no	___XaX(b)Xc____	move left
5	no	____Xa(X)bXc___	move left
5	no	_____X(a)XbXc__	move left
5	no	_____(X)aXbXc_	move left
5	no	_____(_)XaXbXc	move right, go to state 1
1	no	_____(X)aXbXc_	move right
1	no	_____X(a)XbXc__	write X, move right, go to state 2
2	no	____XX(X)bXc___	move right
2	no	___XXX(b)Xc____	write X, move right, go to state 3
3	no	__XXXX(X)c_____	move right
3	no	_XXXXX(c)_____	write X, move right, go to state 4
4	no	XXXXXX(_)_____	move left, go to state 5
5	no	_XXXXX(X)_____	move left
5	no	__XXXX(X)X_____	move left
5	no	___XXX(X)XX____	move left
5	no	____XX(X)XXX___	move left
5	no	_____X(X)XXXX__	move left
5	no	_____(X)XXXXX_	move left
5	no	_____(_)XXXXXX	move right, go to state 1
1	no	_____(X)XXXXX_	move right

State	Accepting?	Tape contents	Action
1	no	_____X(X)XXXX__	move right
1	no	___XX(X)XXX___	move right
1	no	___XXX(X)XX____	move right
1	no	__XXXX(X)X_____	move right
1	no	_XXXXX(X)_____	move right
1	no	XXXXXX(_)_____	move left, go to state 6
6	yes	_XXXXX(X)_____	—

This machine works because of the exact choice of rules during the scanning stages. For example, while the machine is in state 3—scanning right and looking for a c—it only has rules for moving the head past bs and Xs. If it hits some other character (e.g., an unexpected a), then it has no rule to follow, in which case it'll go into an implicit stuck state and stop executing, thereby rejecting that input.

 We're keeping things simple by assuming that the input can only ever contain the characters a, b, and c, but this machine won't work properly if that's not true; for example, it will accept the string 'XaXXbXXXc' even though it should be rejected. To correctly handle that sort of input, we'd need to add more states and rules that scan over the whole string to check that it doesn't contain any unexpected characters before the machine starts crossing anything off.

Determinism

For a particular Turing machine design to be deterministic, it has to obey the same constraints as a deterministic pushdown automaton (see "Determinism" on page 111), although this time we don't have to worry about free moves, because Turing machines don't have them.

A Turing machine's next action is chosen according to its current state and the character currently underneath its tape head, so a deterministic machine can only have one rule for each combination of state and character—the "no contradictions" rule—in order to prevent any ambiguity over what its next action will be. For simplicity, we'll relax the "no omissions" rule, just as we did for DPDAs, and assume there's an implicit stuck state that the machine can go into when no rule applies, instead of insisting that it must have a rule for every possible situation.

Simulation

Now that we have a good idea of how a deterministic Turing machine should work, let's build a Ruby simulation of one so we can see it in action.

The first step is to implement a Turing machine tape. This implementation obviously has to store the characters that are written on the tape, but it also needs to remember the current position of the tape head so that the simulated machine can read the current character, write a new character at the current position, and move the head left and right to reach other positions.

An elegant way of doing this is to split up the tape into three separate parts—all the characters to the left of the tape head, the single character directly underneath it, and all the characters to its right—and store each part separately. This makes it very easy to read and write the current character, and moving the tape head can be achieved by shuffling characters between all three parts; moving one square to the right, for instance, means that the current character becomes the last character to the left of the head, and the first character to the right of the head becomes the current one.

Our implementation must also maintain the illusion that the tape is infinitely long and filled with blank squares, but fortunately, we don't need an infinitely large data structure to do this. The only tape location that can be read at any given moment is the one that's beneath the head, so we just need to arrange for a new blank character to appear there whenever the head is moved beyond the finite number of nonblank characters already written on the tape. To make this work, we need to know in advance which character represents a blank square, and then we can make that character automatically appear underneath the tape head whenever it moves into an unexplored part of the tape.

So, the basic representation of a tape looks like this:

```
class Tape < Struct.new(:left, :middle, :right, :blank)
  def inspect
    "#<Tape #{left.join}(#{middle})#{right.join}>"
  end
end
```

This lets us create a tape and read the character beneath the tape head:

```
>> tape = Tape.new(['1', '0', '1'], '1', [], '_')
=> #<Tape 101(1)>
>> tape.middle
=> "1"
```

We can add operations to write to the current tape position[1] and move the head left and right:

```
class Tape
  def write(character)
    Tape.new(left, character, right, blank)
  end

  def move_head_left
    Tape.new(left[0..-2], left.last || blank, [middle] + right, blank)
  end
end
```

1. Tape, like Stack, is purely functional: writing to the tape and moving the head are nondestructive operations that return a new Tape object rather than updating the existing one.

```
    def move_head_right
      Tape.new(left + [middle], right.first || blank, right.drop(1), blank)
    end
  end
```

Now we can write onto the tape and move the head around:

```
>> tape
=> #<Tape 101(1)>
>> tape.move_head_left
=> #<Tape 10(1)1>
>> tape.write('0')
=> #<Tape 101(0)>
>> tape.move_head_right
=> #<Tape 1011(_)>
>> tape.move_head_right.write('0')
=> #<Tape 1011(0)>
```

In Chapter 4, we used the word *configuration* to refer to the combination of a pushdown automaton's state and stack, and the same idea is useful here. We can say that a *Turing machine configuration* is the combination of a state and a tape, and implement Turing machine rules that deal directly with those configurations:

```
class TMConfiguration < Struct.new(:state, :tape)
end

class TMRule < Struct.new(:state, :character, :next_state,
                          :write_character, :direction)
  def applies_to?(configuration)
    state == configuration.state && character == configuration.tape.middle
  end
end
```

A rule only applies when the machine's current state and the character currently underneath the tape head match its expectations:

```
>> rule = TMRule.new(1, '0', 2, '1', :right)
=> #<struct TMRule
      state=1,
      character="0",
      next_state=2,
      write_character="1",
      direction=:right
   >
>> rule.applies_to?(TMConfiguration.new(1, Tape.new([], '0', [], '_')))
=> true
>> rule.applies_to?(TMConfiguration.new(1, Tape.new([], '1', [], '_')))
=> false
>> rule.applies_to?(TMConfiguration.new(2, Tape.new([], '0', [], '_')))
=> false
```

Once we know that a rule applies to a particular configuration, we need the ability to update that configuration by writing a new character, moving the tape head, and changing the machine's state in accordance with the rule:

```
class TMRule
  def follow(configuration)
    TMConfiguration.new(next_state, next_tape(configuration))
  end

  def next_tape(configuration)
    written_tape = configuration.tape.write(write_character)

    case direction
    when :left
      written_tape.move_head_left
    when :right
      written_tape.move_head_right
    end
  end
end
```

That code seems to work fine:

```
>> rule.follow(TMConfiguration.new(1, Tape.new([], '0', [], '_')))
=> #<struct TMConfiguration state=2, tape=#<Tape 1(_)>>
```

The implementation of DTMRulebook is almost the same as DFARulebook and DPDARulebook, except #next_configuration doesn't take a character argument, because there's no external input to read characters from (only the tape, which is already part of the configuration):

```
class DTMRulebook < Struct.new(:rules)
  def next_configuration(configuration)
    rule_for(configuration).follow(configuration)
  end

  def rule_for(configuration)
    rules.detect { |rule| rule.applies_to?(configuration) }
  end
end
```

Now we can make a DTMRulebook for the "increment a binary number" Turing machine and use it to manually step through a few configurations:

```
>> rulebook = DTMRulebook.new([
     TMRule.new(1, '0', 2, '1', :right),
     TMRule.new(1, '1', 1, '0', :left),
     TMRule.new(1, '_', 2, '1', :right),
     TMRule.new(2, '0', 2, '0', :right),
     TMRule.new(2, '1', 2, '1', :right),
     TMRule.new(2, '_', 3, '_', :left)
   ])
=> #<struct DTMRulebook rules=[…]>
>> configuration = TMConfiguration.new(1, tape)
=> #<struct TMConfiguration state=1, tape=#<Tape 101(1)>>
>> configuration = rulebook.next_configuration(configuration)
=> #<struct TMConfiguration state=1, tape=#<Tape 10(1)0>>
>> configuration = rulebook.next_configuration(configuration)
=> #<struct TMConfiguration state=1, tape=#<Tape 1(0)00>>
```

```
>> configuration = rulebook.next_configuration(configuration)
=> #<struct TMConfiguration state=2, tape=#<Tape 11(0)0>>
```

It's convenient to wrap all this up in a DTM class so we can have #step and #run methods, just like we did with the small-step semantics implementation in Chapter 2:

```ruby
class DTM < Struct.new(:current_configuration, :accept_states, :rulebook)
  def accepting?
    accept_states.include?(current_configuration.state)
  end

  def step
    self.current_configuration = rulebook.next_configuration(current_configuration)
  end

  def run
    step until accepting?
  end
end
```

We now have a working simulation of a deterministic Turing machine, so let's give it some input and try it out:

```
>> dtm = DTM.new(TMConfiguration.new(1, tape), [3], rulebook)
=> #<struct DTM …>
>> dtm.current_configuration
=> #<struct TMConfiguration state=1, tape=#<Tape 101(1)>>
>> dtm.accepting?
=> false
>> dtm.step; dtm.current_configuration
=> #<struct TMConfiguration state=1, tape=#<Tape 10(1)0>>
>> dtm.accepting?
=> false
>> dtm.run
=> nil
>> dtm.current_configuration
=> #<struct TMConfiguration state=3, tape=#<Tape 110(0)_>>
>> dtm.accepting?
=> true
```

As with our DPDA simulation, we need to do a bit more work to gracefully handle a Turing machine becoming stuck:

```
>> tape = Tape.new(['1', '2', '1'], '1', [], '_')
=> #<Tape 121(1)>
>> dtm = DTM.new(TMConfiguration.new(1, tape), [3], rulebook)
=> #<struct DTM …>
>> dtm.run
NoMethodError: undefined method `follow' for nil:NilClass
```

This time we don't need a special representation of a stuck state. Unlike a PDA, a Turing machine doesn't have an external input, so we can tell it's stuck just by looking at its rulebook and current configuration:

```ruby
class DTMRulebook
  def applies_to?(configuration)
```

```
        !rule_for(configuration).nil?
      end
    end

    class DTM
      def stuck?
        !accepting? && !rulebook.applies_to?(current_configuration)
      end

      def run
        step until accepting? || stuck?
      end
    end
```

Now the simulation will notice it's stuck and stop automatically:

```
>> dtm = DTM.new(TMConfiguration.new(1, tape), [3], rulebook)
=> #<struct DTM …>
>> dtm.run
=> nil
>> dtm.current_configuration
=> #<struct TMConfiguration state=1, tape=#<Tape 1(2)00>>
>> dtm.accepting?
=> false
>> dtm.stuck?
=> true
```

Just for fun, here's the Turing machine we saw earlier, for recognizing strings like
'aaabbbccc':

```
>> rulebook = DTMRulebook.new([
    # state 1: scan right looking for a
    TMRule.new(1, 'X', 1, 'X', :right), # skip X
    TMRule.new(1, 'a', 2, 'X', :right), # cross out a, go to state 2
    TMRule.new(1, '_', 6, '_', :left),  # find blank, go to state 6 (accept)

    # state 2: scan right looking for b
    TMRule.new(2, 'a', 2, 'a', :right), # skip a
    TMRule.new(2, 'X', 2, 'X', :right), # skip X
    TMRule.new(2, 'b', 3, 'X', :right), # cross out b, go to state 3

    # state 3: scan right looking for c
    TMRule.new(3, 'b', 3, 'b', :right), # skip b
    TMRule.new(3, 'X', 3, 'X', :right), # skip X
    TMRule.new(3, 'c', 4, 'X', :right), # cross out c, go to state 4

    # state 4: scan right looking for end of string
    TMRule.new(4, 'c', 4, 'c', :right), # skip c
    TMRule.new(4, '_', 5, '_', :left),  # find blank, go to state 5

    # state 5: scan left looking for beginning of string
    TMRule.new(5, 'a', 5, 'a', :left),  # skip a
    TMRule.new(5, 'b', 5, 'b', :left),  # skip b
    TMRule.new(5, 'c', 5, 'c', :left),  # skip c
    TMRule.new(5, 'X', 5, 'X', :left),  # skip X
    TMRule.new(5, '_', 1, '_', :right)  # find blank, go to state 1
```

```
  ])
=> #<struct DTMRulebook rules=[…]>
>> tape = Tape.new([], 'a', ['a', 'a', 'b', 'b', 'b', 'c', 'c', 'c'], '_')
=> #<Tape (a)aabbbccc>
>> dtm = DTM.new(TMConfiguration.new(1, tape), [6], rulebook)
=> #<struct DTM …>
>> 10.times { dtm.step }; dtm.current_configuration
=> #<struct TMConfiguration state=5, tape=#<Tape XaaXbbXc(c)_>>
>> 25.times { dtm.step }; dtm.current_configuration
=> #<struct TMConfiguration state=5, tape=#<Tape _XXa(X)XbXXc_>>
>> dtm.run; dtm.current_configuration
=> #<struct TMConfiguration state=6, tape=#<Tape _XXXXXXXX(X)_>>
```

This implementation was pretty easy to build—it's not hard to simulate a Turing machine as long as we've got data structures to represent tapes and rulebooks. Of course, Alan Turing specifically intended them to be simple so they would be easy to build and to reason about, and we'll see later (in "General-Purpose Machines" on page 154) that this ease of implementation is an important property.

Nondeterministic Turing Machines

In "Equivalence" on page 94, we saw that nondeterminism makes no difference to what a finite automaton is capable of, while "Nonequivalence" on page 125 showed us that a nondeterministic pushdown automaton can do more than a deterministic one. That leaves us with an obvious question about Turing machines: does adding nondeterminism[2] make a Turing machine more powerful?

In this case the answer is no: a nondeterministic Turing machine can't do any more than a deterministic one. Pushdown automata are the exception here, because both DFAs and DTMs have enough power to simulate their nondeterministic counterparts. A single state of a finite automaton can be used to represent a combination of many states, and a single Turing machine tape can be used to store the contents of many tapes, but a single pushdown automaton stack can't represent many possible stacks at once.

So, just as with finite automata, a deterministic Turing machine can simulate a nondeterministic one. The simulation works by using the tape to store a queue of suitably encoded Turing machine configurations, each one containing a possible current state and tape of the simulated machine. When the simulation starts, there's only one configuration stored on the tape, representing the starting configuration of the simulated machine. Each step of the simulated computation is performed by reading the configuration at the front of the queue, finding each rule that applies to it, and using that rule to generate a new configuration that is written onto the tape at the back of the queue. Once this has been done for every applicable rule, the frontmost configuration is erased

---

2. For a Turing machine, "nondeterminism" means allowing more than one rule per combination of state and character, so that multiple execution paths are possible from a single starting configuration.

and the process starts again with the next configuration in the queue. The simulated machine step is repeated until the configuration at the front of the queue represents a machine that has reached an accept state.

This technique allows a deterministic Turing machine to explore all possible configurations of a simulated machine in breadth-first order; if there is any way for the nondeterministic machine to reach an accept state, the simulation will find it, even if other execution paths lead to infinite loops. Actually implementing the simulation as a rulebook requires a lot of detail, so we won't try to do it here, but the fact that it's possible means that we can't make a Turing machine any more powerful just by adding nondeterminism.

Maximum Power

Deterministic Turing machines represent a dramatic tipping point from limited computing machines to full-powered ones. In fact, any attempt to upgrade the specification of Turing machines to make them more powerful is doomed to failure, because they're already capable of *simulating* any potential enhancement.[3] While adding certain features can make Turing machines smaller or more efficient, there's no way to give them fundamentally new capabilities.

We've already seen why this is true for nondeterminism. Let's look at four other extensions to conventional Turing machines—internal storage, subroutines, multiple tapes, and multidimensional tape—and see why none of them provides an increase in computational power. While some of the simulation techniques involved are complicated, in the end, they're all just a matter of programming.

Internal Storage

Designing a rulebook for a Turing machine can be frustrating because of the lack of arbitrary internal storage. For instance, we often want the machine to move the tape head to a particular position, read the character that's stored there, then move to a different part of the tape and perform some action that depends on which character it read earlier. Superficially, this seems impossible, because there's nowhere for the machine to "remember" that character—it's still written on the tape, of course, and we can move the head back over there and read it again whenever we like, but once the head moves away from that square, we can no longer trigger a rule based on its contents.

---

3. Strictly speaking, this is only true for enhancements that we actually know how to implement. A Turing machine *would* become more powerful if we gave it the magical ability to instantly deduce the answers to questions that no conventional Turing machine can answer (see Chapter 8), but in practice, there's no way of doing that.

It would be more convenient if a Turing machine had some temporary internal storage —call it "RAM," "registers," "local variables," or whatever—where it could save the character from the current tape square and refer back to it later, even after the head has moved to a different part of the tape entirely. In fact, if a Turing machine had that capability, we wouldn't need to limit it to storing characters from the tape: it could store any relevant information, like the intermediate result of some calculation the machine is performing, and free us from the chore of having to move the head around to write scraps of data onto the tape. This extra flexibility feels like it could give a Turing machine the ability to perform new kinds of tasks.

Well, as with nondeterminism, adding extra internal storage to a Turing machine certainly would make certain tasks easier to perform, but it wouldn't enable the machine to do anything it can't already do. The desire to store intermediate results inside the machine instead of on the tape is relatively easy to dismiss, because the tape works just fine for storing that kind of information, even if it takes a while for the head to move back and forth to access it. But we have to take the character-remembering point more seriously, because a Turing machine would be very limited if it couldn't make use of the contents of a tape square after moving the head somewhere else.

Fortunately, a Turing machine already has perfectly good internal storage: its current state. There is no upper limit to the number of states available to a Turing machine, although for any particular set of rules, that number must be finite and decided in advance, because there's no way to create new states during a computation. If necessary, we can design a machine with a hundred states, or a thousand, or a billion, and use its current state to retain arbitrary amounts of information from one step to the next.

This inevitably means duplicating rules to accommodate multiple states whose meanings are identical except for the information they are "remembering." Instead of having a single state that means "scan right looking for a blank square," a machine can have one state for "scan right looking for a blank square (remembering that I read an a earlier)," another for "scan right looking for a blank square (remembering that I read a b earlier)," and so on for all possible characters—although the number of characters is finite too, so this duplication always has a limit.

Here's a simple Turing machine that uses this technique to copy a character from the beginning of a string to the end:

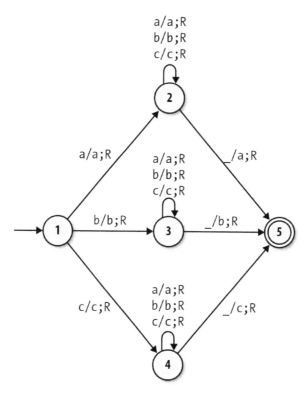

```ruby
>> rulebook = DTMRulebook.new([
    # state 1: read the first character from the tape
    TMRule.new(1, 'a', 2, 'a', :right), # remember a
    TMRule.new(1, 'b', 3, 'b', :right), # remember b
    TMRule.new(1, 'c', 4, 'c', :right), # remember c

    # state 2: scan right looking for end of string (remembering a)
    TMRule.new(2, 'a', 2, 'a', :right), # skip a
    TMRule.new(2, 'b', 2, 'b', :right), # skip b
    TMRule.new(2, 'c', 2, 'c', :right), # skip c
    TMRule.new(2, '_', 5, 'a', :right), # find blank, write a

    # state 3: scan right looking for end of string (remembering b)
    TMRule.new(3, 'a', 3, 'a', :right), # skip a
    TMRule.new(3, 'b', 3, 'b', :right), # skip b
    TMRule.new(3, 'c', 3, 'c', :right), # skip c
    TMRule.new(3, '_', 5, 'b', :right), # find blank, write b

    # state 4: scan right looking for end of string (remembering c)
    TMRule.new(4, 'a', 4, 'a', :right), # skip a
    TMRule.new(4, 'b', 4, 'b', :right), # skip b
```

```
        TMRule.new(4, 'c', 4, 'c', :right), # skip c
        TMRule.new(4, '_', 5, 'c', :right)  # find blank, write c
      ])
 => #<struct DTMRulebook rules=[…]>
 >> tape = Tape.new([], 'b', ['c', 'b', 'c', 'a'], '_')
 => #<Tape (b)cbca>
 >> dtm = DTM.new(TMConfiguration.new(1, tape), [5], rulebook)
 => #<struct DTM …>
 >> dtm.run; dtm.current_configuration.tape
 => #<Tape bcbcab(_)>
```

States 2, 3, and 4 of this machine are almost identical, except they each represent a machine that is remembering a different character from the beginning of the string, and in this case, they all do something different when they reach the end.

 The machine only works for strings made up of the characters a, b, and c; if we wanted it to work for strings containing *any* alphabetic characters (or alphanumeric characters, or whatever larger set we chose), we'd have to add a lot more states—one for each character that might need to be remembered—and a lot more rules to go with them.

Exploiting the current state in this way allows us to design Turing machines that can remember any finite combination of facts while the tape head moves back and forth, effectively giving us the same capabilities as a machine with explicit "registers" for internal storage, at the expense of using a large number of states.

Subroutines

A Turing machine's rulebook is a long, hardcoded list of extremely low-level instructions, and it can be difficult to write these rules without losing sight of the high-level task that the machine is meant to perform. Designing a rulebook would be easier if there was a way of calling a *subroutine*: if some part of the machine could store all the rules for, say, incrementing a number, then our rulebook could just say "now increment a number" instead of having to manually string together the instructions to make that happen. And again, perhaps that extra flexibility would allow us to design machines with new capabilities.

But this is another feature that is really just about convenience, not overall power. Just like the finite automata that implement individual fragments of a regular expression (see "Semantics" on page 83), several small Turing machines can be connected together to make a larger one, with each small machine effectively acting as a subroutine. The binary-increment machine we saw earlier can have its states and rules built into a larger machine that adds two binary numbers together, and that adder can itself be built into an even larger machine that performs multiplication.

When the smaller machine only needs to be "called" from a single state of the larger one, this is easy to arrange: just include a copy of the smaller machine, merging its start and accept states with the states of the larger machine where the subroutine call should begin and end. This is how we'd expect to use the incrementing machine as part of an adding machine, because the overall design of the rulebook would be to repeat the single task "if the first number isn't zero, decrement the first number and increment the second number" as many times as possible. There'd only be one place in the machine where incrementing would need to happen, and only one place for execution to continue after the incrementing work had completed.

The only difficulty comes when we want to call a particular subroutine from more than one place in the overall machine. A Turing machine has no way to store a "return address" to let the subroutine know which state to move back into once it has finished, so superficially, we can't support this more general kind of code reuse. But we can solve this problem with duplication, just like we did in "Internal Storage" on page 148: rather than incorporating a single copy of the smaller machine's states and rules, we can build in many copies, one for each place where it needs to be used in the larger machine.

For example, the easiest way to turn the "increment a number" machine into an "add three to a number" machine is to connect three copies together to achieve an overall design of "increment the number, then increment the number, then increment the number." This takes the larger machine through several intermediate states that track its progress toward the final goal, with each use of "increment the number" originating from and returning to a different intermediate state:

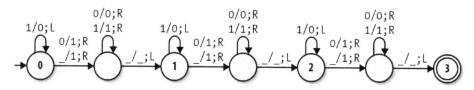

```
>> def increment_rules(start_state, return_state)
     incrementing = start_state
     finishing = Object.new
     finished = return_state

     [
       TMRule.new(incrementing, '0', finishing,     '1', :right),
       TMRule.new(incrementing, '1', incrementing, '0', :left),
       TMRule.new(incrementing, '_', finishing,     '1', :right),
       TMRule.new(finishing,    '0', finishing,     '0', :right),
       TMRule.new(finishing,    '1', finishing,     '1', :right),
       TMRule.new(finishing,    '_', finished,      '_', :left)
     ]
   end
=> nil
>> added_zero, added_one, added_two, added_three = 0, 1, 2, 3
=> [0, 1, 2, 3]
>> rulebook = DTMRulebook.new(
     increment_rules(added_zero, added_one) +
     increment_rules(added_one, added_two) +
```

```
    increment_rules(added_two, added_three)
  )
=> #<struct DTMRulebook rules=[…]>
>> rulebook.rules.length
=> 18
>> tape = Tape.new(['1', '0', '1'], '1', [], '_')
=> #<Tape 101(1)>
>> dtm = DTM.new(TMConfiguration.new(added_zero, tape), [added_three], rulebook)
=> #<struct DTM …>
>> dtm.run; dtm.current_configuration.tape
=> #<Tape 111(0)_>
```

The ability to compose states and rules in this way allows us to build Turing machine rulebooks of arbitrary size and complexity, without needing any explicit support for subroutines, as long as we're prepared to accept the increase in machine size.

Multiple Tapes

The power of a machine can sometimes be increased by expanding its external storage. For example, a pushdown automaton becomes more powerful when we give it access to a second stack, because two stacks can be used to simulate an infinite tape: each stack stores the characters from one half of the simulated tape, and the PDA can pop and push characters between the stacks to simulate the motion of the tape head, just like our Tape implementation in "Simulation" on page 141. Any finite state machine with access to an infinite tape is effectively a Turing machine, so just adding an extra stack makes a pushdown automaton significantly more powerful.

It's therefore reasonable to expect that a Turing machine might be made more powerful by adding one or more extra tapes, each with its own independent tape head, but again that's not the case. A single Turing machine tape has enough space to store the contents of any number of tapes by interleaving them: three tapes containing abc, def, and ghi can be stored together as adgbehcfi. If we leave a blank square alongside each inter-leaved character, the machine has space to write markers indicating where all of the simulated tape heads are located: by using X characters to mark the current position of each head, we can represent both the contents and the head positions of the tapes ab(c), (d)ef, and g(h)i with the single tape a_dXg_b_e_hXcXf_i_.

Programming a Turing machine to use multiple simulated tapes is complicated, but the fiddly details of reading, writing, and moving the heads of the tapes can be wrapped up in dedicated states and rules ("subroutines") so that the main logic of the machine doesn't become too convoluted. In any case, however inconvenient the programming turns out to be, a single-tape Turing machine is ultimately capable of performing any task that a multitape machine can, so adding extra tapes to a Turing machine doesn't give it any new abilities.

Multidimensional Tape

Finally, it's tempting to try giving a Turing machine a more spacious storage device. Instead of using a linear tape, we could provide an infinite two-dimensional grid of squares and allow the tape head to move up and down as well as left and right. That would be useful for any situation where we want the machine to quickly access a particular part of its external storage without having to move the head past everything else on it, and it would allow us to leave an unlimited amount of blank space around multiple strings so that each of them can easily grow longer, rather than having to manually shuffle information along the whole tape to make space whenever we want to insert a character.

Inevitably, though, a grid can be simulated with one-dimensional tape. The easiest way is to use *two* one-dimensional tapes: a primary tape for actually storing data, and a secondary tape to use as scratch space. Each row of the simulated grid[4] is stored on the primary tape, top row first, with a special character marking the end of each row.

The primary tape head is positioned over the current character as usual, so to move left and right on the simulated grid, the machine simply moves the head left and right. If the head hits an end-of-row marker, a subroutine is used to shuffle everything along the tape to make the grid one space wider.

To move up or down on the simulated grid, the tape head must move a complete row to the left or right respectively. The machine can do this by first moving the tape head to the beginning or end of the current row, using the secondary tape to record the distance travelled, and then moving the head to the same offset in the previous or next row. If the head moves off the top or bottom of the simulated grid, a subroutine can be used to allocate a new empty row for the head to move into.

This simulation does require a machine with two tapes, but we know how to simulate that too, so we end up with a simulated grid stored on two simulated tapes that are themselves stored on a single native tape. The two layers of simulation introduce a lot of extra rules and states, and require the underlying machine to take many steps to perform a single step of the simulated one, but the added size and slowness don't prevent it from (eventually) doing what it's supposed to do.

General-Purpose Machines

All the machines we've seen so far have a serious shortcoming: their rules are hardcoded, leaving them unable to adapt to different tasks. A DFA that accepts all the strings that match a particular regular expression can't learn to accept a different set of strings; an NPDA that recognizes palindromes will only ever recognize palindromes; a Turing machine that increments a binary number will never be useful for anything else.

---

4. Although the grid itself is infinite, it can only ever have a finite number of characters written onto it, so we only need to store the rectangular area containing all the nonblank characters.

This isn't how most real-world computers work. Rather than being specialized for a particular job, modern digital computers are designed to be *general purpose* and can be programmed to perform many different tasks. Although the instruction set and CPU design of a programmable computer is fixed, it's able to use *software* to control its hardware and adapt its behavior to whatever job its user wants it to do.

Can any of our simple machines do that? Instead of having to design a new machine every time we want to do a different job, can we design a *single* machine that can read a program from its input and then do whatever job the program specifies?

Perhaps unsurprisingly, a Turing machine is powerful enough to read the description of a simple machine from its tape—a deterministic finite automaton, say—and then run a simulation of that machine to find out what it does. In "Simulation" on page 66, we wrote some Ruby code to simulate a DFA from its description, and with a bit of work, the ideas from that code can be turned into the rulebook of a Turing machine that runs the same simulation.

 There's an important difference between a Turing machine that simulates a *particular* DFA and one that can simulate *any* DFA.

Designing a Turing machine to reproduce the behavior of a specific DFA is very easy—after all, a Turing machine is just a deterministic finite automaton with a tape attached. Every rule from the DFA's rulebook can be converted directly into an equivalent Turing machine rule; instead of reading from the DFA's external input stream, each converted rule reads a character from the tape and moves the head to the next square. But this isn't especially interesting, since the resulting Turing machine is no more useful than the original DFA.

More interesting is a Turing machine that performs a *general* DFA simulation. This machine can read a DFA design from the tape—rules, start state, and accept states—and walk through each step of that DFA's execution, using another part of the tape to keep track of the simulated machine's current state and remaining input. The general simulation is much harder to implement, but it gives us a single Turing machine that can adapt itself to any job that a DFA can do, just by being fed a description of that DFA as input.

The same applies to our deterministic Ruby simulations of NFAs, DPDAs and NPDAs, each of which can be turned into a Turing machine capable of simulating any automaton of that type. But crucially, it also works for our simulation of Turing machines themselves: by reimplementing `Tape`, `TMRule`, `DTMRulebook`, and `DTM` as Turing machine rules, we are able to design a machine that can simulate any other DTM by reading its rules, accept states, and initial configuration from the tape and stepping through its execution, essentially acting as a Turing machine rulebook interpreter. A machine that does this is called a *universal Turing machine* (UTM).

This is exciting, because it makes the maximum computational power of Turing machines available in a single programmable device. We can write software—an encoded description of a Turing machine—onto a tape, feed that tape to the UTM, and have our software executed to produce the behavior we want. Finite automata and push-down automata can't simulate their own kind in this way, so Turing machines not only mark the transition from limited to powerful computing machines, but also from single-purpose devices to fully programmable ones.

Let's look briefly at how a universal Turing machine works. There are a lot of fiddly and uninteresting technical details involved in actually building a UTM, so our exploration will be relatively superficial, but we should at least be able to convince ourselves that such a thing is possible.

Encoding

Before we can design a UTM's rulebook, we have to decide how to represent an entire Turing machine as a sequence of characters on a tape. A UTM has to read in the rules, accept states, and starting configuration of an arbitrary Turing machine, then repeatedly update the simulated machine's current configuration as the simulation progresses, so we need a practical way of storing all this information in a way that the UTM can work with.

One challenge is that every Turing machine has a finite number of states and a finite number of different characters it can store on its tape, with both of these numbers being fixed in advance by its rulebook, and a UTM is no exception. If we design a UTM that can handle 10 different tape characters, how can it simulate a machine whose rules use 11 characters? If we're more generous and design it to handle a hundred different characters, what happens when we want to simulate a machine that uses a thousand? However many characters we decide to use for the UTM's own tape, it'll never be enough to directly represent every possible Turing machine.

There's also the risk of unintentional character collisions between the simulated machine and the UTM. To store Turing machine rules and configurations on a tape, we need to be able to mark their boundaries with characters that will have special meaning to the UTM, so that it can tell where one rule ends and another begins. But if we choose, say, X as the special marker between rules, we'll run into problems if any of the simulated rules contain the character X. Even if we set aside a super-special set of reserved characters that only a universal Turing machine is allowed to use, they'd still cause problems if we ever tried to simulate the UTM with itself, so the machine wouldn't be truly universal. This suggests we need to do some kind of escaping to prevent ordinary characters from the simulated machine getting incorrectly interpreted as special characters by the UTM.

We can solve both of these problems by coming up with a scheme that uses a fixed repertoire of characters to encode the tape contents of a simulated machine. If the encoding scheme only uses certain characters, then we can be sure it's safe for the UTM to use other characters for special purposes, and if the scheme can accommodate any number of simulated states and characters, then we don't need to worry about the size and complexity of the machine being simulated.

The precise details of the encoding scheme aren't important as long as it meets these goals. To give an example, one possible scheme uses a *unary*[5] representation to encode different values as different-sized strings of a single repeated character (e.g., 1): if the simulated machine uses the characters a, b, and c, these could be encoded in unary as 1, 11, and 111. Another character, say 0, can be used as a marker to delimit unary values: the string acbc might be represented as 101110110111. This isn't a very space-efficient scheme, but it can scale up to accommodate any number of encoded characters simply by storing longer and longer strings of 1s on the tape.

Once we've decided how to encode individual characters, we need a way to represent the rules of the simulated Turing machine. We can do that by encoding the separate parts of the rule (state, character, next state, character to write, direction to move) and concatenating them together on the tape, using special separator characters where necessary. In our example encoding scheme, we could represent states in unary too—state 1 is 1, state 2 is 11, and so on—although we're free to use dedicated characters to represent left and right (say, L and R), since we know there will only ever be two directions.

We can concatenate individual rules together to represent an entire rulebook; similarly, we can encode the current configuration of the simulated machine by concatenating the representation of its current state with the representation of its current tape contents.[6] And that gives us what we want: a complete Turing machine written as a sequence of characters on another Turing machine's tape, ready to be brought to life by a simulation.

Simulation

Fundamentally a universal Turing machine works in the same way as the Ruby simulation we built in "Simulation" on page 141, just much more laboriously.

The description of the simulated machine—its rulebook, accept states, and starting configuration—is stored in encoded form on the UTM's tape. To perform a single step of the simulation, the UTM moves its head back and forth between the rules, current state, and tape of the simulated machine in search of a rule that applies to the current configuration. When it finds one, it updates the simulated tape according to the character and direction specified by that rule, and puts the simulated machine into its new state.

---

5. Binary is base two, unary is base one.

6. We've glossed over exactly how a tape should be represented, but that's not difficult either, and we always have the option of storing it on a simulated second tape by using the technique from "Multiple Tapes" on page 153.

That process is repeated until the simulated machine enters an accept state, or gets stuck by reaching a configuration to which no rule applies.

Computation and Computability

Throughout the first part of this book we've played around with familiar examples of computation: imperative programming languages, state machines, and general-purpose computers. Those examples have showed us that computation is—more or less—the process of using a system to manipulate information and answer questions.

Now, in this second part, we're going to be a bit more adventurous. We'll start by looking for computation in unfamiliar places, and finish by exploring the fundamental limits of what computing machines can do.

As programmers we work with languages and machines that are designed to fit our mental models of the world, and we expect them to come equipped with features that make it easy to translate our ideas into implementations. These human-centered designs are motivated by convenience rather than necessity; even the simple design of a Turing machine is meant to remind us of a mathematician working with pencil and paper.

But friendly, familiar machines aren't the only places where computation can happen. More unusual systems can be just as computationally powerful, even if their inner workings aren't as easy for humans to control or to understand. We'll investigate this idea in Chapter 6 by trying to write programs in an extremely minimal language that doesn't seem to have any useful features at all, and follow the thread further in Chapter 7, where we'll survey a variety of simple systems and see how they're able to perform the same computations as more complex machines.

Once we've convinced ourselves that full-powered computation can happen in many different kinds of system, we'll spend Chapter 8 examining what computation itself is actually capable of. It's natural to assume that computers can solve essentially any problem as long as enough time and effort is spent on writing a suitable program, but there turn out to be hard theoretical constraints: certain problems just can't be solved by any computer, no matter how fast and efficient it is.

Unfortunately some of these insoluble problems are concerned with predicting the behavior of programs, which is exactly the kind of thing that programmers would like computers to help them with. We'll look at some strategies for coping with these hard limits of the computational universe, and conclude in Chapter 9 by exploring how to use abstraction to squeeze approximate answers out of unanswerable questions.

## CHAPTER 6

Programming with Nothing

*If you wish to make an apple pie from scratch, you must
first invent the universe.*

—Carl Sagan

In this book, we've been trying to understand computation by building models of it.
So far, we've modelled computation by designing simple imaginary machines with
various constraints, and seen that different constraints produce systems with different
amounts of computational power.

The Turing machines from Chapter 5 are interesting because they're able to implement
complex behavior without relying on complex features. Equipped with just a tape, a
read/write head, and a fixed set of rules, Turing machines have enough flexibility to
simulate the behavior of machines with better storage capabilities, or nondeterministic
execution, or any other fancy feature we might want. This tells us that full-blown computation doesn't require a machine with a lot of underlying complexity, just the ability
to store values, retrieve them, and use them to make simple decisions.

Models of computation don't have to look like machines; they can look like programming languages instead. The SIMPLE programming language from Chapter 2 can certainly perform computation, but it's not elegant in the way that a Turing machine is.
It already has plenty of syntax—numbers, Booleans, binary expressions, variables, assignments, sequences, conditionals, loops—and we haven't even started to add the
features that would make it suitable for writing real programs: strings, data structures,
procedure calls, and so on.

To turn SIMPLE into a genuinely useful programming language would be hard work, and
the resulting design would contain a lot of incidental detail and not reveal very much
about the basic nature of computation. It would be more interesting to start from
scratch and create something minimal, a Turing machine of the programming language
world, so that we can see which features are essential for computation and which are
just incidental noise.

In this chapter, we're going to investigate an extremely minimal programming language called the *untyped lambda calculus*. First, we'll experiment with writing programs in a dialect of Ruby that approximates the lambda calculus by using as few language features as possible; this will still just be Ruby programming, but imposing imaginary constraints gives us an easy way to explore a restricted semantics without having to learn a whole new language. Then, once we've seen what this very limited feature set is capable of, we'll take those features and implement them as a standalone language— with its own parser, abstract syntax, and operational semantics—using the techniques we've learned in earlier chapters.

Impersonating the Lambda Calculus

To see how programming in a minimal language can work, let's try solving a problem in Ruby without taking advantage of its many helpful features. Naturally, that means no gems, no standard library, and no modules, methods, classes, or objects, but since we're trying to be as minimal as possible, we'll also avoid the use of control structures, assignment, arrays, strings, numbers, and Booleans.

Of course, there won't be a language left to program in if we avoid absolutely *every* feature of Ruby, so here are the ones we're going to keep:

- Referring to variables
- Creating procs
- Calling procs

That means we can only write Ruby code that looks like this:

```ruby
-> x { -> y { x.call(y) } }
```

 This is roughly how untyped lambda calculus programs look, and that's a good enough approximation for our purposes. We'll look at the lambda calculus itself in more detail in "Implementing the Lambda Calculus" on page 197.

To make our code shorter and easier to read, we're also going to allow ourselves to use constants as abbreviations: if we create a complex expression, we can assign it to a constant to give it a short name that we can reuse later. Referring to the name is no different from retyping the original expression again—the name just makes the code less verbose—so we won't be making ourselves dependent upon Ruby's assignment features. At any time, we can decide to be more strict and undo the abbreviations by replacing each constant with the proc it refers to, at the expense of making our programs much longer.

Working with Procs

Since we're going to be building entire programs out of procs, let's spend a minute looking at their properties before we dive into using them.

 For the moment, we're still using full-featured Ruby to illustrate the general behavior of procs. We won't impose the restrictions until we start writing code to tackle "The Problem" on page 164.

Plumbing

Procs are plumbing for moving values around programs. Consider what happens when we call a proc:

```
-> x { x + 2 }.call(1)
```

The value that's provided as an argument to the call, in this case 1, flows *into* the parameter of the block, in this case x, and then flows *out of* the parameter to all the places where it's used, so Ruby ends up evaluating 1 + 2. It's the rest of the language that does the actual work; procs just connect parts of the program together and make values flow to where they're needed.

This already doesn't bode well for our experiment in minimal Ruby. If procs can only move values between the pieces of Ruby that actually do something with them, how are we ever going to be able to build useful programs out of procs alone? We'll get to that once we've explored some other properties of procs.

Arguments

Procs can take multiple arguments, but this isn't an essential feature. If we've got a proc that takes multiple arguments...

```
-> x, y {
  x + y
}.call(3, 4)
```

...we can always rewrite it as nested single-argument procs:

```
-> x {
  -> y {
    x + y
  }
}.call(3).call(4)
```

Here, the outer proc takes one argument, x, and returns the inner proc, which also takes one argument, y. We can call the outer proc with a value for x and then call the inner proc with a value for y, and we get the same result as in the multiargument case.[1]

---

1. This is called *currying*, and we can use Proc#curry to do this transformation automatically.

Since we're trying to remove as many features of Ruby as possible, let's restrict ourselves to creating and calling *single-argument* procs; it won't make things much worse.

Equality

The only way to find out about the code inside a proc is to call it, so two procs are interchangeable if they produce identical results when called with the same arguments, even if their internal code is different. This idea of treating two things as equal based on their externally visible behavior is called *extensional equality*.

For example, say we have a proc p:

```
>> p = -> n { n * 2 }
=> #<Proc (lambda)>
```

We can make another proc, q, which takes an argument and simply calls p with it:

```
>> q = -> x { p.call(x) }
=> #<Proc (lambda)>
```

p and q are obviously two different procs, but they're extensionally equal, because they do exactly the same thing for any argument:

```
>> p.call(5)
=> 10
>> q.call(5)
=> 10
```

Knowing that p is equivalent to -> x { p.call(x) } opens up new opportunities for refactoring. If we see the general pattern -> x { p.call(x) } in our program, we may choose to eliminate it by replacing the whole expression with just p, and under certain circumstances (which we'll see later), we might decide to go in the other direction too.

Syntax

Ruby provides a choice of syntax for creating and calling procs. From this point onward, we'll use -> *arguments* { *body* } to create a proc and square brackets to call it:

```
>> -> x { x + 5 }[6]
=> 11
```

This makes it easy to see the body and argument of the proc without too much extra syntax getting in the way.

The Problem

Our goal is to write the well-known FizzBuzz program:

> Write a program that prints the numbers from 1 to 100. But for multiples of three, print "Fizz" instead of the number, and for the multiples of five, print "Buzz." For numbers that are multiples of both three and five, print "FizzBuzz."

—Imran Ghory, *Using FizzBuzz to Find Developers who Grok Coding* (*http://imranontech .com/2007/01/24/using-fizzbuzz-to-find-developers-who-grok-coding/*)

This is an intentionally simple problem, designed to test whether an interview candidate has any programming experience at all. Anybody who knows how to program should be able to solve it without much difficulty.

Here's an implementation of FizzBuzz in full-featured Ruby:

```ruby
(1..100).each do |n|
  if (n % 15).zero?
    puts 'FizzBuzz'
  elsif (n % 3).zero?
    puts 'Fizz'
  elsif (n % 5).zero?
    puts 'Buzz'
  else
    puts n.to_s
  end
end
```

This isn't the cleverest implementation of FizzBuzz—there are plenty of clever ones out there (*http://redd.it/10d7w*)—but it's a straightforward one that anyone could write without thinking about it.

However, this program contains some `puts` statements, and we have no way to print text to the console using only procs,[2] so we're going to replace it with a roughly equivalent program that returns an array of strings rather than printing them:

```ruby
(1..100).map do |n|
  if (n % 15).zero?
    'FizzBuzz'
  elsif (n % 3).zero?
    'Fizz'
  elsif (n % 5).zero?
    'Buzz'
  else
    n.to_s
  end
end
```

This is still a meaningful solution to the FizzBuzz problem, but now it's one that we have a chance of implementing using only procs.

Despite its simplicity, this is quite an ambitious program if we don't have any of the features of a programming language: it creates a range, maps over it, evaluates a big conditional, does some arithmetic with the modulo operator, uses the `Fixnum#zero?` predicate, uses some string literals, and turns numbers into strings with `Fixnum#to_s`.

---

2. We could certainly *model* printing to the console by introducing a proc to represent standard output and devising a convention for how to send text to it, but that would complicate the exercise in an uninteresting way. FizzBuzz isn't about printing, it's about arithmetic and control flow.

That's a fair amount of built-in Ruby functionality, and we're going to have to strip it all out and reimplement it with procs.

Numbers

We're going to start by focusing on the numbers that appear in FizzBuzz. How can we possibly represent numbers without using `Fixnums` or any of the other datatypes that Ruby provides?

If we're going to try to implement numbers[3] from scratch, we'd better have a solid understanding of what we're implementing. What is a *number*, anyway? It's hard to come up with a concrete definition that doesn't accidentally assume some aspect of what we're trying to define; for example, "something that tells us how many…" is not very useful, because "how many" is really just another way of saying "number."

Here's one way of characterizing numbers: imagine we have a bag of apples and a bag of oranges. We take an apple out of one bag, an orange out of the other, and put them aside; then we keep taking out an apple and an orange together until at least one of the bags is empty.

If both bags become empty at the same time, we've learned something interesting: in spite of containing different things, those bags had some shared property that meant they became empty at the same time; at every point during the procedure of repeatedly removing an item from each bag, either both bags were nonempty or both bags were empty. This abstract property shared by the bags is what we can call a number (although we don't know *which* number!), and we can compare these bags with any other bag in the world to see if it has the same "number" as them.

So one way to characterize numbers is by repetition (or *iteration*) of some action, in this case, taking an item from a bag. Each number corresponds to a unique way of repeating an action: the number one corresponds to just performing the action; the number two corresponds to performing it and then performing it again; and so on. The number zero, unsurprisingly, corresponds to not performing the action at all.

Since making and calling procs are the only "actions" our program can perform, we can try implementing a number n with code that repeats the action of calling a proc n times.

For example, if we were allowed to define methods—which we're not, but play along —then we could define #one as a method that takes a proc and some arbitrary second argument, and then calls the proc with that argument once:

```
def one(proc, x)
  proc[x]
end
```

---

3. To be more specific, what we want to implement here are the *nonnegative integers*: zero, one, two, three, and so on.

We could also define #two, which calls the proc once and then calls it again with whatever the result of calling it the first time was:[4]

```
def two(proc, x)
  proc[proc[x]]
end
```

And so on:

```
def three(proc, x)
  proc[proc[proc[x]]]
end
```

Following this pattern, it's natural to define #zero as a method that takes a proc and some other argument, ignores the proc entirely (i.e., calls it zero times), and returns the second argument untouched:

```
def zero(proc, x)
  x
end
```

All of these implementations can be translated into methodless representations; for example, we can replace the method #one with a proc that takes two arguments[5] and then calls the first argument with the second one. They look like this:

```
ZERO  = -> p { -> x {        x    } }
ONE   = -> p { -> x {      p[x]   } }
TWO   = -> p { -> x {    p[p[x]]  } }
THREE = -> p { -> x { p[p[p[x]]] } }
```

This avoids functionality that we're not allowed to use, and instead gives names to procs by assigning them to constants.

 This technique of representing data as pure code is named *Church encoding* after Alonzo Church, the inventor of the lambda calculus (*http: //dx.doi.org/10.2307/2371045*). The encoded numbers are *Church numerals*, and we'll shortly be seeing examples of *Church Booleans* and *Church pairs*.

Now, although we're eschewing Ruby's features *inside* our FizzBuzz solution, it would be useful to translate these foreign representations of numbers into native Ruby values once they're *outside* our code—so that they can be usefully inspected on the console or asserted against in tests, or at least so that we can convince ourselves that they really do represent numbers in the first place.

---

4. This is called "iterating the function."

5. Actually, "takes two arguments" is inaccurate, because we're restricting ourselves to single-argument procs (see "Arguments" on page 163). To be technically correct, we should say "takes one argument and returns a new proc that takes another argument," but that's too long-winded, so we'll stick with the shorthand and just remember what we really mean.

Fortunately we can write a #to_integer method that performs this conversion:

```
def to_integer(proc)
  proc[-> n { n + 1 }][0]
end
```

This method takes a proc that represents a number and calls it with another proc (which just increments its argument) and the native Ruby number 0. If we call #to_integer with ZERO then, because of ZERO's definition, the incrementing proc doesn't get called at all and we get an untouched Ruby 0 back:

```
>> to_integer(ZERO)
=> 0
```

And if we call #to_integer with THREE, the incrementing proc gets called three times and we get a Ruby 3 back:

```
>> to_integer(THREE)
=> 3
```

So these proc-based representations really do encode numbers, and we can convert them into a more practical representation whenever we want to.

For FizzBuzz, we need the numbers five, fifteen, and one hundred, which can all be implemented with the same technique:

```
FIVE    = -> p { -> x { p[p[p[p[p[x]]]]] } }
FIFTEEN = -> p { -> x { p[p[p[p[p[p[p[p[p[p[p[p[p[p[p[x]]]]]]]]]]]]]]] } }
HUNDRED = -> p { -> x { p[p[p[p[p[p[p[p[p[p[p[p[p[p[p[p[p[p[p[p[p[p[p[p[p[p[p[p[p[↵
p[p[p[p[p[p[p[p[p[p[p[p[p[p[p[p[p[p[p[p[p[p[p[p[p[p[p[p[p[p[p[p[p[p[p[p[p[p[p[↵
p[p[p[p[p[p[p[p[p[p[p[p[p[p[p[p[p[p[p[p[p[p[p[p[p[p[p[p[p[p[p[x]]]]]]]]]]]]]]]]]]]]]]]]]]]]]]]]↵
]]]]]]]]]]]]]]]]]]]]]]]]]]]]]]]]]]]]]]]]]]]]]]]]]]]]]]]]]]]]]]]]]]]]]]]] } }
```

These aren't very compact definitions, but they work, as we can confirm with #to_inte ger:

```
>> to_integer(FIVE)
=> 5
>> to_integer(FIFTEEN)
=> 15
>> to_integer(HUNDRED)
=> 100
```

So, going back to the FizzBuzz program, all of the Ruby numbers can be replaced with their proc-based implementations:

```
(ONE..HUNDRED).map do |n|
  if (n % FIFTEEN).zero?
    'FizzBuzz'
  elsif (n % THREE).zero?
    'Fizz'
  elsif (n % FIVE).zero?
    'Buzz'
  else
    n.to_s
```

```
      end
  end
```

 As promised, we're writing `ONE` instead of `-> p { -> x { p[x] } }`, and so on, to make the code clearer.

Unfortunately, this program doesn't work anymore, because we're now using operations like `..` and `%` on the proc-based implementations of numbers. Because Ruby doesn't know how to treat these as numbers it'll just blow up: `TypeError: can't iterate from Proc`, `NoMethodError: undefined method `%' for #<Proc (lambda)>`, and so on. We need to replace all of the operations to work with these representations—and we can only use procs to do it.

Before we can reimplement any of the operations, though, we need implementations of `true` and `false`.

Booleans

How can we represent Booleans using only procs? Well, Booleans exist solely to be used in conditional statements, and in general, a conditional says "if some Boolean then *this* else *that*":

```
>> success = true
=> true
>> if success then 'happy' else 'sad' end
=> "happy"
>> success = false
=> false
>> if success then 'happy' else 'sad' end
=> "sad"
```

So the real job of a Boolean is to allow us to choose between two options, and we can take advantage of this by representing a Boolean as a proc that chooses one of two values. Instead of thinking of a Boolean as a lifeless piece of data that can be read by some future code to decide which of two options to choose, we'll just implement it directly as a piece of code that, when called with two options, either chooses the first option or chooses the second option.

Implemented as methods, then, `#true` and `#false` could be:

```
def true(x, y)
  x
end

def false(x, y)
  y
end
```

#true is a method that takes two arguments and returns the first one, and #false takes two arguments and returns the second. This is enough to give us crude conditional behavior:

```
>> success = :true
=> :true
>> send(success, 'happy', 'sad')
=> "happy"
>> success = :false
=> :false
>> send(success, 'happy', 'sad')
=> "sad"
```

As before, it's straightforward to translate these methods into procs:

```
TRUE  = -> x { -> y { x } }
FALSE = -> x { -> y { y } }
```

And just as we defined #to_integer as a sanity check, to make sure it was possible to convert proc-based numbers into Ruby numbers, so we can define a #to_boolean method that can turn the TRUE and FALSE procs into Ruby's native true and false objects:

```
def to_boolean(proc)
  proc[true][false]
end
```

This works by taking a proc that represents a Boolean and calling it with true as its first argument and false as its second. TRUE just returns its first argument, so to_boolean(TRUE) will return true, and likewise for FALSE:

```
>> to_boolean(TRUE)
=> true
>> to_boolean(FALSE)
=> false
```

So representing Booleans with procs is surprisingly easy, but for FizzBuzz, we don't just need Booleans, we need a proc-only implementation of Ruby's if-elsif-else. In fact, because of the way these Boolean implementations work, it's easy to write an #if method too:

```
def if(proc, x, y)
  proc[x][y]
end
```

And that's easy to translate into a proc:

```
IF =
  -> b {
    -> x {
      -> y {
        b[x][y]
      }
    }
  }
```

Clearly IF doesn't need to do any useful work, because the Boolean itself picks the right argument—IF is just sugar—but it looks more natural than calling the Boolean directly:

```
>> IF[TRUE]['happy']['sad']
=> "happy"
>> IF[FALSE]['happy']['sad']
=> "sad"
```

Incidentally, this means we can revise the definition of #to_boolean to use IF:

```
def to_boolean(proc)
  IF[proc][true][false]
end
```

While we're refactoring, it's worth noting that the implementation of IF can be cleaned up significantly, because it contains some procs that are equivalent to simpler ones, as discussed in "Equality" on page 164. For example, look at IF's innermost proc:

```
-> y {
  b[x][y]
}
```

This code means:

1. Take an argument y.
2. Call b with x to get a proc.
3. Call that proc with y.

Steps 1 and 3 are dead wood: when we call this proc with an argument, it just passes it on to another proc. So the whole thing is equivalent to just step 2, b[x], and we can remove the dead wood in the implementation of IF to make it simpler:

```
IF =
  -> b {
    -> x {
      b[x]
    }
  }
```

We can see the same pattern again in what's now the innermost proc:

```
-> x {
  b[x]
}
```

For the same reason, this proc is the same as just b, so we can simplify IF even further:

```
IF = -> b { b }
```

We're not going to be able to simplify it any more than that.

IF doesn't do anything useful—it's TRUE and FALSE that do all the work —so we *could* simplify further by getting rid of it altogether. But our goal is to translate the original FizzBuzz solution into procs as faithfully as possible, so it's convenient to use IF to remind us where the if-elsif-else expression appeared in the original, even though it's purely decorative.

Anyway, now that we have IF, we can go back to the FizzBuzz program and replace the Ruby if-elsif-else with nested calls to IF:

```
(ONE..HUNDRED).map do |n|
  IF[(n % FIFTEEN).zero?][
    'FizzBuzz'
  ][IF[(n % THREE).zero?][
    'Fizz'
  ][IF[(n % FIVE).zero?][
    'Buzz'
  ][
    n.to_s
  ]]]
end
```

Predicates

Our next job is to replace Fixnum#zero? with a proc-based implementation that will work with proc-based numbers. The underlying algorithm of #zero? for Ruby values is something like this:

```
def zero?(n)
  if n == 0
    true
  else
    false
  end
end
```

(This is more verbose than is necessary, but it's explicit about what happens: compare the number with 0; if it's equal, then return true; otherwise, return false.)

How can we adapt this to handle procs instead of Ruby numbers? Look at our implementation of numbers again:

```
ZERO  = -> p { -> x {        x     } }
ONE   = -> p { -> x {      p[x]    } }
TWO   = -> p { -> x {    p[p[x]]   } }
THREE = -> p { -> x {  p[p[p[x]]]  } }
⋮
```

Notice that ZERO is the only number that doesn't call p—it just returns x—whereas all of the other numbers call p at least once. We can take advantage of this: if we call an unknown number with TRUE as its second argument, it'll return TRUE immediately if the number is ZERO. If it's not ZERO, then it'll return whatever calling p returns, so if we make p a proc that always returns FALSE, we'll get the behavior we want:

```
def zero?(proc)
  proc[-> x { FALSE }][TRUE]
end
```

Again, it's easy to rewrite this as a proc:

```
IS_ZERO = -> n { n[-> x { FALSE }][TRUE] }
```

We can use #to_boolean on the console to check that it works:

```
>> to_boolean(IS_ZERO[ZERO])
=> true
>> to_boolean(IS_ZERO[THREE])
=> false
```

That's working fine, so in FizzBuzz, we can replace all of the calls to #zero? with IS_ZERO:

```
(ONE..HUNDRED).map do |n|
  IF[IS_ZERO[n % FIFTEEN]][
    'FizzBuzz'
  ][IF[IS_ZERO[n % THREE]][
    'Fizz'
  ][IF[IS_ZERO[n % FIVE]][
    'Buzz'
  ][
    n.to_s
  ]]]
end
```

Pairs

We have usable data in the form of numbers and Booleans, but we don't have any data *structures* for storing more than one value in an organized way. We'll soon need some kind of data structure in order to implement more complex functionality, so let's pause briefly to introduce one.

The simplest data structure is a *pair*, which is like a two-element array. Pairs are quite easy to implement:

```
PAIR  = -> x { -> y { -> f { f[x][y] } } }
LEFT  = -> p { p[-> x { -> y { x } } ] }
RIGHT = -> p { p[-> x { -> y { y } } ] }
```

The purpose of a pair is to store two values and provide them again later on request. To construct a pair, we call PAIR with two values, an x and a y, and it returns its inner proc:

```
-> f { f[x][y] }
```

This is a proc that, when called with another proc f, will call it back with the earlier values of x and y as arguments. LEFT and RIGHT are the operations that pick out the left and the right element of a pair by calling it with a proc that returns its first or second argument respectively. It all works simply enough:

```
>> my_pair = PAIR[THREE][FIVE]
=> #<Proc (lambda)>
>> to_integer(LEFT[my_pair])
=> 3
>> to_integer(RIGHT[my_pair])
=> 5
```

This very simple data structure is enough to get us started; we'll use pairs later, in "Lists" on page 181, as a building block for more complex structures.

Numeric Operations

Now that we have numbers, Booleans, conditionals, predicates, and pairs, we're almost ready to reimplement the modulo operator.

Before we can do anything as ambitious as taking the modulo of two numbers, we need to be able to perform simpler operations like incrementing and decrementing a single number. Incrementing is fairly straightforward:

```
INCREMENT = -> n { -> p { -> x { p[n[p][x]] } } }
```

Look at how INCREMENT works: we call it with a proc-based number n, and it'll return a new proc that takes some other proc p and some arbitrary second argument x, just like numbers do.

What does this new proc do when we call it? First it calls n with p and x—since n is a number, this means "call p, n times, on x," just as the original number would have done —and then calls p one more time on the result. Overall, then, this is a proc whose first argument gets called n + 1 times on its second argument, which is exactly how to represent the number n + 1.

But what about decrementing? This looks like a much harder problem: once a proc has already been called n times, it's easy enough to add an extra call so that it's been called n + 1 times, but there's no obvious way to "undo" one of them to make n - 1 calls.

One solution is to design a proc that, when called n times on some initial argument, returns the number n - 1. Fortunately, pairs give us a way of doing exactly that. Think about what this Ruby method does:

```
def slide(pair)
  [pair.last, pair.last + 1]
end
```

When we call slide with a two-element array of numbers, it returns a new two-element array containing the second number and the number that's one greater than it; if the input array contains *consecutive* numbers, the effect is that of "sliding" a narrow window up the number line:

```
>> slide([3, 4])
=> [4, 5]
>> slide([8, 9])
=> [9, 10]
```

This is useful to us, because by starting that window at -1, we can arrange a situation where the first number in the array is *one less than* the number of times we've called slide on it, even though we're only ever incrementing numbers:

```
>> slide([-1, 0])
=> [0, 1]
>> slide(slide([-1, 0]))
=> [1, 2]
>> slide(slide(slide([-1, 0])))
=> [2, 3]
>> slide(slide(slide(slide([-1, 0]))))
=> [3, 4]
```

We can't do exactly this with proc-based numbers, because we don't have a way of representing -1, but what's interesting about slide is that it only looks at the second number in the array anyway, so we can put any dummy value—say, 0—in place of -1 and still get exactly the same result:

```
>> slide([0, 0])
=> [0, 1]
>> slide(slide([0, 0]))
=> [1, 2]
>> slide(slide(slide([0, 0])))
=> [2, 3]
>> slide(slide(slide(slide([0, 0]))))
=> [3, 4]
```

This is the key to making DECREMENT work: we can turn slide into a proc, use the proc representation of the number n to call slide n times on a pair of ZEROs, and then use LEFT to pull out the left number from the resulting pair.

```
SLIDE     = -> p { PAIR[RIGHT[p]][INCREMENT[RIGHT[p]]] }
DECREMENT = -> n { LEFT[n[SLIDE][PAIR[ZERO][ZERO]]] }
```

Here's DECREMENT in action:

```
>> to_integer(DECREMENT[FIVE])
=> 4
>> to_integer(DECREMENT[FIFTEEN])
=> 14
>> to_integer(DECREMENT[HUNDRED])
=> 99
>> to_integer(DECREMENT[ZERO])
=> 0
```

The result of DECREMENT[ZERO] is actually just the dummy left element from the initial PAIR[ZERO][ZERO] value, which doesn't get SLIDE called on it at all in this case. Since we don't have negative numbers, 0 is the closest reasonable answer we can give for DECREMENT[ZERO], so using ZERO as the dummy value is a good idea.

Now that we have INCREMENT and DECREMENT, it's possible to implement more useful numeric operations like addition, subtraction, multiplication, and exponentiation:

```
ADD      = -> m { -> n { n[INCREMENT][m] } }
SUBTRACT = -> m { -> n { n[DECREMENT][m] } }
MULTIPLY = -> m { -> n { n[ADD[m]][ZERO] } }
POWER    = -> m { -> n { n[MULTIPLY[m]][ONE] } }
```

These implementations are largely self-explanatory. If we want to add m and n, that's just "starting with m, INCREMENT it n times," and likewise for subtraction; once we have ADD, we can multiply m and n by saying "starting with ZERO, ADD m to it n times," and similarly for exponentiation with MULTIPLY and ONE.

In "Reducing expressions" on page 202, we'll get Ruby to work through the small-step evaluation of ADD[ONE][ONE] to show how it produces TWO.

That should be enough arithmetic to get us started, but before we can implement % with procs, we need to know an algorithm for performing the modulo operation. Here's one that works on Ruby's numbers:

```
def mod(m, n)
  if n <= m
    mod(m - n, n)
  else
    m
  end
end
```

For example, to calculate 17 modulo 5:

- If 5 is less than or equal to 17, which it is, then subtract 5 from 17 and call #mod again with the result, i.e. try 12 modulo 5.
- 5 is less than or equal to 12, so try 7 modulo 5.
- 5 is less than or equal to 7, so try 2 modulo 5.
- 5 is *not* less than or equal to 2, so return the result 2.

But we can't implement #mod with procs yet, because it uses another operator, <=, for which we don't yet have an implementation, so we need to digress briefly to implement <= with procs.

We can begin with what looks like a pointlessly circular implementation of #less_or_equal? for Ruby numbers:

```
def less_or_equal?(m, n)
  m - n <= 0
end
```

This isn't very useful, because it begs the question by relying on <=, but it does at least recast the problem in terms of two other problems we've already looked at: subtraction and comparison with zero. Subtraction we've already dealt with, and we've done comparison for *equality* with zero, but how do we implement *less-than-or-equal-to* zero?

As it happens we don't need to worry about it, because zero is already the smallest number we know how to implement—recall that our proc-based numbers are the nonnegative integers—so "less than zero" is a meaningless concept in our number system. If we use SUBTRACT to subtract a larger number from a smaller one, it'll just return ZERO, because there's no way for it to return a negative number, and ZERO is the closest it can get:[6]

```
>> to_integer(SUBTRACT[FIVE][THREE])
=> 2
>> to_integer(SUBTRACT[THREE][FIVE])
=> 0
```

We've already written IS_ZERO, and since SUBTRACT[m][n] will return ZERO if m is less than or equal to n (i.e., if n is at least as large as m), we have enough to implement #less_or_equal? with procs:

```
def less_or_equal?(m, n)
  IS_ZERO[SUBTRACT[m][n]]
end
```

And let's turn that method into a proc:

```
IS_LESS_OR_EQUAL =
  -> m { -> n {
    IS_ZERO[SUBTRACT[m][n]]
  } }
```

Does it work?

```
>> to_boolean(IS_LESS_OR_EQUAL[ONE][TWO])
=> true
>> to_boolean(IS_LESS_OR_EQUAL[TWO][TWO])
=> true
>> to_boolean(IS_LESS_OR_EQUAL[THREE][TWO])
=> false
```

Looks good.

---

6. You might protest that 3 - 5 = 0 isn't called "subtraction" where you come from, and you'd be right: the technical name for this operation is "monus," because the nonnegative integers under addition form a commutative monoid instead of a proper abelian group.

This gives us the missing piece for our implementation of #mod, so we can rewrite it with procs:

```
def mod(m, n)
  IF[IS_LESS_OR_EQUAL[n][m]][
    mod(SUBTRACT[m][n], n)
  ][
    m
  ]
end
```

And replace the method definition with a proc:

```
MOD =
  -> m { -> n {
    IF[IS_LESS_OR_EQUAL[n][m]][
      MOD[SUBTRACT[m][n]][n]
    ][
      m
    ]
  } }
```

Great! Does it work?

```
>> to_integer(MOD[THREE][TWO])
SystemStackError: stack level too deep
```

No.

Ruby dives off into an infinite recursive loop when we call MOD, because our translation of Ruby's native functionality into procs has missed something important about the semantics of conditionals. In languages like Ruby, the if-else statement is nonstrict (or *lazy*): we give it a condition and two blocks, and it evaluates the condition to decide which of the two blocks to evaluate and return—it never evaluates both.

The problem with our IF implementation is that we can't take advantage of the lazy behavior that's built into Ruby if-else; we just say "call a proc, IF, with two other procs," so Ruby charges ahead and evaluates both arguments before IF gets a chance to decide which one to return.

Look again at MOD:

```
MOD =
  -> m { -> n {
    IF[IS_LESS_OR_EQUAL[n][m]][
      MOD[SUBTRACT[m][n]][n]
    ][
      m
    ]
  } }
```

When we call MOD with values for m and n, and Ruby starts evaluating the body of the inner proc, it reaches the recursive call to MOD[SUBTRACT[m][n]][n] and immediately starts evaluating it as an argument to pass to IF, regardless of whether

IS_LESS_OR_EQUAL[n][m] evaluated to TRUE or FALSE. This second call to MOD results in another unconditional recursive call, and so on, hence the infinite recursion.

To fix this, we need a way of telling Ruby to defer evaluation of IF's second argument until we're sure we need it. Evaluation of any expression in Ruby can be deferred by wrapping it in a proc, but wrapping an arbitrary Ruby value in a proc will generally change its meaning (e.g., the result of 1 + 2 does not equal -> { 1 + 2 }), so we might need to be more clever.

Fortunately we don't, because this is a special case: we know that the result of calling MOD will be a single-argument proc, because *all* of our values are single-argument procs, and we already know (from "Equality" on page 164) that wrapping any proc p with another proc that takes the same arguments as p and immediately calls p with them will produce a value that is indistinguishable from just p, so we can use that trick here to defer the recursive call without affecting the meaning of the value being passed into IF:

```
MOD =
  -> m { -> n {
    IF[IS_LESS_OR_EQUAL[n][m]][
      -> x {
        MOD[SUBTRACT[m][n]][n][x]
      }
    ][
      m
    ]
  } }
```

This wraps the recursive MOD call in -> x { ...[x] } to defer it; Ruby now won't try to evaluate the body of that proc when it calls IF, but if the proc gets chosen by IF and returned as the result, it can be called by its recipient to finally trigger the (now definitely required) recursive call to MOD.

Does MOD work *now*?

```
>> to_integer(MOD[THREE][TWO])
=> 1
>> to_integer(MOD[
     POWER[THREE][THREE]
   ][
     ADD[THREE][TWO]
   ])
=> 2
```

Yes! Hooray!

But don't celebrate yet, because there's another, more insidious problem: we are defining the constant MOD *in terms of the constant MOD*, so this definition is *not* just an innocent abbreviation. This time we're not merely assigning a complex proc to a constant in order to reuse it later; in fact, we're relying on Ruby's assignment semantics in order to assume that, even though MOD has obviously not yet been defined while we're still defining it, we can nonetheless refer to it in MOD's implementation and expect it to have *become* defined by the time we evaluate it later.

That's cheating, because in principle, we should be able to undo all of the abbreviations —"where we said MOD, what we actually meant was this long proc"—but that's impossible as long as MOD is defined in terms of itself.

We can solve this problem with the *Y combinator*, a famous piece of helper code designed for exactly this purpose: defining a recursive function without cheating. Here's what it looks like:

```
Y = -> f { -> x { f[x[x]] } }[-> x { f[x[x]] } ] }
```

The Y combinator is hard to explain accurately without lots of detail, but here's a (technically inaccurate) sketch: when we call the Y combinator with a proc, it will call that proc *with the proc itself as the first argument*. So, if we write a proc that expects an argument and then call the Y combinator with that proc, then the proc will get itself as that argument and therefore can use that argument whenever it wants to call itself.

Sadly, for the same reason that MOD was looping forever, the Y combinator will loop forever in Ruby too, so we need a modified version. It's the expression x[x] that causes the problem, and we can again fix the problem by wrapping the occurrences of that expression in inert -> y { …[y] } procs to defer their evaluation:

```
Z = -> f { -> x { f[-> y { x[x][y] }] } }[-> x { f[-> y { x[x][y] }] } ] }
```

This is the *Z combinator*, which is just the Y combinator adapted for strict languages like Ruby.

We can now finally make a satisfactory implementation of MOD by giving it an extra argument, f, wrapping a call to the Z combinator around it, and calling f where we used to call MOD:

```
MOD =
  Z[-> f { -> m { -> n {
    IF[IS_LESS_OR_EQUAL[n][m]][
      -> x {
        f[SUBTRACT[m][n]][n][x]
      }
    ][
      m
    ]
  } } }]
```

Thankfully this noncheating version of MOD still works:

```
>> to_integer(MOD[THREE][TWO])
=> 1
>> to_integer(MOD[
     POWER[THREE][THREE]
   ][
     ADD[THREE][TWO]
   ])
=> 2
```

Now we can replace all of the occurrences of % in the FizzBuzz program with calls to MOD:

```
(ONE..HUNDRED).map do |n|
  IF[IS_ZERO[MOD[n][FIFTEEN]]][
    'FizzBuzz'
  ][IF[IS_ZERO[MOD[n][THREE]]][
    'Fizz'
  ][IF[IS_ZERO[MOD[n][FIVE]]][
    'Buzz'
  ][
    n.to_s
  ]]]
end
```

Lists

We only have a few Ruby features left to reimplement for FizzBuzz: the range, the #map, the string literals, and the Fixnum#to_s. We've seen lots of detail for the other values and operations we've implemented, so we'll go through the remaining ones quickly and in as little detail as possible. (Don't worry about understanding everything; we'll just be getting a flavor.)

To be able to implement ranges and #map, we need an implementation of lists, and the easiest way to build lists is to use pairs. The implementation works like a linked list, where each pair stores a value and a pointer to the next pair in the list; in this case, we use nested pairs instead of pointers. The standard list operations look like this:

```
EMPTY    = PAIR[TRUE][TRUE]
UNSHIFT  = -> l { -> x {
             PAIR[FALSE][PAIR[x][l]]
           } }
IS_EMPTY = LEFT
FIRST    = -> l { LEFT[RIGHT[l]] }
REST     = -> l { RIGHT[RIGHT[l]] }
```

And they work like this:

```
>> my_list =
     UNSHIFT[
       UNSHIFT[
         UNSHIFT[EMPTY][THREE]
       ][TWO]
     ][ONE]
=> #<Proc (lambda)>
>> to_integer(FIRST[my_list])
=> 1
>> to_integer(FIRST[REST[my_list]])
=> 2
>> to_integer(FIRST[REST[REST[my_list]]])
=> 3
>> to_boolean(IS_EMPTY[my_list])
=> false
>> to_boolean(IS_EMPTY[EMPTY])
=> true
```

Using FIRST and REST to pull out individual elements of lists is quite clumsy, so as with numbers and Booleans we can write a #to_array method to help us on the console:

```
def to_array(proc)
  array = []

  until to_boolean(IS_EMPTY[proc])
    array.push(FIRST[proc])
    proc = REST[proc]
  end

  array
end
```

This makes it easier to inspect lists:

```
>> to_array(my_list)
=> [#<Proc (lambda)>, #<Proc (lambda)>, #<Proc (lambda)>]
>> to_array(my_list).map { |p| to_integer(p) }
=> [1, 2, 3]
```

How can we implement ranges? In fact, instead of finding a way to explicitly represent ranges as procs, let's just write a proc that can build a list of all the elements in a range. For native Ruby numbers and "lists" (i.e., arrays), we can write it like this:

```
def range(m, n)
  if m <= n
    range(m + 1, n).unshift(m)
  else
    []
  end
end
```

This algorithm is slightly contrived in anticipation of the available list operations, but it makes sense: the list of all the numbers from m to n is the same as the list of all the numbers from m + 1 to n with m unshifted onto the front; if m is greater than n, then the list of numbers is empty.

Happily, we already have everything we need to translate this method directly into procs:

```
RANGE =
  Z[-> f {
    -> m { -> n {
      IF[IS_LESS_OR_EQUAL[m][n]][
        -> x {
          UNSHIFT[f[INCREMENT[m]][n]][m][x]
        }
      ][
        EMPTY
      ]
    } }
  }]
```

Note the use of the Z combinator for recursion, and a deferring -> x { … [x] } proc around the TRUE branch of the conditional.

Does this work?

```
>> my_range = RANGE[ONE][FIVE]
=> #<Proc (lambda)>
>> to_array(my_range).map { |p| to_integer(p) }
=> [1, 2, 3, 4, 5]
```

Yes, so let's use it in FizzBuzz:

```
RANGE[ONE][HUNDRED].map do |n|
  IF[IS_ZERO[MOD[n][FIFTEEN]]][
    'FizzBuzz'
  ][IF[IS_ZERO[MOD[n][THREE]]][
    'Fizz'
  ][IF[IS_ZERO[MOD[n][FIVE]]][
    'Buzz'
  ][
    n.to_s
  ]]]
end
```

To implement #map, we can use a helper called FOLD, which is a bit like Ruby's Enumerable#inject:

```
FOLD =
  Z[-> f {
    -> l { -> x { -> g {
      IF[IS_EMPTY[l]][
        x
      ][
        -> y {
          g[f[REST[l]][x][g]][FIRST[l]][y]
        }
      ]
    } } }
  }]
```

FOLD makes it easier to write procs that process every item in a list:

```
>> to_integer(FOLD[RANGE[ONE][FIVE]][ZERO][ADD])
=> 15
>> to_integer(FOLD[RANGE[ONE][FIVE]][ONE][MULTIPLY])
=> 120
```

Once we have FOLD, we can write MAP concisely:

```
MAP =
  -> k { -> f {
    FOLD[k][EMPTY][
      -> l { -> x { UNSHIFT[l][f[x]] } }
```

```
    ]
  } }
```

Does MAP work?

```
>> my_list = MAP[RANGE[ONE][FIVE]][INCREMENT]
=> #<Proc (lambda)>
>> to_array(my_list).map { |p| to_integer(p) }
=> [2, 3, 4, 5, 6]
```

Yes. So we can replace #map in FizzBuzz:

```
MAP[RANGE[ONE][HUNDRED]][-> n {
  IF[IS_ZERO[MOD[n][FIFTEEN]]][
    'FizzBuzz'
  ][IF[IS_ZERO[MOD[n][THREE]]][
    'Fizz'
  ][IF[IS_ZERO[MOD[n][FIVE]]][
    'Buzz'
  ][
    n.to_s
  ]]]
}]
```

Nearly finished! All that remains is to deal with the strings.

Strings

Strings are easy to handle: we can just represent them as lists of numbers, as long as we agree on an encoding that determines which number represents which character.

We can choose any encoding we want, so instead of using a general-purpose one like ASCII, let's design a new one that's more convenient for FizzBuzz. We only need to encode digits and the strings 'FizzBuzz', 'Fizz', and 'Buzz', so we can use the numbers 0 to 9 to represent the characters '0' to '9', and the numbers from 10 to 14 to encode the characters 'B', 'F', 'i', 'u', and 'z'.

This already gives us a way to represent the string literals we need (being careful not to clobber the Z combinator):

```
TEN = MULTIPLY[TWO][FIVE]
B   = TEN
F   = INCREMENT[B]
I   = INCREMENT[F]
U   = INCREMENT[I]
ZED = INCREMENT[U]

FIZZ     = UNSHIFT[UNSHIFT[UNSHIFT[UNSHIFT[EMPTY][ZED]][ZED]][I]][F]
BUZZ     = UNSHIFT[UNSHIFT[UNSHIFT[UNSHIFT[EMPTY][ZED]][ZED]][U]][B]
FIZZBUZZ = UNSHIFT[UNSHIFT[UNSHIFT[UNSHIFT[BUZZ][ZED]][ZED]][I]][F]
```

To check that these work, we can write some external methods to convert them into Ruby strings:

```
def to_char(c)
  '0123456789BFiuz'.slice(to_integer(c))
end

def to_string(s)
  to_array(s).map { |c| to_char(c) }.join
end
```

Alright, do the strings work?

```
>> to_char(ZED)
=> "z"
>> to_string(FIZZBUZZ)
=> "FizzBuzz"
```

Great. So we can use them in FizzBuzz:

```
MAP[RANGE[ONE][HUNDRED]][-> n {
  IF[IS_ZERO[MOD[n][FIFTEEN]]][
    FIZZBUZZ
  ][IF[IS_ZERO[MOD[n][THREE]]][
    FIZZ
  ][IF[IS_ZERO[MOD[n][FIVE]]][
    BUZZ
  ][
    n.to_s
  ]]]
}]
```

The very last thing to implement is Fixnum#to_s. For that, we need to be able to split a number into its component digits, and here's one way to do that in Ruby:

```
def to_digits(n)
  previous_digits =
    if n < 10
      []
    else
      to_digits(n / 10)
    end

  previous_digits.push(n % 10)
end
```

We haven't implemented <, but we can dodge that problem by using n <= 9 instead of n < 10. Unfortunately, we can't dodge implementing Fixnum#/ and Array#push, so here they are:

```
DIV =
  Z[-> f { -> m { -> n {
    IF[IS_LESS_OR_EQUAL[n][m]][
      -> x {
        INCREMENT[f[SUBTRACT[m][n]][n]][x]
      }
    ][
      ZERO
    ]
  } } }]
```

```
PUSH =
  -> l {
    -> x {
      FOLD[l][UNSHIFT[EMPTY][x]][UNSHIFT]
    }
  }
```

Now we can translate #to_digits into a proc:

```
TO_DIGITS =
  Z[-> f { -> n { PUSH[
    IF[IS_LESS_OR_EQUAL[n][DECREMENT[TEN]]][
      EMPTY
    ][
      -> x {
        f[DIV[n][TEN]][x]
      }
    ]
  ][MOD[n][TEN]] } }]
```

Does it work?

```
>> to_array(TO_DIGITS[FIVE]).map { |p| to_integer(p) }
=> [5]
>> to_array(TO_DIGITS[POWER[FIVE][THREE]]).map { |p| to_integer(p) }
=> [1, 2, 5]
```

Yes. And because we had the foresight to design a string encoding where 1 represents
'1' and so on, the arrays produced by TO_DIGITS are already valid strings:

```
>> to_string(TO_DIGITS[FIVE])
=> "5"
>> to_string(TO_DIGITS[POWER[FIVE][THREE]])
=> "125"
```

So we can replace #to_s with TO_DIGITS in FizzBuzz:

```
MAP[RANGE[ONE][HUNDRED]][-> n {
  IF[IS_ZERO[MOD[n][FIFTEEN]]][
    FIZZBUZZ
  ][IF[IS_ZERO[MOD[n][THREE]]][
    FIZZ
  ][IF[IS_ZERO[MOD[n][FIVE]]][
    BUZZ
  ][
    TO_DIGITS[n]
  ]]]
}]
```

The Solution

We've finally finished! (This would've been the longest, most awkward job interview
ever.) We now have an implementation of FizzBuzz written entirely with procs. Let's
run it to make sure it works properly:

```
>> solution =
     MAP[RANGE[ONE][HUNDRED]][-> n {
       IF[IS_ZERO[MOD[n][FIFTEEN]]][
         FIZZBUZZ
       ][IF[IS_ZERO[MOD[n][THREE]]][
         FIZZ
       ][IF[IS_ZERO[MOD[n][FIVE]]][
         BUZZ
       ][
         TO_DIGITS[n]
       ]]]
     }]
=> #<Proc (lambda)>
>> to_array(solution).each do |p|
     puts to_string(p)
   end; nil
1
2
Fizz
4
Buzz
Fizz
7
⋮
94
Buzz
Fizz
97
98
Fizz
Buzz
=> nil
```

Having gone to so much trouble to make sure that every constant is just an abbreviation
of some longer expression, we owe it to ourselves to replace each constant with its
definition so we can see the complete program:

```
-> k { -> f { -> f { -> x { f[-> y { x[x][y] }] }][-> x { f[-> y { x[x][y] }] }] }
[-> f { -> l { -> x { -> g { -> b { b }[-> p { p[-> x { -> y { x } }] }[1]][x]
[-> y { g[f[-> l { -> p { p[-> x { -> y { y } }] }[-> p { p[-> x { -> y { y } }] }]
[1]] }[1]][x][g]][-> l { -> p { p[-> x { -> y { x } }] }[-> p { p[-> x { -> y
{ y } }] }[1]] }[1]][y] }] } } }][k][-> x { -> y { -> f { f[x][y] } } }[-> x
{ -> y { x } }][-> x { -> y { x } }]][-> l { -> x { -> l { -> x { -> x { -> y
{ -> f { f[x][y] } } }[-> x { -> y { y } }][-> x { -> y { -> f { f[x][y] } } }
[x][1]] } }[1][f[x]] } }] } }][-> f { -> x { f[-> y { x[x][y] }] }][-> x { f[-> y
{ x[x][y] }] }] }][-> f { -> m { -> n { -> b { b }[-> m { -> n { -> n { n[-> x
{ -> x { -> y { y } } }]][-> x { -> y { x } }] }] }[-> m { -> n { n[-> n { -> p { p[-
> x { -> y { x } }] }[n[-> p { -> x { -> y { -> f { f[x][y] } } }[-> p { p[-> x
{ -> y { y } }] }[p]][-> n { -> p { -> x { p[n[p][x]] } } }[-> p { p[-> x { ->
y { y } }] }[p]]] }][-> x { -> y { -> f { f[x][y] } } }[-> p { -> x { x } }][-
> p { -> x { x } }]]] }][m] } }[m][n]] } }[m][n]][-> x { -> l { -> x { -> x { -
```

> y { -> f { f[x][y] } } }][-> x { -> y { y } }][-> x { -> y { -> f { f[x][y] } } }
[x][1]] } }[f[-> n { -> p { -> x { p[n[p][x]] } } }[m]][n]][m][x] }][-> x { ->
y { -> f { f[x][y] } } }][-> x { -> y { x } }][-> x { -> y { x } }]] } } }][-> p
{   ->   x   {   p[x]   }   }][->   p   {   ->   x
{ p[p[p[p[p[p[p[p[p[p[p[p[p[p[p[p[p[p[p[p[p[p[p[p[p[p[p[p[p[p[p[p[p[p[p[p[p[p[
p[p[p[p[p[p[p[p[p[p[p[p[p[p[p[p[p[p[p[p[p[p[p[p[p[p[p[p[p[p[p[p[p[p[p[p[p[p[p[
p[p[p[p[p[p[p[p[p[p[p[p[p[p[p[p[p[p[p[p[p[p[x]]]]]]]]]]]]]]]]]]]]]]]]]]]]]]]]]
]]] } }][->
n { -> b { b }[-> n { n[-> x { -> x { -> y { y } } }][-> x { -> y { x } }] }[-
> f { -> x { f[-> y { x[x][y] }] }][-> x { f[-> y { x[x][y] }] }] }][-> f { -> m
{ -> n { -> b { b }[-> m { -> n { -> n { n[-> x { -> x { -> y { y } } }][-> x
{ -> y { x } }] }[-> m { -> n { n[-> n { -> p { p[-> x { -> y { x } }] }[n[-> p
{ -> x { -> y { -> f { f[x][y] } } }][-> p { p[-> x { -> y { y } }] }[p]][-> n
{ -> p { -> x { p[n[p][x]] } } }][-> p { p[-> x { -> y { y } }] }[p]]] }][-> x
{ -> y { -> f { f[x][y] } } }][-> p { -> x { x } }][-> p { -> x { x } }]]] }]
[m] } }[m][n]] }[n][m]][-> x { f[-> m { -> n { n[-> n { -> p { p[-> x { -> y
{ x } }] }[n[-> p { -> x { -> y { -> f { f[x][y] } } }][-> p { p[-> x { -> y
{ y } }] }[p]][-> n { -> p { -> x { p[n[p][x]] } } }][-> p { p[-> x { -> y
{ y } }] }[p]]] }][-> x { -> y { -> f { f[x][y] } } }][-> p { -> x { x } }][-> p
{ -> x { x } }]]] }][m] } }[m][n]][n][x] }][m] } } }][n][-> p { -> x
{ p[p[p[p[p[p[p[p[p[p[p[p[p[p[x]]]]]]]]]]]]]] } }]]][-> l { -> x { -> x { -
> y { -> f { f[x][y] } } }][-> x { -> y { y } }][-> x { -> y { -> f { f[x][y] } } }
[x][1]] } }[-> l { -> x { -> x { -> y { -> f { f[x][y] } } }][-> x { -> y { y } }]
[-> x { -> y { -> f { f[x][y] } } }[x][1]] } }[-> l { -> x { -> x { -> y { -> f
{ f[x][y] } } }][-> x { -> y { y } }][-> x { -> y { -> f { f[x][y] } } }[x][1]] } }
[-> l { -> x { -> x { -> y { -> f { f[x][y] } } }][-> x { -> y { y } }][-> x { -
> y { -> f { f[x][y] } } }[x][1]] } }[-> l { -> x { -> x { -> y { -> f { f[x]
[y] } } }][-> x { -> y { y } }][-> x { -> y { -> f { f[x][y] } } }[x][1]] } }[-
> l { -> x { -> x { -> y { -> f { f[x][y] } } }][-> x { -> y { y } }][-> x { ->
y { -> f { f[x][y] } } }[x][1]] } }[-> l { -> x { -> x { -> y { -> f { f[x]
[y] } } }][-> x { -> y { y } }][-> x { -> y { -> f { f[x][y] } } }[x][1]] } }[-
> l { -> x { -> x { -> y { -> f { f[x][y] } } }][-> x { -> y { y } }][-> x { ->
y { -> f { f[x][y] } } }[x][1]] } }[-> x { -> y { -> f { f[x][y] } } }][-> x { -
> y { x } }][-> x { -> y { x } }]][-> n { -> p { -> x { p[n[p][x]] } } }][-> n
{ -> p { -> x { p[n[p][x]] } } }][-> n { -> p { -> x { p[n[p][x]] } } }][-> n { -
> p { -> x { p[n[p][x]] } } }][-> m { -> n { n[-> m { -> n { n[-> n { -> p { ->
x { p[n[p][x]] } } }][m] } }[m]][-> p { -> x { x } }] } }[-> p { -> x
{ p[p[x]] } }][-> p { -> x { p[p[p[p[x]]]] } }]]]]]]][-> n { -> p { -> x
{ p[n[p][x]] } } }][-> n { -> p { -> x { p[n[p][x]] } } }][-> n { -> p { -> x
{ p[n[p][x]] } } }][-> n { -> p { -> x { p[n[p][x]] } } }][-> m { -> n { n[-> m
{ -> n { n[-> n { -> p { -> x { p[n[p][x]] } } }][m] } }[m]][-> p { -> x
{ x } }] } }][-> p { -> x { p[p[x]] } }][-> p { -> x { p[p[p[p[x]]]] } }]]]]]]]
[-> n { -> p { -> x { p[n[p][x]] } } }][-> n { -> p { -> x { p[n[p][x]] } } }][-

> n { -> p { -> x { p[n[p][x]] } } }[-> m { -> n { n[-> m { -> n { n[-> n { ->
p { -> x { p[n[p][x]] } } }][m] } }[m]][-> p { -> x { x } }] } } }[-> p { -> x
{ p[p[x]] } }][-> p { -> x { p[p[p[p[p[x]]]]] } }]]]]][-> m { -> n { n[-> m { -
> n { n[-> n { -> p { -> x { p[n[p][x]] } } }][m] } }[m]][-> p { -> x { x } }] } }
[-> p { -> x { p[p[x]] } }][-> p { -> x { p[p[p[p[p[x]]]]] } }]]][-> n { -> p
{ -> x { p[n[p][x]] } } }[-> n { -> p { -> x { p[n[p][x]] } } }[-> n { -> p { -
> x { p[n[p][x]] } } }[-> n { -> p { -> x { p[n[p][x]] } } }[-> m { -> n { n[-
> m { -> n { n[-> n { -> p { -> x { p[n[p][x]] } } }][m] } }[m]][-> p { -> x
{ x } }] } }[-> p { -> x { p[p[x]] } }][-> p { -> x { p[p[p[p[p[x]]]]] } }]]]]]]]
[-> n { -> p { -> x { p[n[p][x]] } } }[-> n { -> p { -> x { p[n[p][x]] } } }[-
> n { -> p { -> x { p[n[p][x]] } } }[-> n { -> p { -> x { p[n[p][x]] } } }[-> m
{ -> n { n[-> m { -> n { n[-> n { -> p { -> x { p[n[p][x]] } } }][m] } }[m]][-
> p { -> x { x } }] } } }[-> p { -> x { p[p[x]] } }][-> p { -> x
{ p[p[p[p[p[x]]]]] } }]]]]]]][-> n { -> p { -> x { p[n[p][x]] } } }[-> n { -> p
{ -> x { p[n[p][x]] } } }[-> m { -> n { n[-> m { -> n { n[-> n { -> p { -> x
{ p[n[p][x]] } } }][m] } }[m]][-> p { -> x { x } }] } }[-> p { -> x { p[p[x]] } }]
[-> p { -> x { p[p[p[p[p[x]]]]] } }]]]]][-> n { -> p { -> x { p[n[p][x]] } } }
[-> m { -> n { n[-> m { -> n { n[-> n { -> p { -> x { p[n[p][x]] } } }][m] } }
[m]][-> p { -> x { x } }] } }[-> p { -> x { p[p[x]] } }][-> p { -> x
{ p[p[p[p[p[x]]]]] } }]]]][-> b { b }[-> n { n[-> x { -> x { -> y { y } } }][-
> x { -> y { x } }] }[-> f { -> x { f[-> y { x[x][y] }] }[-> x { f[-> y { x[x]
[y] }] }] }[-> f { -> m { -> n { -> b { b }[-> m { -> n { -> n { n[-> x { -> x
{ -> y { y } } }][-> x { -> y { x } }] }[-> m { -> n { n[-> n { -> p { p[-> x
{ -> y { x } }] }[n[-> p { -> x { -> y { -> f { f[x][y] } } }][-> p { p[-> x { -
> y { y } }] }][p]][-> n { -> p { -> x { p[n[p][x]] } } }[-> p { p[-> x { -> y
{ y } }] }][p]]] }][-> x { -> y { -> f { f[x][y] } } }][-> p { -> x { x } }][-> p
{ -> x { x } }]]] }][m] } }[m][n]] } }[n][m]][-> x { f[-> m { -> n { n[-> n { -
> p { p[-> x { -> y { x } }] }[n[-> p { -> x { -> y { -> f { f[x][y] } } }][-> p
{ p[-> x { -> y { y } }] }][p]][-> n { -> p { -> x { p[n[p][x]] } } }[-> p { p[-
> x { -> y { y } }] }][p]]] }][-> x { -> y { -> f { f[x][y] } } }][-> p { -> x
{ x } }][-> p { -> x { x } }]]] }][m] } }[m][n]][n][x] }][m] } } }][n][-> p { -
> x { p[p[x]] } } }]]]][-> 1 { -> x { -> x { -> y { -> f { f[x][y] } } }[-> x
{ -> y { y } } }][-> x { -> y { -> f { f[x][y] } } }[x][1]] } }[-> 1 { -> x { ->
x { -> y { -> f { f[x][y] } } }[-> x { -> y { y } }][-> x { -> y { -> f { f[x]
[y] } } }[x][1]] } }[-> 1 { -> x { -> x { -> y { -> f { f[x][y] } } }[-> x { -
> y { y } }][-> x { -> y { -> f { f[x][y] } } }[x][1]] } }[-> 1 { -> x { -> x
{ -> y { -> f { f[x][y] } } }[-> x { -> y { y } }][-> x { -> y { -> f { f[x]
[y] } } }[x][1]] } }[-> x { -> y { -> f { f[x][y] } } }[-> x { -> y { x } }][-
> x { -> y { x } }]][-> n { -> p { -> x { p[n[p][x]] } } }[-> n { -> p { -> x
{ p[n[p][x]] } } }[-> n { -> p { -> x { p[n[p][x]] } } }[-> n { -> p { -> x
{ p[n[p][x]] } } }[-> m { -> n { n[-> m { -> n { n[-> n { -> p { -> x { p[n[p]
[x]] } } }][m] } }[m]][-> p { -> x { x } }] } }[-> p { -> x { p[p[x]] } }][-> p
{ -> x { p[p[p[p[p[x]]]]] } }]]]]]]][-> n { -> p { -> x { p[n[p][x]] } } }[-> n

```
{ -> p { -> x { p[n[p][x]] } } }[-> n { -> p { -> x { p[n[p][x]] } } }[-> n { -
> p { -> x { p[n[p][x]] } } }[-> m { -> n { n[-> m { -> n { n[-> n { -> p { ->
x { p[n[p][x]] } } }][m] } }[m]][-> p { -> x { x } }] } }[-> p { -> x
{ p[p[x]] } }][-> p { -> x { p[p[p[p[p[x]]]]] } }]]]]]]][-> n { -> p { -> x
{ p[n[p][x]] } } }[-> n { -> p { -> x { p[n[p][x]] } } }[-> m { -> n { n[-> m
{ -> n { n[-> n { -> p { -> x { p[n[p][x]] } } }][m] } }[m]][-> p { -> x
{ x } }] } }[-> p { -> x { p[p[x]] } }][-> p { -> x { p[p[p[p[p[x]]]]] } }]]]]]
[-> n { -> p { -> x { p[n[p][x]] } } }[-> m { -> n { n[-> m { -> n { n[-> n { -
> p { -> x { p[n[p][x]] } } }][m] } }[m]][-> p { -> x { x } }] } }[-> p { -> x
{ p[p[x]] } }][-> p { -> x { p[p[p[p[p[x]]]]] } }]]]][-> b { b }[-> n { n[-> x
{ -> x { -> y { y } } }][-> x { -> y { x } }] } }[-> f { -> x { f[-> y { x[x]
[y] }] }[-> x { f[-> y { x[x][y] }] }] }] }[-> f { -> m { -> n { -> b { b }[-> m
{ -> n { -> n { n[-> x { -> x { -> y { y } } }][-> x { -> y { x } }] } }[-> m { -
> n { n[-> n { -> p { p[-> x { -> y { x } }] }[n[-> p { -> x { -> y { -> f { f[x]
[y] } } }[-> p { p[-> x { -> y { y } }] }[p]][-> n { -> p { -> x { p[n[p][x]] } } }
[-> p { p[-> x { -> y { y } }] }[p]]] }][-> x { -> y { -> f { f[x][y] } } }[->
p { -> x { x } }][-> p { -> x { x } }]]] }][m] } }[m][n]] } }[n][m]][-> x { f[-
> m { -> n { n[-> n { -> p { p[-> x { -> y { x } }] }[n[-> p { -> x { -> y { -
> f { f[x][y] } } }[-> p { p[-> x { -> y { y } }] }[p]][-> n { -> p { -> x
{ p[n[p][x]] } } }[-> p { p[-> x { -> y { y } }] }[p]]] }][-> x { -> y { -> f
{ f[x][y] } } }[-> p { -> x { x } }][-> p { -> x { x } }]]] }][m] } }[m][n]][n]
[x] }][m] } } }[n][-> p { -> x { p[p[p[p[p[x]]]]] } }]]]][-> l { -> x { -> x { -
> y { -> f { f[x][y] } } }[-> x { -> y { y } }][-> x { -> y { -> f { f[x][y] } } }
[x][l]] } }[-> l { -> x { -> x { -> y { -> f { f[x][y] } } }[-> x { -> y { y } }]
[-> x { -> y { -> f { f[x][y] } } }[x][l]] } }[-> l { -> x { -> x { -> y { -> f
{ f[x][y] } } }[-> x { -> y { y } }][-> x { -> y { -> f { f[x][y] } } }[x][l]] } }
[-> l { -> x { -> x { -> y { -> f { f[x][y] } } }[-> x { -> y { y } }][-> x { -
> y { -> f { f[x][y] } } }[x][l]] } }[-> x { -> y { -> f { f[x][y] } } }[-> x
{ -> y { x } }][-> x { -> y { x } }]]][-> n { -> p { -> x { p[n[p][x]] } } }[-> n
{ -> p { -> x { p[n[p][x]] } } }[-> n { -> p { -> x { p[n[p][x]] } } }[-> n
{ -> p { -> x { p[n[p][x]] } } }[-> m { -> n { n[-> m { -> n { n[-> n { -> p { -
> x { p[n[p][x]] } } }][m] } }[m]][-> p { -> x { x } }] } }[-> p { -> x
{ p[p[x]] } }][-> p { -> x { p[p[p[p[p[x]]]]] } }]]]]]]][-> n { -> p { -> x
{ p[n[p][x]] } } }[-> n { -> p { -> x { p[n[p][x]] } } }[-> n { -> p { -> x
{ p[n[p][x]] } } }[-> n { -> p { -> x { p[n[p][x]] } } }[-> m { -> n { n[-> m
{ -> n { n[-> n { -> p { -> x { p[n[p][x]] } } }][m] } }[m]][-> p { -> x
{ x } }] } }[-> p { -> x { p[p[x]] } }][-> p { -> x { p[p[p[p[p[x]]]]] } }]]]]]]]
[-> n { -> p { -> x { p[n[p][x]] } } }[-> n { -> p { -> x { p[n[p][x]] } } }[-
> n { -> p { -> x { p[n[p][x]] } } }[-> m { -> n { n[-> m { -> n { n[-> n { ->
p { -> x { p[n[p][x]] } } }][m] } }[m]][-> p { -> x { x } }] } }[-> p { -> x
{ p[p[x]] } }][-> p { -> x { p[p[p[p[p[x]]]]] } }]]]]]][-> m { -> n { n[-> m { -
> n { n[-> n { -> p { -> x { p[n[p][x]] } } }][m] } }[m]][-> p { -> x { x } }] } }
[-> p { -> x { p[p[x]] } }][-> p { -> x { p[p[p[p[p[x]]]]] } }]]]][-> f { -> x
```

{ f[-> y { x[x][y] }] }[-> x { f[-> y { x[x][y] }] }] }[-> f { -> n { -> l { -
> x { -> f { -> x { f[-> y { x[x][y] }] }[-> x { f[-> y { x[x][y] }] }] }[-> f
{ -> l { -> x { -> g { -> b { b }[-> p { p[-> x { -> y { x } }] }[1]][x][-> y
{ g[f[-> l { -> p { p[-> x { -> y { y } }] }[-> p { p[-> x { -> y { y } }] }] }
[1]] }[1]][x][g]][-> l { -> p { p[-> x { -> y { y } }] }[-> p { p[-> x { -> y
{ y } }] }[1]] }[1]][y] }] } } } }][1][-> l { -> x { -> x { -> y { -> f { f[x]
[y] } } }[-> x { -> y { y } }][-> x { -> y { -> f { f[x][y] } } }[x][1]] } }[-
> x { -> y { -> f { f[x][y] } } }[-> x { -> y { x } }][-> x { -> y { x } }]][x]]
[-> l { -> x { -> x { -> y { -> f { f[x][y] } } }[-> x { -> y { y } }][-> x { -
> y { -> f { f[x][y] } } }[x][1]] } }] } }[-> b { b }[-> m { -> n { -> n { n[-
> x { -> x { -> y { y } } }][-> x { -> y { x } }] }[-> m { -> n { n[-> n { -> p
{ p[-> x { -> y { x } }] }[n[-> p { -> x { -> y { -> f { f[x][y] } } }[-> p { p[-
> x { -> y { y } }] }[p]][-> n { -> p { -> x { p[n[p][x]] } } }[-> p { p[-> x
{ -> y { y } }] }[p]]] }][-> x { -> y { -> f { f[x][y] } } }[-> p { -> x { x } }]
[-> p { -> x { x } }]]] }][m] } }[m][n]] } }[n][-> n { -> p { p[-> x { -> y
{ x } }] }[n[-> p { -> x { -> y { -> f { f[x][y] } } }[-> p { p[-> x { -> y
{ y } }] }[p]][-> n { -> p { -> x { p[n[p][x]] } } }[-> p { p[-> x { -> y
{ y } }] }[p]]] }][-> x { -> y { -> f { f[x][y] } } }[-> p { -> x { x } }][-> p
{ -> x { x } }]]] }[-> m { -> n { n[-> m { -> n { n[-> n { -> p { -> x { p[n[p]
[x]] } } }][m] } }[m]][-> p { -> x { x } }] } }[-> p { -> x { p[p[x]] } }][-> p
{ -> x { p[p[p[p[p[x]]]]] } }]]]][-> x { -> y { -> f { f[x][y] } } }[-> x { ->
y { x } }][-> x { -> y { x } }]][-> x { f[-> f { -> x { f[-> y { x[x][y] }] }[-
> x { f[-> y { x[x][y] }] }] }[-> f { -> m { -> n { -> b { b }[-> m { -> n { -
> n { n[-> x { -> x { -> y { y } } }][-> x { -> y { x } }] }[-> m { -> n { n[-
> n { -> p { p[-> x { -> y { x } }] }[n[-> p { -> x { -> y { -> f { f[x][y] } } }
[-> p { p[-> x { -> y { y } }] }[p]][-> n { -> p { -> x { p[n[p][x]] } } }[-> p
{ p[-> x { -> y { y } }] }[p]]] }][-> x { -> y { -> f { f[x][y] } } }[-> p { -
> x { x } }][-> p { -> x { x } }]]] }][m] } }[m][n]] } }[n][m]][-> x { -> n { -
> p { -> x { p[n[p][x]] } } }[f[-> m { -> n { n[-> n { -> p { p[-> x { -> y
{ x } }] }[n[-> p { -> x { -> y { -> f { f[x][y] } } }[-> p { p[-> x { -> y
{ y } }] }[p]][-> n { -> p { -> x { p[n[p][x]] } } }[-> p { p[-> x { -> y
{ y } }] }[p]]] }][-> x { -> y { -> f { f[x][y] } } }[-> p { -> x { x } }][-> p
{ -> x { x } }]]] }][m] } }[m][n]][n]][x] }][-> p { -> x { x } }] } }][n][->
m { -> n { n[-> m { -> n { n[-> n { -> p { -> x { p[n[p][x]] } } }][m] } }[m]]
[-> p { -> x { x } }] } }[-> p { -> x { p[p[x]] } }][-> p { -> x
{ p[p[p[p[p[x]]]]] } }]]][x] }]][-> f { -> x { f[-> y { x[x][y] }] }[-> x { f[-
> y { x[x][y] }] }] }[-> f { -> m { -> n { -> b { b }[-> m { -> n { -> n { n[-
> x { -> x { -> y { y } } }][-> x { -> y { x } }] }[-> m { -> n { n[-> n { -> p
{ p[-> x { -> y { x } }] }[n[-> p { -> x { -> y { -> f { f[x][y] } } }[-> p { p[-
> x { -> y { y } }] }[p]][-> n { -> p { -> x { p[n[p][x]] } } }[-> p { p[-> x
{ -> y { y } }] }[p]]] }][-> x { -> y { -> f { f[x][y] } } }[-> p { -> x { x } }]
[-> p { -> x { x } }]]] }][m] } }[m][n]] } }[n][m]][-> x { f[-> m { -> n { n[-
> n { -> p { p[-> x { -> y { x } }] }[n[-> p { -> x { -> y { -> f { f[x][y] } } }

```
[-> p { p[-> x { -> y { y } }] }[p]][-> n { -> p { -> x { p[n[p][x]] } } }[-> p
{ p[-> x { -> y { y } }] }[p]]] }][-> x { -> y { -> f { f[x][y] } } }[-> p { -
> x { x } }][-> p { -> x { x } }]]] }][m] } }[m][n]][n][x] }][m] } } }][n][-> m
{ -> n { n[-> m { -> n { n[-> n { -> p { -> x { p[n[p][x]] } } }][m] } }[m]][-
> p { -> x { x } }] } }[-> p { -> x { p[p[x]] } }][-> p { -> x
{ p[p[p[p[p[x]]]]] } }]]] } }][n]]]] }]
```

Beautiful.

Advanced Programming Techniques

Constructing programs entirely out of procs takes a lot of effort, but we've seen that
it's possible to get real work done as long as we don't mind applying a bit of ingenuity.
Let's take a quick look at a couple of other techniques for writing code in this minimal
environment.

Infinite streams

Using code to represent data has some interesting advantages. Our proc-based lists
don't have to be static: a list is just code that does the right thing when we pass it to
FIRST and REST, so we can easily implement lists that calculate their contents on the fly,
also known as *streams*. In fact, there's no reason why streams even need to be finite,
because the calculation only has to generate the list contents as they're consumed, so
it can keep producing new values indefinitely.

For example, here's how to implement an infinite stream of zeros:

```
ZEROS = Z[-> f { UNSHIFT[f][ZERO] }]
```

> This is the "no cheating" version of ZEROS = UNSHIFT[ZEROS][ZERO], a
> data structure defined in terms of itself. As programmers, we're gener-
> ally comfortable with the idea of defining a recursive function in terms
> of itself, but defining a data structure in terms of itself might seem weird
> and unusual; in this setting, they're exactly the same thing, and the Z
> combinator makes both completely legitimate.

On the console, we can see that ZEROS behaves just like a list, albeit one with no end in
sight:

```
>> to_integer(FIRST[ZEROS])
=> 0
>> to_integer(FIRST[REST[ZEROS]])
=> 0
>> to_integer(FIRST[REST[REST[REST[REST[REST[ZEROS]]]]]])
=> 0
```

A helper method to turn this stream into a Ruby array would be convenient, but to_array will run forever unless we explicitly stop the conversion process. An optional "maximum size" argument does the trick:

```
def to_array(l, count = nil)
  array = []

  until to_boolean(IS_EMPTY[l]) || count == 0
    array.push(FIRST[l])
    l = REST[l]
    count = count - 1 unless count.nil?
  end

  array
end
```

This lets us retrieve any number of elements from the stream and turn them into an array:

```
>> to_array(ZEROS, 5).map { |p| to_integer(p) }
=> [0, 0, 0, 0, 0]
>> to_array(ZEROS, 10).map { |p| to_integer(p) }
=> [0, 0, 0, 0, 0, 0, 0, 0, 0, 0]
>> to_array(ZEROS, 20).map { |p| to_integer(p) }
=> [0, 0, 0, 0, 0, 0, 0, 0, 0, 0, 0, 0, 0, 0, 0, 0, 0, 0, 0, 0]
```

ZEROS doesn't calculate a new element each time, but that's easy enough to do. Here's a stream that counts upward from a given number:

```
>> UPWARDS_OF = Z[-> f { -> n { UNSHIFT[-> x { f[INCREMENT[n]][x] }][n] } }]
=> #<Proc (lambda)>
>> to_array(UPWARDS_OF[ZERO], 5).map { |p| to_integer(p) }
=> [0, 1, 2, 3, 4]
>> to_array(UPWARDS_OF[FIFTEEN], 20).map { |p| to_integer(p) }
=> [15, 16, 17, 18, 19, 20, 21, 22, 23, 24, 25, 26, 27, 28, 29, 30, 31, 32, 33, 34]
```

A more elaborate stream contains all the multiples of a given number:

```
>> MULTIPLES_OF =
     -> m {
       Z[-> f {
         -> n { UNSHIFT[-> x { f[ADD[m][n]][x] }][n] }
       }][m]
     }
=> #<Proc (lambda)>
>> to_array(MULTIPLES_OF[TWO], 10).map { |p| to_integer(p) }
=> [2, 4, 6, 8, 10, 12, 14, 16, 18, 20]
>> to_array(MULTIPLES_OF[FIVE], 20).map { |p| to_integer(p) }
=> [5, 10, 15, 20, 25, 30, 35, 40, 45, 50, 55, 60, 65, 70, 75, 80, 85, 90, 95, 100]
```

Remarkably, we can manipulate these infinite streams like any other list. For example, we can make a new stream by mapping a proc over an existing one:

```
>> to_array(MULTIPLES_OF[THREE], 10).map { |p| to_integer(p) }
=> [3, 6, 9, 12, 15, 18, 21, 24, 27, 30]
>> to_array(MAP[MULTIPLES_OF[THREE]][INCREMENT], 10).map { |p| to_integer(p) }
```

```
=> [4, 7, 10, 13, 16, 19, 22, 25, 28, 31]
>> to_array(MAP[MULTIPLES_OF[THREE]][MULTIPLY[TWO]], 10).map { |p| to_integer(p) }
=> [6, 12, 18, 24, 30, 36, 42, 48, 54, 60]
```

We can even write procs that combine two streams to make a third:

```
>> MULTIPLY_STREAMS =
     Z[-> f {
       -> k { -> l {
         UNSHIFT[-> x { f[REST[k]][REST[l]][x] }][MULTIPLY[FIRST[k]][FIRST[l]]]
       } }
     }]
=> #<Proc (lambda)>
>> to_array(MULTIPLY_STREAMS[UPWARDS_OF[ONE]][MULTIPLES_OF[THREE]], 10).
     map { |p| to_integer(p) }
=> [3, 12, 27, 48, 75, 108, 147, 192, 243, 300]
```

Since the contents of a stream can be generated by any computation, there's nothing to stop us creating an infinite list of the Fibonacci series, or the prime numbers, or all possible strings in alphabetical order, or anything else computable. This abstraction is a powerful one and doesn't require any clever features on top of what we already have.

Native Ruby Streams

Ruby has an Enumerator class that can be used to build infinite streams without relying on procs. Here's how to implement the "multiples of a given number" stream:

```
def multiples_of(n)
  Enumerator.new do |yielder|
    value = n
    loop do
      yielder.yield(value)
      value = value + n
    end
  end
end
```

This method returns an Enumerator that performs one iteration of the loop each time we call #next on it, returning the yielded value each time:

```
>> multiples_of_three = multiples_of(3)
=> #<Enumerator: #<Enumerator::Generator>:each>
>> multiples_of_three.next
=> 3
>> multiples_of_three.next
=> 6
>> multiples_of_three.next
=> 9
```

The Enumerator class includes the Enumerable module, so we can also call methods like #first, #take, and #detect:

```
>> multiples_of(3).first
=> 3
>> multiples_of(3).take(10)
=> [3, 6, 9, 12, 15, 18, 21, 24, 27, 30]
>> multiples_of(3).detect { |x| x > 100 }
=> 102
```

Other `Enumerable` methods like `#map` and `#select` won't work properly on this `Enumerator`, because they'll try to process every item in the infinite stream. However, Ruby 2.0's `Enumerator::Lazy` class reimplements some `Enumerable` methods so that they work even when the underlying `Enumerator` goes on forever. We can get an `Enumerator::Lazy` by calling `#lazy` on an `Enumerator`, and then we can manipulate these infinite streams just as we could with the proc versions:

```
>> multiples_of(3).lazy.map { |x| x * 2 }.take(10).force
=> [6, 12, 18, 24, 30, 36, 42, 48, 54, 60]
>> multiples_of(3).lazy.map { |x| x * 2 }.select { |x| x > 100 }.take(10).force
=> [102, 108, 114, 120, 126, 132, 138, 144, 150, 156]
>> multiples_of(3).lazy.zip(multiples_of(4)).map { |a, b| a * b }.take(10).force
=> [12, 48, 108, 192, 300, 432, 588, 768, 972, 1200]
```

This isn't quite as tidy as proc-based lists—we have to write special code to work with infinite streams, instead of just treating them like conventional `Enumerables`—but it shows that Ruby does have a built-in way of handling these unusual data structures.

Avoiding arbitrary recursion

During the FizzBuzz exercise, we used recursive functions like MOD and RANGE to demonstrate the use of the Z combinator. This is convenient, because it lets us translate from an unconstrained recursive Ruby implementation to a proc-only one without changing the structure of the code, but technically, we can implement these functions without the Z combinator by taking advantage of the behavior of Church numerals.

For example, our implementation of `MOD[m][n]` works by repeatedly subtracting n from m as long as n <= m, always checking the condition to decide whether to make the next recursive call. But we can get the same result by blindly performing the action "subtract n from m if n <= m" a fixed number of times instead of using recursion to dynamically control the repetition. We don't know exactly how many times we need to repeat it, but we do know that m times is definitely enough (for the worst case where n is 1), and it doesn't hurt to do it more times than necessary:

```
def decrease(m, n)
  if n <= m
    m - n
  else
    m
  end
end

>> decrease(17, 5)
=> 12
>> decrease(decrease(17, 5), 5)
=> 7
>> decrease(decrease(decrease(17, 5), 5), 5)
=> 2
>> decrease(decrease(decrease(decrease(17, 5), 5), 5), 5)
=> 2
>> decrease(decrease(decrease(decrease(decrease(17, 5), 5), 5), 5), 5)
=> 2
```

We can therefore rewrite MOD to make use of a proc that takes a number and either subtracts n from it (if it's greater than n) or returns it untouched. This proc gets called m times on m itself to give the final answer:

```
MOD =
  -> m { -> n {
    m[-> x {
      IF[IS_LESS_OR_EQUAL[n][x]][
        SUBTRACT[x][n]
      ][
        x
      ]
    }][m]
  } }
```

This version of MOD works just as well as the recursive one:

```
>> to_integer(MOD[THREE][TWO])
=> 1
>> to_integer(MOD[
     POWER[THREE][THREE]
   ][
     ADD[THREE][TWO]
   ])
=> 2
```

Although this implementation is arguably simpler than the original, it is both harder to read and less efficient in general, because it always performs a worst-case number of repeated calls instead of stopping as soon as possible. It's also not extensionally equal to the original, because the old version of MOD would loop forever if we asked it to divide by ZERO (the condition n <= m would never become false), whereas this implementation just returns its first argument:

```
>> to_integer(MOD[THREE][ZERO])
=> 3
```

RANGE is slightly more challenging, but we can use a trick similar to the one that makes DECREMENT work: design a function that, when called n times on some initial argument, returns a list of n numbers from the desired range. As with DECREMENT, the secret is to use a pair to store both the resulting list and the information needed by the next iteration:

```
def countdown(pair)
  [pair.first.unshift(pair.last), pair.last - 1]
end

>> countdown([[], 10])
=> [[10], 9]
>> countdown(countdown([[], 10]))
=> [[9, 10], 8]
>> countdown(countdown(countdown([[], 10])))
=> [[8, 9, 10], 7]
>> countdown(countdown(countdown(countdown([[], 10]))))
=> [[7, 8, 9, 10], 6]
```

This is easy to rewrite with procs:

```
COUNTDOWN = -> p { PAIR[UNSHIFT[LEFT[p]][RIGHT[p]]][DECREMENT[RIGHT[p]]] }
```

Now we just need to implement RANGE so that it calls COUNTDOWN the right number of times (the range from m to n always has m - n + 1 elements) and unpacks the result list from the final pair:

```
RANGE = -> m { -> n { LEFT[INCREMENT[SUBTRACT[n][m]][COUNTDOWN][PAIR[EMPTY][n]]] } }
```

Again, this combinator-free version works just fine:

```
>> to_array(RANGE[FIVE][TEN]).map { |p| to_integer(p) }
=> [5, 6, 7, 8, 9, 10]
```

 We're able to implement MOD and RANGE by performing a predetermined number of iterations—rather than executing an arbitrary loop that runs until its condition becomes true—because they're *primitive recursive* functions. See "Partial Recursive Functions" on page 210 for more about this.

Implementing the Lambda Calculus

Our FizzBuzz experiment has given us a sense of how it feels to write programs in the untyped lambda calculus. The constraints forced us to implement a lot of basic functionality from scratch rather than relying on features of the language, but we did eventually manage to build all of the data structures and algorithms we needed to solve the problem we were given.

Of course, we haven't *really* been writing lambda calculus programs, because we don't have a lambda calculus interpreter; we've just written Ruby programs in the style of the lambda calculus to get a feel for how such a minimal language can work. But we already have all the knowledge we need to build a lambda calculus interpreter and use it to evaluate actual lambda calculus expressions, so let's give that a try.

Syntax

The untyped lambda calculus is a programming language with only three kinds of expression: variables, function definitions, and calls. Rather than introduce a new concrete syntax for lambda calculus expressions, we'll stick with the Ruby conventions—variables look like x, functions look like -> x { x }, and calls look like x[y]—and try not to get the two languages confused.

Why "lambda calculus"?

In this context, the word *calculus* means a system of rules for manipulating strings of symbols.[7] The native syntax of the lambda calculus uses the Greek letter lambda (λ) in place of Ruby's -> symbol; for instance, ONE is written as λp.λx.p x.

We can implement LCVariable, LCFunction, and LCCall syntax classes in the usual way:

```
class LCVariable < Struct.new(:name)
  def to_s
    name.to_s
  end

  def inspect
    to_s
  end
end

class LCFunction < Struct.new(:parameter, :body)
  def to_s
    "-> #{parameter} { #{body} }"
  end

  def inspect
    to_s
  end
end

class LCCall < Struct.new(:left, :right)
  def to_s
    "#{left}[#{right}]"
  end

  def inspect
    to_s
  end
end
```

These classes let us build abstract syntax trees of lambda calculus expressions, just like we did with SIMPLE in Chapter 2 and regular expressions in Chapter 3:

```
>> one =
    LCFunction.new(:p,
      LCFunction.new(:x,
        LCCall.new(LCVariable.new(:p), LCVariable.new(:x))
      )
    )
=> -> p { -> x { p[x] } }
>> increment =
    LCFunction.new(:n,
```

---

7. Most people associate it with the *differential and integral calculus*, a system concerned with rates of change and accumulation of quantities in mathematical functions.

```
      LCFunction.new(:p,
        LCFunction.new(:x,
          LCCall.new(
            LCVariable.new(:p),
            LCCall.new(
              LCCall.new(LCVariable.new(:n), LCVariable.new(:p)),
              LCVariable.new(:x)
            )
          )
        )
      )
    )
=> -> n { -> p { -> x { p[n[p][x]] } } }
>> add =
     LCFunction.new(:m,
       LCFunction.new(:n,
         LCCall.new(LCCall.new(LCVariable.new(:n), increment), LCVariable.new(:m))
       )
     )
=> -> m { -> n { n[-> n { -> p { -> x { p[n[p][x]] } } }][m] } }
```

Because the language has such minimal syntax, those three classes are enough to represent any lambda calculus program.

Semantics

Now we're going to give a small-step operational semantics for the lambda calculus by implementing a #reduce method on each syntax class. Small-step is an attractive choice, because it allows us to see the individual steps of evaluation, which is something we can't easily do for Ruby expressions.

Replacing variables

Before we can implement #reduce, we need another operation called #replace, which finds occurrences of a particular variable inside an expression and replaces them with some other expression:

```
class LCVariable
  def replace(name, replacement)
    if self.name == name
      replacement
    else
      self
    end
  end
end

class LCFunction
  def replace(name, replacement)
    if parameter == name
      self
    else
      LCFunction.new(parameter, body.replace(name, replacement))
```

```
      end
    end
  end

  class LCCall
    def replace(name, replacement)
      LCCall.new(left.replace(name, replacement), right.replace(name, replacement))
    end
  end
```

This works in the obvious way on variables and calls:

```
>> expression = LCVariable.new(:x)
=> x
>> expression.replace(:x, LCFunction.new(:y, LCVariable.new(:y)))
=> -> y { y }
>> expression.replace(:z, LCFunction.new(:y, LCVariable.new(:y)))
=> x
>> expression =
     LCCall.new(
       LCCall.new(
         LCCall.new(
           LCVariable.new(:a),
           LCVariable.new(:b)
         ),
         LCVariable.new(:c)
       ),
       LCVariable.new(:b)
     )
=> a[b][c][b]
>> expression.replace(:a, LCVariable.new(:x))
=> x[b][c][b]
>> expression.replace(:b, LCFunction.new(:x, LCVariable.new(:x)))
=> a[-> x { x }][c][-> x { x }]
```

For functions, the situation is more complicated. #replace only acts on the body of a
function, and it only replaces *free variables*—that is, variables that haven't been
bound to the function by being named as its parameter:

```
>> expression =
     LCFunction.new(:y,
       LCCall.new(LCVariable.new(:x), LCVariable.new(:y))
     )
=> -> y { x[y] }
>> expression.replace(:x, LCVariable.new(:z))
=> -> y { z[y] }
>> expression.replace(:y, LCVariable.new(:z))
=> -> y { x[y] }
```

This lets us replace occurrences of a variable throughout an expression without accidentally changing unrelated variables that happen to have the same name:

```
>> expression =
     LCCall.new(
       LCCall.new(LCVariable.new(:x), LCVariable.new(:y)),
       LCFunction.new(:y, LCCall.new(LCVariable.new(:y), LCVariable.new(:x)))
```

```
        )
=> x[y][-> y { y[x] }]
>> expression.replace(:x, LCVariable.new(:z))
=> z[y][-> y { y[z] }] ❶
>> expression.replace(:y, LCVariable.new(:z))
=> x[z][-> y { y[x] }] ❷
```

❶ Both occurrences of x are free in the original expression, so they both get replaced.

❷ Only the first occurrence of y is a free variable, so only that one is replaced. The second y is a function parameter, not a variable, and the third y is a variable that belongs to that function and shouldn't be touched.

Our simple #replace implementation won't work on certain inputs. It doesn't properly handle replacements that contain free variables:

```
>> expression =
     LCFunction.new(:x,
       LCCall.new(LCVariable.new(:x), LCVariable.new(:y))
     )
=> -> x { x[y] }
>> replacement = LCCall.new(LCVariable.new(:z), LCVariable.new(:x))
=> z[x]
>> expression.replace(:y, replacement)
=> -> x { x[z[x]] }
```

It's not okay to just paste z[x] into the body of -> x { … } like that, because the x in z[x] is a free variable and should remain free afterward, but here it gets accidentally *captured* by the function parameter with the same name.[8]

We can ignore this deficiency, because we'll only be evaluating expressions that don't contain any free variables, so it won't actually cause a problem, but beware that a more sophisticated implementation is needed in the general case.

Calling functions

The whole point of #replace is to give us a way to implement the semantics of function calls. In Ruby, when a proc is called with one or more arguments, the body of the proc gets evaluated in an environment where each argument has been assigned to a local variable, so each use of that variable behaves like the argument itself: in a metaphorical sense, calling the proc -> x, y { x + y } with the arguments 1 and 2 produces the intermediate expression 1 + 2, and that's what gets evaluated to produce the final result.

We can apply the same idea more literally in the lambda calculus by actually replacing variables in a function's body when we evaluate a call. To do this, we can define a LCFunction#call method that does the replacement and returns the result:

8. The correct behavior is to automatically rename the function's parameter so that it doesn't clash with any free variables: rewrite -> x { x[y] } as the equivalent expression -> w { w[y] }, say, and then safely perform the replacement to get -> w { w[z[x]] }, leaving x free.

```
class LCFunction
  def call(argument)
    body.replace(parameter, argument)
  end
end
```

This lets us simulate the moment when a function gets called:

```
>> function =
     LCFunction.new(:x,
       LCFunction.new(:y,
         LCCall.new(LCVariable.new(:x), LCVariable.new(:y))
       )
     )
=> -> x { -> y { x[y] } }
>> argument = LCFunction.new(:z, LCVariable.new(:z))
=> -> z { z }
>> function.call(argument)
=> -> y { -> z { z }[y] }
```

Reducing expressions

Function calls are the only thing that actually *happens* when a lambda calculus program
is evaluated, so now we're ready to implement #reduce. It'll find a place in the expression where a function call can occur, then use #call to make it happen. We just need
to be able to identify which expressions are actually callable...

```
class LCVariable
  def callable?
    false
  end
end

class LCFunction
  def callable?
    true
  end
end

class LCCall
  def callable?
    false
  end
end
```

...and then we can write #reduce:

```
class LCVariable
  def reducible?
    false
  end
end

class LCFunction
  def reducible?
    false
```

```ruby
      end
  end

  class LCCall
    def reducible?
      left.reducible? || right.reducible? || left.callable?
    end

    def reduce
      if left.reducible?
        LCCall.new(left.reduce, right)
      elsif right.reducible?
        LCCall.new(left, right.reduce)
      else
        left.call(right)
      end
    end
  end
```

In this implementation, function calls are the only kind of syntax that can be reduced. Reducing LCCall works a bit like reducing Add or Multiply from SIMPLE: if either of its subexpressions is reducible, we reduce that; if not, we actually perform the call by calling the left subexpression (which should be a LCFunction) with the right one as its argument. This strategy is known as *call-by-value* evaluation—first we reduce the argument to an irreducible value, then we perform the call.

Let's test our implementation by using the lambda calculus to calculate one plus one:

```
>> expression = LCCall.new(LCCall.new(add, one), one)
=> -> m { -> n { n[-> n { -> p { -> x { p[n[p][x]] } } }][m] } }[-> p { -> x { p[x] } ↵
}][-> p { -> x { p[x] } }]
>> while expression.reducible?
     puts expression
     expression = expression.reduce
   end; puts expression
-> m { -> n { n[-> n { -> p { -> x { p[n[p][x]] } } }][m] } }[-> p { -> x { p[x] } }]↵
[-> p { -> x { p[x] } }]
-> n { n[-> n { -> p { -> x { p[n[p][x]] } } }][-> p { -> x { p[x] } }] }[-> p { -> x ↵
{ p[x] } }]
-> p { -> x { p[x] } }[-> n { -> p { -> x { p[n[p][x]] } } }][-> p { -> x { p[x] } }]
-> x { -> n { -> p { -> x { p[n[p][x]] } } }[x] }[-> p { -> x { p[x] } }]
-> n { -> p { -> x { p[n[p][x]] } } }[-> p { -> x { p[x] } }]
-> p { -> x { p[-> p { -> x { p[x] } }[p][x]] } }
=> nil
```

Well, something definitely happened, but we didn't get quite the result we wanted: the final expression is -> p { -> x { p[-> p { -> x { p[x] } }[p][x]] } }, but the lambda calculus representation of the number two is supposed to be -> p { -> x { p[p[x]] } })]. What went wrong?

The mismatch is caused by the evaluation strategy we're using. There are still reducible function calls buried within the result—the call -> p { -> x { p[x] } }[p] could be reduced to -> x { p[x] }, for instance—but #reduce doesn't touch them, because they appear inside the body of a function, and our semantics doesn't treat functions as reducible.[9]

However, as discussed in "Equality" on page 164, two expressions with different syntax can still be considered equal if they have the same behavior. We know how the lambda calculus representation of the number two is supposed to behave: if we give it two arguments, it calls the first argument twice on the second argument. So let's try calling our expression with two made-up variables, inc and zero,[10] and see what it actually does:

```
>> inc, zero = LCVariable.new(:inc), LCVariable.new(:zero)
=> [inc, zero]
>> expression = LCCall.new(LCCall.new(expression, inc), zero)
=> -> p { -> x { p[-> p { -> x { p[x] } }[p][x]] } }[inc][zero]
>> while expression.reducible?
     puts expression
     expression = expression.reduce
   end; puts expression
-> p { -> x { p[-> p { -> x { p[x] } }[p][x]] } }[inc][zero]
-> x { inc[-> p { -> x { p[x] } }[inc][x]] }[zero]
inc[-> p { -> x { p[x] } }[inc][zero]]
inc[-> x { inc[x] }[zero]]
inc[inc[zero]]
=> nil
```

That's exactly how we expect the number two to behave, so -> p { -> x { p[-> p { -> x { p[x] } }[p][x]] } } is the right result after all, even though it looks slightly different than the expression we were expecting.

Parsing

Now that we've got a working semantics, let's finish things off by building a parser for lambda calculus expressions. As usual, we can use Treetop to write a grammar:

```
grammar LambdaCalculus
  rule expression
    calls / variable / function
  end

  rule calls
    first:(variable / function) rest:('[' expression ']')+ {
      def to_ast
        arguments.map(&:to_ast).inject(first.to_ast) { |l, r| LCCall.new(l, r) }
      end
```

9. We could fix this by reimplementing #reduce to use a more aggressive evaluation strategy (like *applicative order* or *normal order* evaluation) that performs reduction on the bodies of functions, but a function body taken in isolation usually contains free variables, so that would require a more robust implementation of #replace.

10. We're taking a risk by evaluating an expression containing the free variables inc and zero, but fortunately, none of the functions in the expression have arguments with those names, so in this specific case, there's no danger of either variable being accidentally captured.

```
      def arguments
        rest.elements.map(&:expression)
      end
    }
  end

  rule variable
    [a-z]+ {
      def to_ast
        LCVariable.new(text_value.to_sym)
      end
    }
  end

  rule function
    '-> ' parameter:[a-z]+ ' { ' body:expression ' }' {
      def to_ast
        LCFunction.new(parameter.text_value.to_sym, body.to_ast)
      end
    }
  end
end
```

 As discussed in "Implementing Parsers" on page 58, Treetop grammars typically generate right-associative trees, so this grammar has to do extra work to accommodate the lambda calculus's left-associative function call syntax. The `calls` rule matches one or more consecutive calls (like `a[b][c][d]`), and the `#to_ast` method on the resulting concrete syntax tree node uses `Enumerable#inject` to roll up the arguments of those calls into a left-associative abstract syntax tree.

The parser and operational semantics together give us a complete implementation of the lambda calculus, allowing us to read expressions and evaluate them:

```
>> require 'treetop'
=> true
>> Treetop.load('lambda_calculus')
=> LambdaCalculusParser
>> parse_tree = LambdaCalculusParser.new.parse('-> x { x[x] }[-> y { y }]')
=> SyntaxNode+Calls2+Calls1 offset=0, "…}[-> y { y }]" (to_ast,arguments,first,rest):
     SyntaxNode+Function1+Function0 offset=0, "… x { x[x] }" (to_ast,parameter,body):
       SyntaxNode offset=0, "-> "
       SyntaxNode offset=3, "x":
         SyntaxNode offset=3, "x"
       SyntaxNode offset=4, " { "
       SyntaxNode+Calls2+Calls1 offset=7, "x[x]" (to_ast,arguments,first,rest):
         SyntaxNode+Variable0 offset=7, "x" (to_ast):
           SyntaxNode offset=7, "x"
         SyntaxNode offset=8, "[x]":
           SyntaxNode+Calls0 offset=8, "[x]" (expression):
             SyntaxNode offset=8, "["
             SyntaxNode+Variable0 offset=9, "x" (to_ast):
```

```
                      SyntaxNode offset=9, "x"
                  SyntaxNode offset=10, "]"
              SyntaxNode offset=11, " }"
          SyntaxNode offset=13, "[-> y { y }]":
            SyntaxNode+Calls0 offset=13, "[-> y { y }]" (expression):
              SyntaxNode offset=13, "["
              SyntaxNode+Function1+Function0 offset=14, "… { y }" (to_ast,parameter,body):
                SyntaxNode offset=14, "-> "
                SyntaxNode offset=17, "y":
                  SyntaxNode offset=17, "y"
                SyntaxNode offset=18, " { "
                SyntaxNode+Variable0 offset=21, "y" (to_ast):
                  SyntaxNode offset=21, "y"
                SyntaxNode offset=22, " }"
              SyntaxNode offset=24, "]"
```

>> expression = parse_tree.to_ast
=> -> x { x[x] }[-> y { y }]
>> expression.reduce
=> -> y { y }[-> y { y }]

## CHAPTER 7

Universality Is Everywhere

Most of the complexity we see in the world comes from complicated systems—mammals, microprocessors, the economy, the weather—so it's natural to assume that a simple system can only do simple things. But in this book, we've seen that simple systems can have impressive capabilities: Chapter 6 showed that even a very minimal programming language has enough power to do useful work, and Chapter 5 sketched the design of a universal Turing machine that can read an encoded description of another machine and then simulate its execution.

The existence of the universal Turing machine is extremely significant. Even though any individual Turing machine has a hardcoded rulebook, the universal Turing machine demonstrates that it's possible to design a device that can adapt to arbitrary tasks by reading instructions from a tape. These instructions are effectively a piece of software that controls the operation of the machine's hardware, just like in the general-purpose programmable computers we use every day.[1] Finite and pushdown automata are slightly *too* simple to support this kind of full-blown programmability, but a Turing machine has just enough complexity to make it work.

In this chapter, we'll take a tour of several simple systems and see that they're all universal—all capable of simulating a Turing machine, and therefore all capable of executing an arbitrary program provided as input instead of hardcoded into the rules of the system—which suggests that universality is a lot more common than we might expect.

Lambda Calculus

We've seen that the lambda calculus is a usable programming language, but we haven't yet explored whether it's as powerful as a Turing machine. In fact, the lambda calculus

---

1. "Hardware" means the read/write head, the tape, and the rulebook. They're not literally hardware since a Turing machine is usually a thought experiment rather than a physical object, but they're "hard" in the sense that they're a fixed part of the system, as opposed to the ever-changing "soft" information that exists as characters written on the tape.

must be at least that powerful, because it turns out to be capable of simulating any Turing machine, including (of course) a *universal* Turing machine.

Let's get a taste of how that works by quickly implementing part of a Turing machine —the tape—in the lambda calculus.

 As in Chapter 6, we're going to take the convenient shortcut of representing lambda calculus expressions as Ruby code, as long as that code does nothing except make procs, call procs, and use constants as abbreviations.

It's a little risky to bring Ruby into play when it's not the language we're supposed to be investigating, but in exchange, we get a familiar syntax for expressions and an easy way to evaluate them, and our discoveries will still be valid as long as we stay within the constraints.

A Turing machine tape has four attributes: the list of characters appearing on the left of the tape, the character in the middle of the tape (where the machine's read/write head is), the list of characters on the right, and the character to be treated as a blank. We can represent those four values as a pair of pairs:

```
TAPE        = -> l { -> m { -> r { -> b { PAIR[PAIR[l][m]][PAIR[r][b]] } } } }
TAPE_LEFT   = -> t { LEFT[LEFT[t]] }
TAPE_MIDDLE = -> t { RIGHT[LEFT[t]] }
TAPE_RIGHT  = -> t { LEFT[RIGHT[t]] }
TAPE_BLANK  = -> t { RIGHT[RIGHT[t]] }
```

TAPE acts as a constructor that takes the four tape attributes as arguments and returns a proc representing a tape, and TAPE_LEFT, TAPE_MIDDLE, TAPE_RIGHT, and TAPE_BLANK are the accessors that can take one of those tape representations and pull the corresponding attribute out again.

Once we have this data structure, we can implement TAPE_WRITE, which takes a tape and a character and returns a new tape with that character written in the middle position:

```
TAPE_WRITE = -> t { -> c { TAPE[TAPE_LEFT[t]][c][TAPE_RIGHT[t]][TAPE_BLANK[t]] } }
```

We can also define operations to move the tape head. Here's a TAPE_MOVE_HEAD_RIGHT proc for moving the head one square to the right, converted directly from the unrestricted Ruby implementation of Tape#move_head_right in "Simulation" on page 141:[2]

```
TAPE_MOVE_HEAD_RIGHT =
  -> t {
    TAPE[
      PUSH[TAPE_LEFT[t]][TAPE_MIDDLE[t]]
    ][
      IF[IS_EMPTY[TAPE_RIGHT[t]]][
```

---

2. The implementation of TAPE_MOVE_HEAD_LEFT is similar, although it requires some extra list-manipulation functions that didn't get defined in "Lists" on page 181.

```
      TAPE_BLANK[t]
    ][
      FIRST[TAPE_RIGHT[t]]
    ]
  ][
    IF[IS_EMPTY[TAPE_RIGHT[t]]][
      EMPTY
    ][
      REST[TAPE_RIGHT[t]]
    ]
  ][
    TAPE_BLANK[t]
  ]
}
```

Taken together, these operations give us everything we need to create a tape, read from it, write onto it, and move its head around. For example, we can start with a blank tape and write a sequence of numbers into consecutive squares:

```
>> current_tape = TAPE[EMPTY][ZERO][EMPTY][ZERO]
=> #<Proc (lambda)>
>> current_tape = TAPE_WRITE[current_tape][ONE]
=> #<Proc (lambda)>
>> current_tape = TAPE_MOVE_HEAD_RIGHT[current_tape]
=> #<Proc (lambda)>
>> current_tape = TAPE_WRITE[current_tape][TWO]
=> #<Proc (lambda)>
>> current_tape = TAPE_MOVE_HEAD_RIGHT[current_tape]
=> #<Proc (lambda)>
>> current_tape = TAPE_WRITE[current_tape][THREE]
=> #<Proc (lambda)>
>> current_tape = TAPE_MOVE_HEAD_RIGHT[current_tape]
=> #<Proc (lambda)>
>> to_array(TAPE_LEFT[current_tape]).map { |p| to_integer(p) }
=> [1, 2, 3]
>> to_integer(TAPE_MIDDLE[current_tape])
=> 0
>> to_array(TAPE_RIGHT[current_tape]).map { |p| to_integer(p) }
=> []
```

We'll skip over the rest of the details, but it's not difficult to continue like this, building proc-based representations of states, configurations, rules, and rulebooks. Once we have all those pieces, we can write proc-only implementations of DTM#step and DTM#run: STEP simulates a single step of a Turing machine by applying a rulebook to one configuration to produce another, and RUN simulates a machine's full execution by using the Z combinator to repeatedly call STEP until no rule applies or the machine reaches a halting state.

In other words, RUN is a lambda calculus program that can simulate any Turing machine.[3] It turns out that the reverse is also possible: a Turing machine can act as an

---

3. The term *Turing complete* is often used to describe a system or programming language that can simulate any Turing machine.

interpreter for the lambda calculus by storing a representation of a lambda calculus expression on the tape and repeatedly updating it according to a set of reduction rules, just like the operational semantics from "Semantics" on page 199.

 Since every Turing machine can be simulated by a lambda calculus program, and every lambda calculus program can be simulated by a Turing machine, the two systems are exactly equivalent in power. That's a surprising result, because Turing machines and lambda calculus programs work in completely different ways and there's no prior reason to expect them to have identical capabilities.

This means there's at least one way to simulate the lambda calculus in itself: first implement a Turing machine in the lambda calculus, then use that simulated machine to run a lambda calculus interpreter. This simulation-inside-a-simulation is a very inefficient way of doing things, and we can get the same result more elegantly by designing data structures to represent lambda calculus expressions and then implementing an operational semantics directly, but it does show that the lambda calculus must be universal without having to build anything new. A self-interpreter is the lambda calculus version of the universal Turing machine: even though the underlying interpreter program is fixed, we can make it do any job by supplying a suitable lambda calculus expression as input.

As we've seen, the real benefit of a universal system is that it can be programmed to perform different tasks, rather than always being hardcoded to perform a single one. In particular, a universal system can be programmed to simulate any other universal system; a universal Turing machine can evaluate lambda calculus expressions, and a lambda calculus interpreter can simulate the execution of a Turing machine.

Partial Recursive Functions

In much the same way that lambda calculus expressions consist entirely of creating and calling procs, *partial recursive functions* are programs that are constructed from four fundamental building blocks in different combinations. The first two building blocks are called `zero` and `increment`, and we can implement them here as Ruby methods:

```
def zero
  0
end

def increment(n)
  n + 1
end
```

These are straightforward methods that return the number zero and add one to a number respectively:

```
>> zero
=> 0
>> increment(zero)
=> 1
>> increment(increment(zero))
=> 2
```

We can use #zero and #increment to define some new methods, albeit not very interesting ones:

```
>> def two
     increment(increment(zero))
   end
=> nil
>> two
=> 2
>> def three
     increment(two)
   end
=> nil
>> three
=> 3
>> def add_three(x)
     increment(increment(increment(x)))
   end
=> nil
>> add_three(two)
=> 5
```

The third building block, #recurse, is more complicated:

```
def recurse(f, g, *values)
  *other_values, last_value = values

  if last_value.zero?
    send(f, *other_values)
  else
    easier_last_value = last_value - 1
    easier_values = other_values + [easier_last_value]

    easier_result = recurse(f, g, *easier_values)
    send(g, *easier_values, easier_result)
  end
end
```

#recurse takes two method names as arguments, f and g, and uses them to perform a recursive calculation on some input values. The immediate result of a call to #recurse is computed by delegating to either f or g depending on what the last input value is:

- If the last input value is zero, #recurse calls the method named by f, passing the rest of the values as arguments.
- If the last input value is not zero, #recurse decrements it, calls itself with the updated input values, and then calls the method named by g with those same values and the result of the recursive call.

This sounds more complicated than it is; #recurse is just a template for defining a certain kind of recursive function. For example, we can use it to define a method called #add that takes two arguments, x and y, and adds them together. To build this method with #recurse, we need to implement two other methods that answer these questions:

- Given the value of x, what is the value of add(x, 0)?
- Given the values of x, y - 1, and add(x, y - 1), what is the value of add(x, y)?

The first question is easy: adding zero to a number doesn't change it, so if we know the value of x, the value of add(x, 0) will be identical. We can implement this as a method called #add_zero_to_x that simply returns its argument:

```
def add_zero_to_x(x)
  x
end
```

The second question is slightly harder, but still simple enough to answer: if we already have the value of add(x, y - 1), we just need to increment it to get the value of add(x, y).[4] This means we need a method that increments its third argument (#recurse calls it with x, y - 1, and add(x, y - 1)). Let's call it #increment_easier_result:

```
def increment_easier_result(x, easier_y, easier_result)
  increment(easier_result)
end
```

Putting these together gives us a definition of #add built out of #recurse and #increment:

```
def add(x, y)
  recurse(:add_zero_to_x, :increment_easier_result, x, y)
end
```

 The same spirit applies here as in Chapter 6: we may only use method definitions to give convenient names to expressions, not to sneak recursion into them.[5] If we want to write a recursive method, we have to use #recurse.

Let's check that #add does what it's supposed to:

```
>> add(two, three)
=> 5
```

Looks good. We can use the same strategy to implement other familiar examples, like #multiply...

---

4. Because subtraction is the *inverse* of addition, (x + (y – 1)) + 1 = (x + (y + –1)) + 1. Because addition is *associative*, (x + (y + –1)) + 1 = (x + y) + (–1 + 1). And because –1 + 1 = 0, which is the *identity element* for addition, (x + y) + (–1 + 1) = x + y.

5. Of course the underlying implementation of #recurse itself uses a recursive method definition, but that's allowed, because we're treating #recurse as one of the four built-in primitives of the system, not a user-defined method.

```
def multiply_x_by_zero(x)
  zero
end

def add_x_to_easier_result(x, easier_y, easier_result)
  add(x, easier_result)
end

def multiply(x, y)
  recurse(:multiply_x_by_zero, :add_x_to_easier_result, x, y)
end
```

...and #decrement...

```
def easier_x(easier_x, easier_result)
  easier_x
end

def decrement(x)
  recurse(:zero, :easier_x, x)
end
```

...and #subtract:

```
def subtract_zero_from_x(x)
  x
end

def decrement_easier_result(x, easier_y, easier_result)
  decrement(easier_result)
end

def subtract(x, y)
  recurse(:subtract_zero_from_x, :decrement_easier_result, x, y)
end
```

These implementations all work as expected:

```
>> multiply(two, three)
=> 6
>> def six
     multiply(two, three)
   end
=> nil
>> decrement(six)
=> 5
>> subtract(six, two)
=> 4
>> subtract(two, six)
=> 0
```

The programs that we can assemble out of #zero, #increment, and #recurse are called the *primitive* recursive functions.

All primitive recursive functions are *total*: regardless of their inputs, they always halt and return an answer. This is because #recurse is the only legitimate way to define a recursive method, and #recurse always halts: each recursive call makes the last argument closer to zero, and when it inevitably reaches zero, the recursion will stop.

#zero, #increment, and #recurse are enough to construct many useful functions, including all the operations needed to perform a single step of a Turing machine: the contents of a Turing machine tape can be represented as a large number, and primitive recursive functions can be used to read the character at the tape head's current position, write a new character onto the tape, and move the tape head left or right. However, we can't simulate the full execution of an arbitrary Turing machine with primitive recursive functions, because some Turing machines loop forever, so primitive recursive functions aren't universal.

To get a truly universal system we have to add a fourth fundamental operation, #mini mize:

```
def minimize
  n = 0
  n = n + 1 until yield(n).zero?
  n
end
```

#minimize takes a block and calls it repeatedly with a single numeric argument. For the first call, it provides 0 as the argument, then 1, then 2, and keeps calling the block with larger and larger numbers until it returns zero.

By adding #minimize to #zero, #increment, and #recurse, we can build many more functions—all the *partial* recursive functions—including ones that don't always halt. For example, #minimize gives us an easy way to implement #divide:

```
def divide(x, y)
  minimize { |n| subtract(increment(x), multiply(y, increment(n))) }
end
```

 The expression subtract(increment(x), multiply(y, increment(n))) is designed to return zero for values of n that make y * (n + 1) greater than x. If we're trying to divide 13 by 4 (x = 13, y = 4), look at the values of y * (n + 1) as n increases:

n	x	y * (n + 1)	Is y * (n + 1) greater than x?
0	13	4	no
1	13	8	no
2	13	12	no
3	13	16	yes
4	13	20	yes

n	x	y * (n + 1)	Is y * (n + 1) greater than x?
5	13	24	yes

The first value of n that satisfies the condition is 3, so the block we pass to #minimize will return zero for the first time when n reaches 3, and we'll get 3 as the result of divide(13, 4).

When #divide is called with sensible arguments, it always returns a result, just like a primitive recursive function:

```
>> divide(six, two)
=> 3
>> def ten
     increment(multiply(three, three))
   end
=> nil
>> ten
=> 10
>> divide(ten, three)
=> 3
```

But #divide doesn't have to return an answer, because #minimize can loop forever. #divide by zero is undefined:

```
>> divide(six, zero)
SystemStackError: stack level too deep
```

It's a little surprising to see a stack overflow here, because the implementation of #minimize is iterative and doesn't directly grow the call stack, but the overflow actually happens during #divide's call to the recursive #multiply method. The depth of recursion in the #multiply call is determined by its second argument, increment(n), and the value of n becomes very large as the #minimize loop tries to run forever, eventually overflowing the stack.

With #minimize, it's possible to fully simulate a Turing machine by repeatedly calling the primitive recursive function that performs a single simulation step. The simulation will continue until the machine halts—and if that never happens, it'll run forever.

SKI Combinator Calculus

The *SKI combinator calculus* is a system of rules for manipulating the syntax of expressions, just like the lambda calculus. Although the lambda calculus is already very simple, it still has three kinds of expression—variables, functions, and calls—and we saw in "Semantics" on page 199 that variables make the reduction rules a bit complicated. The SKI calculus is even simpler, with only two kinds of expression—calls and alphabetic *symbols*—and much easier rules. All of its power comes from the three special symbols S, K, and I (called *combinators*), each of which has its own reduction rule:

- Reduce S[*a*][*b*][*c*] to *a*[*c*][*b*[*c*]], where *a*, *b*, and *c* can be any SKI calculus expressions.

- Reduce K[*a*][*b*] to *a*.

- Reduce I[*a*] to *a*.

For example, here's one way of reducing the expression I[S][K][S][I[K]]:

```
I[S][K][S][I[K]] → S[K][S][I[K]]  (reduce I[S] to S)
                 → S[K][S][K]     (reduce I[K] to K)
                 → K[K][S[K]]     (reduce S[K][S][K] to K[K][S[K]])
                 → K               (reduce K[K][S[K]] to K)
```

Notice that there's no lambda-calculus-style variable replacement going on here, just symbols being reordered, duplicated, and discarded according to the reduction rules.

It's easy to implement the abstract syntax of SKI expressions:

```ruby
class SKISymbol < Struct.new(:name)
  def to_s
    name.to_s
  end

  def inspect
    to_s
  end
end

class SKICall < Struct.new(:left, :right)
  def to_s
    "#{left}[#{right}]"
  end

  def inspect
    to_s
  end
end

class SKICombinator < SKISymbol
end

S, K, I = [:S, :K, :I].map { |name| SKICombinator.new(name) }
```

Here we're defining SKICall and SKISymbol classes to represent calls and symbols generally, then creating the one-off instances S, K, and I to represent those particular symbols that act as combinators.

We could have made S, K, and I direct instances of SKISymbol, but instead, we've used instances of a subclass called SKICombinator. This doesn't help us right now, but it'll make it easier to add methods to all three combinator objects later on.

These classes and objects can be used to build abstract syntax trees of SKI expressions:

```
>> x = SKISymbol.new(:x)
=> x
>> expression = SKICall.new(SKICall.new(S, K), SKICall.new(I, x))
=> S[K][I[x]]
```

We can give the SKI calculus a small-step operational semantics by implementing its reduction rules and applying those rules inside expressions. First, we'll define a method called #call on the SKICombinator instances; S, K, and I each get their own definition of #call that implements their reduction rule:

```
# reduce S[a][b][c] to a[c][b[c]]
def S.call(a, b, c)
  SKICall.new(SKICall.new(a, c), SKICall.new(b, c))
end

# reduce K[a][b] to a
def K.call(a, b)
  a
end

# reduce I[a] to a
def I.call(a)
  a
end
```

Okay, so this gives us a way to apply the rules of the calculus if we already know what arguments a combinator is being called with…

```
>> y, z = SKISymbol.new(:y), SKISymbol.new(:z)
=> [y, z]
>> S.call(x, y, z)
=> x[z][y[z]]
```

…but to use #call with a real SKI expression, we need to extract a combinator and arguments from it. This is a bit fiddly since an expression is represented as a binary tree of SKICall objects:

```
>> expression = SKICall.new(SKICall.new(SKICall.new(S, x), y), z)
=> S[x][y][z]
>> combinator = expression.left.left.left
=> S
>> first_argument = expression.left.left.right
=> x
>> second_argument = expression.left.right
=> y
>> third_argument = expression.right
=> z
>> combinator.call(first_argument, second_argument, third_argument)
=> x[z][y[z]]
```

To make this structure easier to handle, we can define the methods #combinator and #arguments on abstract syntax trees:

```
class SKISymbol
  def combinator
    self
  end

  def arguments
    []
  end
end

class SKICall
  def combinator
    left.combinator
  end

  def arguments
    left.arguments + [right]
  end
end
```

This gives us an easy way to discover which combinator to call and what arguments to pass to it:

```
>> expression
=> S[x][y][z]
>> combinator = expression.combinator
=> S
>> arguments = expression.arguments
=> [x, y, z]
>> combinator.call(*arguments)
=> x[z][y[z]]
```

That works fine for S[x][y][z], but there are a couple of problems in the general case. First, the #combinator method just returns the leftmost *symbol* from an expression, but that symbol isn't necessarily a combinator:

```
>> expression = SKICall.new(SKICall.new(x, y), z)
=> x[y][z]
>> combinator = expression.combinator
=> x
>> arguments = expression.arguments
=> [y, z]
>> combinator.call(*arguments)
NoMethodError: undefined method `call' for x:SKISymbol
```

And second, even if the leftmost symbol *is* a combinator, it isn't necessarily being called with the right number of arguments:

```
>> expression = SKICall.new(SKICall.new(S, x), y)
=> S[x][y]
>> combinator = expression.combinator
=> S
>> arguments = expression.arguments
=> [x, y]
>> combinator.call(*arguments)
ArgumentError: wrong number of arguments (2 for 3)
```

To avoid both these problems, we'll define a #callable? predicate for checking whether it's appropriate to use #call with the results of #combinator and #arguments. A vanilla symbol is never callable, and a combinator is only callable if the number of arguments is correct:

```
class SKISymbol
  def callable?(*arguments)
    false
  end
end

def S.callable?(*arguments)
  arguments.length == 3
end

def K.callable?(*arguments)
  arguments.length == 2
end

def I.callable?(*arguments)
  arguments.length == 1
end
```

Incidentally, Ruby already has a way to ask a method how many arguments it expects (its *arity*):

```
>> def add(x, y)
     x + y
   end
=> nil
>> add_method = method(:add)
=> #<Method: Object#add>
>> add_method.arity
=> 2
```

So we could replace S, K, and I's separate implementations of #callable? with a shared one:

```
class SKICombinator
  def callable?(*arguments)
    arguments.length == method(:call).arity
  end
end
```

Now we can recognize expressions where the reduction rules directly apply:

```
>> expression = SKICall.new(SKICall.new(x, y), z)
=> x[y][z]
>> expression.combinator.callable?(*expression.arguments)
=> false
>> expression = SKICall.new(SKICall.new(S, x), y)
=> S[x][y]
>> expression.combinator.callable?(*expression.arguments)
=> false
>> expression = SKICall.new(SKICall.new(SKICall.new(S, x), y), z)
```

```
=> S[x][y][z]
>> expression.combinator.callable?(*expression.arguments)
=> true
```

We're finally ready to implement the familiar #reducible? and #reduce methods for SKI expressions:

```
class SKISymbol
  def reducible?
    false
  end
end

class SKICall
  def reducible?
    left.reducible? || right.reducible? || combinator.callable?(*arguments)
  end

  def reduce
    if left.reducible?
      SKICall.new(left.reduce, right)
    elsif right.reducible?
      SKICall.new(left, right.reduce)
    else
      combinator.call(*arguments)
    end
  end
end
```

 SKICall#reduce works by recursively looking for a subexpression that we know how to reduce—the S combinator being called with three arguments, for instance—and then applying the appropriate rule with #call.

And that's it! We can now evaluate SKI expressions by repeatedly reducing them until no more reductions are possible. For example, here's the expression S[K[S[I]]][K], which swaps the order of its two arguments, being called with the symbols x and y:

```
>> swap = SKICall.new(SKICall.new(S, SKICall.new(K, SKICall.new(S, I))), K)
=> S[K[S[I]]][K]
>> expression = SKICall.new(SKICall.new(swap, x), y)
=> S[K[S[I]]][K][x][y]
>> while expression.reducible?
     puts expression
     expression = expression.reduce
   end; puts expression
S[K[S[I]]][K][x][y]
K[S[I]][x][K[x]][y]
S[I][K[x]][y]
I[y][K[x][y]]
y[K[x][y]]
y[x]
=> nil
```

The SKI calculus can produce surprisingly complex behavior with its three simple rules —so complex, in fact, that it turns out to be universal. We can prove it's universal by showing how to translate any lambda calculus expression into an SKI expression that does the same thing, effectively using the SKI calculus to give a denotational semantics for the lambda calculus. We already know that the lambda calculus is universal, so if the SKI calculus can completely simulate it, it follows that the SKI calculus is universal too.

At the heart of the translation is a method called #as_a_function_of:

```
class SKISymbol
  def as_a_function_of(name)
    if self.name == name
      I
    else
      SKICall.new(K, self)
    end
  end
end

class SKICombinator
  def as_a_function_of(name)
    SKICall.new(K, self)
  end
end

class SKICall
  def as_a_function_of(name)
    left_function = left.as_a_function_of(name)
    right_function = right.as_a_function_of(name)

    SKICall.new(SKICall.new(S, left_function), right_function)
  end
end
```

The precise details of how #as_a_function_of works aren't important, but roughly speaking, it converts an SKI expression into a new one that turns back into the original when called with an argument. For example, the expression S[K][I] gets converted into S[S[K[S]][K[K]]][K[I]]:

```
>> original = SKICall.new(SKICall.new(S, K), I)
=> S[K][I]
>> function = original.as_a_function_of(:x)
=> S[S[K[S]][K[K]]][K[I]]
>> function.reducible?
=> false
```

When S[S[K[S]][K[K]]][K[I]] is called with an argument, say, the symbol y, it reduces back to S[K][I]:

```
>> expression = SKICall.new(function, y)
=> S[S[K[S]][K[K]]][K[I]][y]
>> while expression.reducible?
     puts expression
```

```
    expression = expression.reduce
  end; puts expression
S[S[K[S]][K[K]]][K[I]][y]
S[K[S]][K[K]][y][K[I][y]]
K[S][y][K[K][y]][K[I][y]]
S[K[K][y]][K[I][y]]
S[K][K[I][y]]
S[K][I]
=> nil
>> expression == original
=> true
```

The name parameter is only used if the original expression contains a symbol with that name. In that case, #as_a_function_of produces something more interesting: an expression that, when called with an argument, reduces to the original expression with that argument in place of the symbol:

```
>> original = SKICall.new(SKICall.new(S, x), I)
=> S[x][I]
>> function = original.as_a_function_of(:x)
=> S[S[K[S]][I]][K[I]]
>> expression = SKICall.new(function, y)
=> S[S[K[S]][I]][K[I]][y]
>> while expression.reducible?
     puts expression
     expression = expression.reduce
   end; puts expression
S[S[K[S]][I]][K[I]][y]
S[K[S]][I][y][K[I][y]]
K[S][y][I[y]][K[I][y]]
S[I[y]][K[I][y]]
S[y][K[I][y]]
S[y][I]
=> nil
>> expression == original
=> false
```

This is an explicit reimplementation of the way that variables get replaced inside the body of a lambda calculus function when it's called. Essentially, #as_a_function_of gives us a way to use an SKI expression as the body of a function: it creates a new expression that behaves just like a function with a particular body and parameter name, even though the SKI calculus doesn't have explicit syntax for functions.

The ability of the SKI calculus to imitate the behavior of functions makes it straightforward to translate lambda calculus expressions into SKI expressions. Lambda calculus variables and calls become SKI calculus symbols and calls, and each lambda calculus function has its body turned into an SKI calculus "function" with #as_a_function_of:

```
class LCVariable
  def to_ski
    SKISymbol.new(name)
  end
end
```

```
class LCCall
  def to_ski
    SKICall.new(left.to_ski, right.to_ski)
  end
end

class LCFunction
  def to_ski
    body.to_ski.as_a_function_of(parameter)
  end
end
```

Let's check this translation by converting the lambda calculus representation of the number two (see "Numbers" on page 166) into the SKI calculus:

```
>> two = LambdaCalculusParser.new.parse('-> p { -> x { p[p[x]] } }').to_ast
=> -> p { -> x { p[p[x]] } }
>> two.to_ski
=> S[S[K[S]][S[K[K]][I]]][S[S[K[S]][S[K[K]][I]]][K[I]]]
```

Does the SKI calculus expression S[S[K[S]][S[K[K]][I]]][S[S[K[S]][S[K[K]][I]]] [K[I]]] do the same thing as the lambda calculus expression -> p { -> x { p[p[x]] } }? Well, it's supposed to call its first argument twice on its second argument, so we can try giving it some arguments to see whether it actually does that, just like we did in "Semantics" on page 199:

```
>> inc, zero = SKISymbol.new(:inc), SKISymbol.new(:zero)
=> [inc, zero]
>> expression = SKICall.new(SKICall.new(two.to_ski, inc), zero)
=> S[S[K[S]][S[K[K]][I]]][S[S[K[S]][S[K[K]][I]]][K[I]]][inc][zero]
>> while expression.reducible?
     puts expression
     expression = expression.reduce
   end; puts expression
S[S[K[S]][S[K[K]][I]]][S[S[K[S]][S[K[K]][I]]][K[I]]][inc][zero]
S[K[S]][S[K[K]][I]][inc][S[S[K[S]][S[K[K]][I]]][K[I]][inc]][zero]
K[S][inc][S[K[K]][I][inc]][S[S[K[S]][S[K[K]][I]]][K[I]][inc]][zero]
S[S[K[K]][I][inc]][S[S[K[S]][S[K[K]][I]]][K[I]][inc]][zero]
S[K[K][inc][I[inc]]][S[S[K[S]][S[K[K]][I]]][K[I]][inc]][zero]
S[K[I[inc]]][S[S[K[S]][S[K[K]][I]]][K[I]][inc]][zero]
S[K[inc]][S[S[K[S]][S[K[K]][I]]][K[I]][inc]][zero]
S[K[inc]][S[K[S]][S[K[K]][I]][inc][K[I][inc]]][zero]
S[K[inc]][K[S][inc][S[K[K]][I][inc]][K[I][inc]]][zero]
S[K[inc]][S[S[K[K]][I][inc]][K[I][inc]]][zero]
S[K[inc]][S[K[K][inc][I[inc]]][K[I][inc]]][zero]
S[K[inc]][S[K[I[inc]]][K[I][inc]]][zero]
S[K[inc]][S[K[inc]][K[I][inc]]][zero]
S[K[inc]][S[K[inc]][I]][zero]
K[inc][zero][S[K[inc]][I][zero]]
inc[S[K[inc]][I][zero]]
inc[K[inc][zero][I[zero]]]
inc[inc[I[zero]]]
inc[inc[zero]]
=> nil
```

Sure enough, calling the converted expression with symbols named `inc` and `zero` has evaluated to `inc[inc[zero]]`, which is exactly what we wanted. The same translation works successfully for any other lambda calculus expression, so the SKI combinator calculus can completely simulate the lambda calculus, and therefore must be universal.

 Although the SKI calculus has three combinators, the I combinator is actually redundant. There are many expressions containing only S and K that do the same thing as I; for instance, look at the behavior of S[K][K]:

```
>> identity = SKICall.new(SKICall.new(S, K), K)
=> S[K][K]
>> expression = SKICall.new(identity, x)
=> S[K][K][x]
>> while expression.reducible?
     puts expression
     expression = expression.reduce
   end; puts expression
S[K][K][x]
K[x][K[x]]
x
=> nil
```

So `S[K][K]` has the same behavior as I, and in fact, that's true for any SKI expression of the form `S[K][whatever]`. The I combinator is syntactic sugar that we can live without; just the two combinators S and K are enough for universality.

Iota

The Greek letter iota (ι) is an extra combinator that can be added to the SKI calculus. Here is its reduction rule: Reduce ι[*a*] to *a*[S][K].

Our implementation of the SKI calculus makes it easy to plug in a new combinator:

```
IOTA = SKICombinator.new('ι')

# reduce ι[a] to a[S][K]
def IOTA.call(a)
  SKICall.new(SKICall.new(a, S), K)
end

def IOTA.callable?(*arguments)
  arguments.length == 1
end
```

Chris Barker proposed a language called Iota (*http://semarch.linguistics.fas.nyu.edu/barker/Iota/*) whose programs *only* use the ι combinator. Although it only has one combinator, Iota is a universal language, because any SKI calculus expression can be converted into it, and we've already seen that the SKI calculus is universal.

We can convert an SKI expression to Iota by applying these substitution rules:

- Replace S with ι[ι[ι[ι[ι]]]].
- Replace K with ι[ι[ι[ι]]].
- Replace I with ι[ι].

It's easy to implement this conversion:

```ruby
class SKISymbol
  def to_iota
    self
  end
end

class SKICall
  def to_iota
    SKICall.new(left.to_iota, right.to_iota)
  end
end

def S.to_iota
  SKICall.new(IOTA, SKICall.new(IOTA, SKICall.new(IOTA, SKICall.new(IOTA, IOTA))))
end

def K.to_iota
  SKICall.new(IOTA, SKICall.new(IOTA, SKICall.new(IOTA, IOTA)))
end

def I.to_iota
  SKICall.new(IOTA, IOTA)
end
```

It's not at all obvious whether the Iota versions of the S, K, and I combinators are equivalent to the originals, so let's investigate by reducing each of them inside the SKI calculus and observing their behavior. Here's what happens when we translate S into Iota and then reduce it:

```
>> expression = S.to_iota
=> ι[ι[ι[ι[ι]]]]
>> while expression.reducible?
     puts expression
     expression = expression.reduce
   end; puts expression
ι[ι[ι[ι[ι]]]]
ι[ι[ι[ι[S][K]]]]
ι[ι[ι[S[S][K][K]]]]
ι[ι[ι[S[K][K[K]]]]]
ι[ι[S[K][K[K]][S][K]]]
ι[ι[K[S][K[K][S]][K]]]
ι[ι[K[S][K][K]]]
ι[ι[S[K]]]
ι[S[K][S][K]]
ι[K[K][S[K]]]
ι[K]
K[S][K]
```

```
S
=> nil
```

So yes, ι[ι[ι[ι[ι]]]] really is equivalent to S. The same thing happens with K:

```
>> expression = K.to_iota
=> ι[ι[ι[ι]]]
>> while expression.reducible?
     puts expression
     expression = expression.reduce
   end; puts expression
ι[ι[ι[ι]]]
ι[ι[ι[S][K]]]
ι[ι[S[S][K][K]]]
ι[ι[S[K][K[K]]]]
ι[S[K][K[K]][S][K]]
ι[K[S][K[K]][S]][K]]
ι[K[S][K][K]]
ι[S[K]]
S[K][S][K]
K[K][S[K]]
K
=> nil
```

Things don't work quite so neatly for I. The ι reduction rule only produces expressions containing the S and K combinators, so there's no chance of ending up with a literal I:

```
>> expression = I.to_iota
=> ι[ι]
>> while expression.reducible?
     puts expression
     expression = expression.reduce
   end; puts expression
ι[ι]
ι[S][K]
S[S][K][K]
S[K][K[K]]
=> nil
```

Now, S[K][K[K]] is obviously not syntactically *equal* to I, but it's another example of an expression that uses the S and K combinators to *do the same thing* as I:

```
>> identity = SKICall.new(SKICall.new(S, K), SKICall.new(K, K))
=> S[K][K[K]]
>> expression = SKICall.new(identity, x)
=> S[K][K[K]][x]
>> while expression.reducible?
     puts expression
     expression = expression.reduce
   end; puts expression
S[K][K[K]][x]
K[x][K[K][x]]
K[x][K]
x
=> nil
```

So the translation into Iota does preserve the individual *behavior* of all three SKI combinators, even though it doesn't quite preserve their syntax. We can test the overall effect by converting a familiar lambda calculus expression into Iota via its SKI calculus representation, then evaluating it to check how it behaves:

```
>> two
=> -> p { -> x { p[p[x]] } }
>> two.to_ski
=> S[S[K[S]][S[K[K]][I]]][S[S[K[S]][S[K[K]][I]]][K[I]]]
>> two.to_ski.to_iota
=> ι[ι[ι[ι[ι]]]][ι[ι[ι[ι[ι]]]]][ι[ι[ι[ι[ι]]]]]][ι[ι[ι[ι[ι]]]]][ι[ι[ι[ι[ι]]]]][ι[↵
ι[ι[ι]]]]][ι[ι[ι]]]][ι[ι[ι[ι[ι]]]]][ι[ι[ι[ι[ι]]]]]][ι[ι[ι[ι[ι]]]]][ι[ι[ι[ι[ι]]]]]↵
]][ι[ι[ι[ι]]]][ι[ι[ι[ι]]]]][ι[ι[ι]]]][ι[ι[ι[ι]]]][ι[ι]]]]
>> expression = SKICall.new(SKICall.new(two.to_ski.to_iota, inc), zero)
=> ι[ι[ι[ι[ι]]]][ι[ι[ι[ι[ι]]]]][ι[ι[ι[ι[ι]]]]]][ι[ι[ι[ι[ι]]]]][ι[ι[ι[ι[ι]]]]][ι[↵
ι[ι[ι]]]]][ι[ι[ι]]]][ι[ι[ι[ι[ι]]]]][ι[ι[ι[ι[ι]]]]]][ι[ι[ι[ι[ι]]]]][ι[ι[ι[ι[ι]]]]]↵
]][ι[ι[ι[ι]]]][ι[ι[ι[ι]]]]][ι[ι[ι]]]][ι[ι[ι[ι]]]][ι[ι]]]][inc][zero]
>> expression = expression.reduce while expression.reducible?
=> nil
>> expression
=> inc[inc[zero]]
```

Again, `inc[inc[zero]]` is the result we expected, so the Iota expression ι[ι[ι[ι[ι]]]] [ι[ι[ι[ι[ι]]]]][ι[ι[ι[ι[ι]]]]]][ι[ι[ι[ι[ι]]]]][ι[ι[ι[ι[ι]]]]][ι[ι]]]] [ι[ι[ι[ι[ι]]]]][ι[ι[ι[ι[ι]]]]]][ι[ι[ι[ι]]]][ι[ι[ι[ι[ι]]]]]]][ι[ι[ι[ι]]]]] [ι[ι[ι[ι]]]]]][ι[ι]]]][ι[ι[ι[ι]]]][ι[ι]]]] really is a working translation of -> p { -> x { p[p[x]] } } into a language with no variables, no functions, and only one combinator; and because we can do this translation for any lambda calculus expression, Iota is yet another universal language.

Tag Systems

A *tag system* is a model of computation that works like a simplified Turing machine: instead of moving a head back and forth over a tape, a tag system operates on a string by repeatedly adding new characters to the end of the string and removing them from the beginning. In some ways, a tag system's string is like a Turing machine's tape, but the tag system is constrained to only operate on the edges of the string, and it only ever "moves" in one direction—toward the end.

A tag system's description has two parts: first, a collection of rules, where each rule specifies some characters to append to the string when a particular character appears at the beginning—"when the character a is at the beginning of the string, append the characters bcd," for instance; and second, a number, called the *deletion number*, which specifies how many characters to delete from the beginning of the string after a rule has been followed.

Here's an example tag system:

- When the string begins with a, append the characters bc.

- When the string begins with b, append the characters caad.
- When the string begins with c, append the characters ccd.
- After following any of the above rules, delete three characters from the beginning of the string—in other words, the deletion number is 3.

We can perform a tag system computation by repeatedly following rules and deleting characters until the first character of the string has no applicable rule, or until the length of the string is less than the deletion number.[6] Let's try running the example tag system with the initial string 'aaaaaa':

Current string	Applicable rule
aaaaaa	When the string begins with a, append the characters bc.
aaabc	When the string begins with a, append the characters bc.
bcbc	When the string begins with b, append the characters caad.
ccaad	When the string begins with c, append the characters ccd.
adccd	When the string begins with a, append the characters bc.
cdbc	When the string begins with c, append the characters ccd.
cccd	When the string begins with c, append the characters ccd.
dccd	—

Tag systems only operate directly on strings, but we can get them to perform sophisticated operations on other kinds of values, like numbers, as long as we have a suitable way to encode those values as strings. One possible way of encoding numbers is this: represent the number n as the string aa followed by n repetitions of the string bb; for example, the number 3 is represented as the string aabbbbbb.

Some aspects of this representation might seem redundant—we could just represent 3 as the string aaa—but using pairs of characters, and having an explicit marker at the beginning of the string, will be useful shortly.

Once we've chosen an encoding scheme for numbers, we can design tag systems that perform operations on numbers by manipulating their string representations. Here's a system that doubles its input number:

- When the string begins with a, append the characters aa.
- When the string begins with b, append the characters bbbb.

6. This second condition prevents us from ever getting into a situation where we need to delete more characters than the string contains.

- After following a rule, delete two characters from the beginning of the string (the deletion number is 2).

Watch how this tag system behaves when started with the string aabbbb, representing the number 2:

```
aabbbb → bbbbaa
       → bbaabbbb
       → aabbbbbbbb (representing the number 4)
       → bbbbbbbbaa
       → bbbbbaabbbb
       → bbbbaabbbbbbbb
       → bbaabbbbbbbbbbbb
       → aabbbbbbbbbbbbbbbb (the number 8)
       → bbbbbbbbbbbbbbbbaa
       → bbbbbbbbbbbbbbaabbbb
       ⋮
```

The doubling is clearly happening, but this tag system runs forever—doubling the number represented by its current string, then doubling it again, then again—which isn't really what we had in mind. To design a system that doubles a number just once and then halts, we need to use different characters to encode the result so that it doesn't trigger another round of doubling. We can do this by relaxing our encoding scheme to allow c and d characters in place of a and b, and then modifying the rules to append cc and dddd instead of aa and bbbb when creating the representation of the doubled number.

With those changes, the computation looks like this:

```
aabbbb → bbbbcc
       → bbccdddd
       → ccddddddd (the number 4, encoded with c and d instead of a and b)
```

The modified system stops when it reaches ccddddddd, because there's no rule for strings beginning with c.

 In this case, we're only depending on the character c to stop the computation at the right point, so we could have safely reused b in the encoding of the result instead of replacing it with d, but there's no harm in using more characters than are strictly needed.

It's generally clearer to use different sets of characters to encode input and output values rather than allowing them to overlap; as we'll see shortly, this also makes it easier to combine several small tag systems into a larger one, by arranging for the output encoding of one system to match up with the input encoding of another.

To simulate a tag system in Ruby, we need an implementation of an individual rule (TagRule), a collection of rules (TagRulebook), and the tag system itself (TagSystem):

```
class TagRule < Struct.new(:first_character, :append_characters)
  def applies_to?(string)
    string.chars.first == first_character
  end

  def follow(string)
    string + append_characters
  end
end

class TagRulebook < Struct.new(:deletion_number, :rules)
  def next_string(string)
    rule_for(string).follow(string).slice(deletion_number..-1)
  end

  def rule_for(string)
    rules.detect { |r| r.applies_to?(string) }
  end
end

class TagSystem < Struct.new(:current_string, :rulebook)
  def step
    self.current_string = rulebook.next_string(current_string)
  end
end
```

This implementation allows us to step through a tag system computation one rule at a time. Let's try that for the original doubling example, this time getting it to double the number 3 (aabbbbbb):

```
>> rulebook = TagRulebook.new(2, [TagRule.new('a', 'aa'), TagRule.new('b', 'bbbb')])
=> #<struct TagRulebook …>
>> system = TagSystem.new('aabbbbbb', rulebook)
=> #<struct TagSystem …>
>> 4.times do
     puts system.current_string
     system.step
   end; puts system.current_string
aabbbbbb
bbbbbbaa
bbbbaabbbb
bbaabbbbbbbb
aabbbbbbbbbbbb
=> nil
```

Because this tag system runs forever, we have to know in advance how many steps to execute before the result appears—four steps, in this case—but if we used the modified version that encodes its result with c and d, we could just let it run until it stops automatically. Let's add the code to support that:

```
class TagRulebook
  def applies_to?(string)
    !rule_for(string).nil? && string.length >= deletion_number
  end
end
```

```
class TagSystem
  def run
    while rulebook.applies_to?(current_string)
      puts current_string
      step
    end

    puts current_string
  end
end
```

Now we can just call TagSystem#run on the halting version of the tag system and let it naturally stop at the right point:

```
>> rulebook = TagRulebook.new(2, [TagRule.new('a', 'cc'), TagRule.new('b', 'dddd')])
=> #<struct TagRulebook ...>
>> system = TagSystem.new('aabbbbbb', rulebook)
=> #<struct TagSystem ...>
>> system.run
aabbbbbb
bbbbbbcc
bbbbccdddd
bbccdddddddd
ccdddddddddddd
=> nil
```

This implementation of tag systems allows us to explore what else they're capable of. With our encoding scheme, it's easy to design systems that perform other numeric operations, like this one for halving a number:

```
>> rulebook = TagRulebook.new(2, [TagRule.new('a', 'cc'), TagRule.new('b', 'd')])
=> #<struct TagRulebook ...>
>> system = TagSystem.new('aabbbbbbbbbbbb', rulebook)
=> #<struct TagSystem ...>
>> system.run
aabbbbbbbbbbbb
bbbbbbbbbbbbcc
bbbbbbbbbbccd
bbbbbbbbccdd
bbbbbbccddd
bbbbccdddd
bbccddddd
ccdddddd
=> nil
```

And this one, which increments a number:

```
>> rulebook = TagRulebook.new(2, [TagRule.new('a', 'ccdd'), TagRule.new('b', 'dd')])
=> #<struct TagRulebook ...>
>> system = TagSystem.new('aabbbb', rulebook)
=> #<struct TagSystem ...>
>> system.run
aabbbb
bbbbccdd
bbccdddd
```

```
ccdddddd
=> nil
```

We can also join two tag systems together, as long as the output encoding of the first system matches the input encoding of the second. Here's a single system that combines the doubling and incrementing rules by using the characters c and d to encode the input to the incrementing rules and e and f to encode their output:

```
>> rulebook = TagRulebook.new(2, [
     TagRule.new('a', 'cc'), TagRule.new('b', 'dddd'), # double
     TagRule.new('c', 'eeff'), TagRule.new('d', 'ff')  # increment
   ])
=> #<struct TagRulebook …>
>> system = TagSystem.new('aabbbb', rulebook)
=> #<struct TagSystem …>
>> system.run
aabbbb  (the number 2)
bbbbcc
bbccdddd
ccdddddddd  (the number 4)  ❶
dddddddddeeff
ddddddeeffff
ddddeeffffff
ddeeffffffff
eeffffffffff  (the number 5)  ❷
=> nil
```

❶ The doubling rules turn 2 into 4, encoded with the characters c and d.

❷ The incrementing rules turn 4 into 5, this time encoded with e and f.

As well as changing numbers into other numbers, tag systems can check their mathematical properties. Here's a tag system that tests whether a number is odd or even:

```
>> rulebook = TagRulebook.new(2, [
     TagRule.new('a', 'cc'), TagRule.new('b', 'd'),
     TagRule.new('c', 'eo'), TagRule.new('d', ''),
     TagRule.new('e', 'e')
   ])
=> #<struct TagRulebook …>
```

If its input represents an even number, this system stops at the single-character string e (which stands for "even"):

```
>> system = TagSystem.new('aabbbbbbbb', rulebook)
=> #<struct TagSystem …>
>> system.run
aabbbbbbbb  (the number 4)
bbbbbbbbcc
bbbbbbccd
bbbbccdd
bbccddd
ccdddd  ❶
ddddeo  ❷
ddeo
eo  ❸
```

```
e ❹
=> nil
```

❶ The a and b rules halve the input; ccdddd represents the number 2.

❷ The c rule deletes the leading cc pair and appends the characters eo, one of which will form the final result.

❸ The empty d rule consumes all of the leading dd pairs, leaving only eo.

❹ The e rule replaces eo with just e, and the system halts.

If the input number is odd, the result is the string o (for "odd"):

```
>> system = TagSystem.new('aabbbbbbbbbb', rulebook)
=> #<struct TagSystem …>
>> system.run
aabbbbbbbbbb  (the number 5)
bbbbbbbbbbcc
bbbbbbbbccd
bbbbbbccdd
bbbbccddd
bbccdddd
ccddddd ❶
dddddeo
dddeo
deo ❷
o ❸
=> nil
```

❶ The number is halved as before, but because it's an odd number this time, the result is a string with an odd number of ds. Our encoding scheme for numbers uses only pairs of characters, so ccddddd doesn't strictly represent anything, but because it contains "two and a half" pairs of d characters, it's reasonable to think of it informally as the number 2.5.

❷ All the leading dd pairs get deleted, leaving a solitary d before the final eo.

❸ The leftover d is deleted and takes the e with it, leaving just o, and the system halts.

> Having a deletion number greater than 1 is essential for making this tag system work. Because every *second* character triggers a rule, we can influence the system's behavior by arranging for certain characters to appear (or not appear) in these trigger positions. This technique of making characters appear in or out of sync with the deletion behavior is the key to designing a powerful tag system.

These number-manipulating techniques can be used to simulate a Turing machine. Building a Turing machine simulation on top of something as simple as a tag system involves a lot of detail, but one way of doing it works (very roughly) like this:

1. As the simplest possible example, take a Turing machine whose tape only uses two characters—we'll call them 0 and 1, with 0 acting as the blank character.

2. Split the Turing machine's tape into two pieces: the left part, consisting of the character underneath the tape head itself and all characters to its left, and the right part, consisting of all characters to the right of the head.

3. Treat the left part of the tape as a binary number: if the initial tape looks like 0001101(0)0011000, the left part is the binary number 11010, which is 26 in decimal.

4. Treat the right part of the tape as a binary number *written backward*: the right part of our example tape is the binary number 1100, or 12 in decimal.

5. Encode those two numbers as a string suitable for use by a tag system. For our example tape, we could use aa followed by 26 copies of bb, then cc followed by 12 copies of dd.

6. Use simple numerical operations—doubling, halving, incrementing, decrementing, and odd/even checking—to simulate reading from the tape, writing to the tape, and moving the tape head. For instance, we can move the head right on our example tape by doubling the number representing the left part and halving the number representing the right part:[7] doubling 26 gives 52, which is 110100 in binary; half of 12 is 6, which is 110 in binary; so the new tape looks like 011010(0)011000. Reading from the tape means checking whether the number representing the left part of the tape is even or odd, and writing a 1 or 0 to the tape means incrementing or decrementing that number.

7. Represent the current state of the simulated Turing machine with the choice of characters used to encode the left and right tape numbers: perhaps when the machine is in state 1, we encode the tape with a, b, c, and d characters, but when it moves into state 2, we use e, f, g, and h instead, and so on.

8. Turn each Turing machine rule into a tag system that rewrites the current string in the appropriate way. A rule that reads a 0, writes a 1, moves the tape head right and goes into state 2 could become a tag system that checks that the left tape number is even, increments it, doubles the left tape number while halving the right tape number, and produces a final string that is encoded with state 2's characters.

9. Combine these individual tag systems to make one large system that simulates every rule of the Turing machine.

---

7. Doubling a number shifts all the digits in its binary representation one place to the left, and halving it shifts them all one place to the right.

For a full explanation of how a tag system simulation of a Turing machine works, see Matthew Cook's elegant construction in section 2.1 of *http://www.complex-systems.com/pdf/15-1-1.pdf*.

Cook's simulation is more sophisticated than the one outlined here. It cleverly uses the "alignment" of the current string to represent the character beneath the simulated tape head instead of incorporating it into one of the tape parts, and can easily be extended to simulate a Turing machine with any number of characters by increasing the tag system's deletion number.

The fact that tag systems can simulate any Turing machine means that they too are universal.

Cyclic Tag Systems

A *cyclic tag system* is a tag system that has been made even simpler by imposing some extra constraints:

- A cyclic tag system's string can contain only two characters, 0 and 1.
- A cyclic tag system rule can only apply when the current string begins with 1, never 0.[8]
- A cyclic tag system's deletion number is always 1.

By themselves, these constraints are too severe to support any kind of useful computation, so cyclic tag systems get an extra feature to compensate: the first rule in a cyclic tag system's rulebook is the *current rule* when execution begins, and after each step of computation, the next rule in the rulebook becomes current, wrapping back to the first rule when the end of the rulebook is reached.

This kind of system is called "cyclic" because of the way the current rule cycles repeatedly through the rulebook. The use of a current rule, combined with the constraint that every rule applies to strings beginning with 1, avoids the overhead of having to search through the rulebook to find an applicable rule at each step of execution; if the first character's a 1, then the current rule applies, otherwise, no rule does.

As an example, let's look at the cyclic tag system with three rules that append the characters 1, 0010, and 10, respectively. Here's what happens when it's started with the string 11:

---

8. A cyclic tag system rule doesn't need to say "when the string begins with 1, append the characters 011," because the first part is assumed—just "append the characters 011" is enough.

Current string	Current rule	Rule applies?
11	append the character 1	yes
11	append the characters 0010	yes
10010	append the characters 10	yes
001010	append the character 1	no
01010	append the characters 0010	no
1010	append the characters 10	yes
01010	append the character 1	no
1010	append the characters 0010	yes
0100010	append the characters 10	no
100010	append the character 1	yes
000101	append the characters 0010	no
00101	append the characters 10	no
0101	append the character 1	no
101	append the characters 0010	yes
010010	append the characters 10	no
10010	append the character 1	yes
00101	append the characters 0010	no
⋮	⋮	⋮

Despite the extreme simplicity of this system, we can see a hint of complex behavior: it's not obvious what will happen next. With a bit of thought we can convince ourselves that the system will run forever rather than dwindle to the empty string, because every rule appends a 1, so as long as the initial string contains a 1, it will never die out entirely.[9] But will the current string keep fitfully growing longer, or will it settle into a repeating pattern of expansion and contraction? Just looking at the rules doesn't answer that question; we need to keep running the system to find out what happens.

We already have a Ruby implementation of a conventional tag system, so simulating a cyclic tag system doesn't require much extra work. We can implement a `CyclicTagRule` simply by subclassing `TagRule` and hardcoding `'1'` as its `first_character`:

```ruby
class CyclicTagRule < TagRule
  FIRST_CHARACTER = '1'

  def initialize(append_characters)
    super(FIRST_CHARACTER, append_characters)
```

9. Unlike a normal tag system, a cyclic tag system keeps going when no rule applies, otherwise it would never get anywhere. The only way for a cyclic tag system to stop running is for its current string to become empty; this always happens when the initial string consists entirely of 0 characters, for example.

```
    end

    def inspect
      "#<CyclicTagRule #{append_characters.inspect}>"
    end
  end
```

#initialize is the *constructor* method that gets called automatically when an instance of a class is created. CyclicTagRule#initialize calls the constructor from the superclass, TagRule, to set the first_charac ter and append_characters attributes.

The rulebook for a cyclic tag system works slightly differently, so we'll build a Cyclic TagRulebook class from scratch, providing new implementations of #applies_to? and #next_string:

```
  class CyclicTagRulebook < Struct.new(:rules)
    DELETION_NUMBER = 1

    def initialize(rules)
      super(rules.cycle)
    end

    def applies_to?(string)
      string.length >= DELETION_NUMBER
    end

    def next_string(string)
      follow_next_rule(string).slice(DELETION_NUMBER..-1)
    end

    def follow_next_rule(string)
      rule = rules.next

      if rule.applies_to?(string)
        rule.follow(string)
      else
        string
      end
    end
  end
```

Unlike a vanilla TagRulebook, a CyclicTagRulebook always applies to any nonempty string, even if the current rule doesn't.

Array#cycle creates an Enumerator (see "Native Ruby Streams" on page 194) that cycles around the elements of an array for-ever:

```
>> numbers = [1, 2, 3].cycle
=> #<Enumerator: [1, 2, 3]:cycle>
>> numbers.next
```

```
=> 1
>> numbers.next
=> 2
>> numbers.next
=> 3
>> numbers.next
=> 1
>> [:a, :b, :c, :d].cycle.take(10)
=> [:a, :b, :c, :d, :a, :b, :c, :d, :a, :b]
```

This is exactly the behavior we want for a cyclic tag system's current
rule, so CyclicTagRulebook#initialize assigns one of these cycling Enu
merators to the rules attribute, and each call to #follow_next_rule uses
rules.next to get the next rule in the cycle.

Now we can create a CyclicTagRulebook full of CyclicTagRules and plug it into a Tag
System to see it working:

```
>> rulebook = CyclicTagRulebook.new([
     CyclicTagRule.new('1'), CyclicTagRule.new('0010'), CyclicTagRule.new('10')
   ])
=> #<struct CyclicTagRulebook …>
>> system = TagSystem.new('11', rulebook)
=> #<struct TagSystem …>
>> 16.times do
     puts system.current_string
     system.step
   end; puts system.current_string
11
11
10010
001010
01010
1010
01010
1010
0100010
100010
000101
00101
0101
101
010010
10010
00101
=> nil
```

That's the same behavior we saw when we stepped through the execution by hand.
Let's keep going:

```
>> 20.times do
     puts system.current_string
     system.step
   end; puts system.current_string
00101
0101
```

```
101
011
11
110
101
010010
10010
00101
0101
101
011
11
110
101
010010
10010
00101
0101
101
=> nil
```

So it turns out that this system *does* settle down into repetitive behavior when it's started with the string 11: after an initial period of instability, a pattern of nine consecutive strings emerges (101, 010010, 10010, 00101, ...) and repeats itself forever. Of course, if we change the initial string or any of the rules, the long-term behavior will be different.

Cyclic tag systems are extremely limited—they have inflexible rules, only two characters, and the lowest possible deletion number—but surprisingly, it's still possible to use them to simulate *any* tag system.

The simulation of a normal tag system by a cyclic tag system works like this:

1. Determine the tag system's *alphabet*—the set of characters it uses.
2. Design an encoding scheme that associates each character with a unique string suitable for use in a cyclic tag system (i.e., containing only 0s and 1s).
3. Convert each of the original system's rules into a cyclic tag system rule by encoding the characters it appends.
4. Pad out the cyclic tag system's rulebook with empty rules to simulate the original tag system's deletion number.
5. Encode the original tag system's input string and use it as input to the cyclic tag system.

Let's make those ideas more concrete by implementing them. First we need to be able to ask a tag system what characters it uses:

```
class TagRule
  def alphabet
    ([first_character] + append_characters.chars.entries).uniq
  end
end
```

```
class TagRulebook
  def alphabet
    rules.flat_map(&:alphabet).uniq
  end
end

class TagSystem
  def alphabet
    (rulebook.alphabet + current_string.chars.entries).uniq.sort
  end
end
```

We can test this on the number-incrementing tag system from "Tag Systems" on page 227. TagSystem#alphabet tells us that this system uses the characters a, b, c, and d:

```
>> rulebook = TagRulebook.new(2, [TagRule.new('a', 'ccdd'), TagRule.new('b', 'dd')])
=> #<struct TagRulebook …>
>> system = TagSystem.new('aabbbb', rulebook)
=> #<struct TagSystem …>
>> system.alphabet
=> ["a", "b", "c", "d"]
```

Next we need a way of encoding each character as a string that the cyclic tag system can use. There's a specific encoding scheme that makes the simulation work: each character is represented as a string of 0s with the same length as the alphabet, with a single 1 character in a position that reflects that character's position in the alphabet.[10]

Our tag system has a four-character alphabet, so each letter gets encoded as a four-character string with a 1 in a different place:

Tag system character	Position in alphabet	Encoded representation
a	0	1000
b	1	0100
c	2	0010
d	3	0001

To implement this encoding scheme, we'll introduce a CyclicTagEncoder that gets constructed with a specific alphabet and then asked to encode strings of characters from that alphabet:

```
class CyclicTagEncoder < Struct.new(:alphabet)
  def encode_string(string)
    string.chars.map { |character| encode_character(character) }.join
  end

  def encode_character(character)
```

10. The resulting sequence of 0s and 1s is *not* meant to represent a binary number. It's just a string of 0 characters with a 1 character marking a particular position.

```
      character_position = alphabet.index(character)
      (0...alphabet.length).map { |n| n == character_position ? '1' : '0' }.join
    end
  end

  class TagSystem
    def encoder
      CyclicTagEncoder.new(alphabet)
    end
  end
```

Now we can use our tag system's `CyclicTagEncoder` to encode any strings made up of a, b, c, and d:

```
>> encoder = system.encoder
=> #<struct CyclicTagEncoder alphabet=["a", "b", "c", "d"]>
>> encoder.encode_character('c')
=> "0010"
>> encoder.encode_string('cab')
=> "001010000100"
```

The encoder gives us a way to convert each tag system rule into a cyclic tag system rule. We just encode the `append_characters` of a `TagRule` and use the resulting string to build a `CyclicTagRule`:

```
  class TagRule
    def to_cyclic(encoder)
      CyclicTagRule.new(encoder.encode_string(append_characters))
    end
  end
```

Let's try that on a single `TagRule`:

```
>> rule = system.rulebook.rules.first
=> #<struct TagRule first_character="a", append_characters="ccdd">
>> rule.to_cyclic(encoder)
=> #<CyclicTagRule "0010001000010001">
```

Alright, so the `append_characters` have been converted, but now we've lost the information about which `first_character` is supposed to trigger the rule—every `CyclicTagRule` is triggered by the character 1 regardless of which `TagRule` it was converted from.

Instead, that information is communicated by the *order* of the rules in the cyclic tag system: the first rule is for the first character in the alphabet, the second rule is for the second character, and so on. Any character without a corresponding rule in the tag system gets a blank rule in the cyclic tag system rulebook.

We can implement a TagRulebook#cyclic_rules method to return the converted rules in the right order:

```ruby
class TagRulebook
  def cyclic_rules(encoder)
    encoder.alphabet.map { |character| cyclic_rule_for(character, encoder) }
  end

  def cyclic_rule_for(character, encoder)
    rule = rule_for(character)

    if rule.nil?
      CyclicTagRule.new('')
    else
      rule.to_cyclic(encoder)
    end
  end
end
```

Here's what #cyclic_rules produces for our tag system:

```ruby
>> system.rulebook.cyclic_rules(encoder)
=> [
     #<CyclicTagRule "0010001000010001">,
     #<CyclicTagRule "00010001">,
     #<CyclicTagRule "">,
     #<CyclicTagRule "">
   ]
```

As expected, the converted a and b rules appear first, followed by two blank rules in the c and d positions.

This arrangement dovetails with the character encoding scheme to make the whole simulation work. If the simulated tag system's input string is the single character b, for instance, it will appear as 0100 in the input string of the cyclic tag system. Watch what happens when the system runs with that input:

Current string	Current rule	Rule applies?
0100	append the characters 0010001000010001 (a rule)	no
100	append the characters 00010001 (b rule)	yes
0000010001	append nothing (c rule)	no
000010001	append nothing (d rule)	no
⋮	⋮	⋮

On the first step of computation, the converted a rule is current, and doesn't get used because the current string begins with a 0. But on the second step, the b rule becomes current just as the leading 0 is deleted from the current string, revealing a leading 1 that triggers the rule. The next two characters are both 0, so the c and d rules don't get used either.

So, by carefully timing the appearances of the character 1 in the input string to coincide with the rotating appearances of rules in the cyclic tag system, we can trigger the right rules at the right times, perfectly simulating the character-matching behavior of conventional tag system rules.

Finally, we need to simulate the deletion number of the original tag system, but that's easily done by inserting extra empty rules into the cyclic tag system's rulebook so that the right number of characters get deleted after a single encoded character has been successfully processed. If the original tag system has n characters in its alphabet, then each character of the original system's string is represented as n characters in the cyclic tag system's string, so we need n blank rules for every additional simulated character that we want to delete:

```
class TagRulebook
  def cyclic_padding_rules(encoder)
    Array.new(encoder.alphabet.length, CyclicTagRule.new('')) * (deletion_number - 1)
  end
end
```

Our tag system has a four-character alphabet and a deletion number of 2, so we need an extra four empty rules to delete one simulated character in addition to the one that already gets deleted by the converted rules:

```
>> system.rulebook.cyclic_padding_rules(encoder)
=> [
     #<CyclicTagRule "">,
     #<CyclicTagRule "">,
     #<CyclicTagRule "">,
     #<CyclicTagRule "">
   ]
```

Now we can put everything together to implement an overall #to_cyclic method for a TagRulebook, then use it in a TagSystem#to_cyclic method that converts both the rulebook and the current string to yield a complete cyclic tag system:

```
class TagRulebook
  def to_cyclic(encoder)
    CyclicTagRulebook.new(cyclic_rules(encoder) + cyclic_padding_rules(encoder))
  end
end

class TagSystem
  def to_cyclic
    TagSystem.new(encoder.encode_string(current_string), rulebook.to_cyclic(encoder))
  end
end
```

Here's what happens when we convert our number-incrementing tag system and run it:

```
>> cyclic_system = system.to_cyclic
=> #<struct TagSystem …>
>> cyclic_system.run
100010000100010001000100 (aabbbb) ❶
000100001000100010001000010001000010001
```

```
001000010001000100010000100010000100001
010000100010001000100010010001000010001
100001000100010001000010001000010001  (abbbbccdd) ❷
000010001000100010000100010000100001
000100010001000100001000100001
001000100010001000010001000010001
010001000100010000100010000100001  (bbbbccdd) ❸
100010001000100001000100001  ❹
000100010001000010001000010001000010001
001000100010000100010001000100001000010001
010001000100001000100001000100001000010001  (bbbccdddd)
100010001000010001000010001000100001
000100010001000100001000100001000010001
001000100001000100001000100001
010001000010001000010001000100001  (bbccdddd)
100010001000100001000100001  ❺
000100001000100001000100010001000100001000010001
001000010001000100001000100010001000010001
010000100010001000100010001000100001000010001  (bccdddddd)
100001000100001000100010001000100001
000010001000100010001000100001000010001
000100010000100010001000100001000010001
001000100001000100010001000100001  (ccdddddd) ❻
010001000010001000100010001000010001
100010000100010001000100001000010001
000100001000100010001000100001  ❼
⋮
001
01
1
❽
=> nil
```

❶ The encoded version of the tag system's **a** rule kicks in here.

❷ The first full character of the simulated string has been processed, so the following four steps use blank rules to delete the next simulated character.

❸ After eight steps of the cyclic tag system, one full step of the simulated tag system is complete.

❹ The encoded **b** rule is triggered here…

❺ …and again here.

❻ Twenty-four steps into the cyclic tag system computation, and we reach the representation of the simulated tag system's final string, **ccdddddd**.

❼ The simulated tag system has no rules for strings beginning with **c** or **d**, so the cyclic tag system's current string keeps getting shorter and shorter…

❽ …until it becomes empty, and the system halts.

This technique can be used to simulate any tag system—including a tag system that itself simulates a Turing machine—which means that cyclic tag systems are also universal.

Conway's Game of Life

In 1970, John Conway invented a universal system called the *Game of Life*. The "game" is played on an infinite two-dimensional grid of square cells, each of which can be *alive* or *dead*. A cell is surrounded by its eight *neighbors*: the three cells above it, the cells to its immediate left and right, and the three cells below it.

The Game of Life proceeds in a series of steps like a finite state machine. At every step, each cell may potentially change from alive to dead, or vice versa, according to rules that are triggered by the current state of the cell itself and the states of its neighbors. The rules are simple: a living cell dies if it has fewer than two living neighbors (underpopulation) or more than three (overpopulation), and a dead cell comes to life if it has exactly three living neighbors (reproduction).

Here are six examples[11] of how the Game of Life rules affect a cell's state over the course of a single step, with living cells shown in black and dead ones in white:

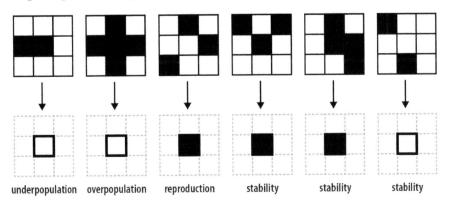

underpopulation   overpopulation   reproduction   stability   stability   stability

 A system like this, consisting of an array of cells and a set of rules for updating a cell's state at each step, is called a *cellular automaton*.

---

11. Out of a possible 512: nine cells are involved, and each cell can be in one of two states, so there are 2 × 2 × 2 × 2 × 2 × 2 × 2 × 2 × 2 = 512 different possibilities.

Like the other systems we've seen in this chapter, the Game of Life exhibits surprising complexity despite the simplicity of its rules. Interesting behavior can arise from specific patterns of living cells, the best-known of which is the *glider*, an arrangement of five living cells that moves itself one square diagonally across the grid every four steps:

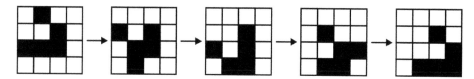

Many other significant patterns have been discovered, including shapes that move around the grid in different ways (*spaceships*), generate a stream of other shapes (*guns*), or even produce complete copies of themselves (*replicators*).

In 1982, Conway showed how to use a stream of gliders to represent streams of binary data, as well as how to design logical AND, OR, and NOT gates to perform digital computation by colliding gliders in creative ways. These constructions showed that it was theoretically possible to simulate a digital computer in the Game of Life, but Conway stopped short of designing a working machine:

> For here on it's just an engineering problem to construct an arbitrarily large finite (and very slow!) computer. Our engineer has been given the tools—let him finish the job! [...] The kind of computer we have simulated is technically known as a *universal machine* because it can be programmed to perform any desired calculation.
>
> —John Conway, *Winning Ways for Your Mathematical Plays*

In 2002, Paul Chapman implemented a particular kind of universal computer (*http://www.igblan.free-online.co.uk/igblan/ca/*) in Life, and in 2010 Paul Rendell constructed a universal Turing machine (*http://rendell-attic.org/gol/utm/*).

Here's a close-up of one small part of Rendell's design:

Rule 110

Rule 110 is another cellular automaton, introduced by Stephen Wolfram in 1983. Each cell can be either alive or dead, just like the cells in Conway's Game of Life, but rule 110 operates on cells arranged in a one-dimensional row instead of a two-dimensional grid. That means each cell only has two neighbors—the cells immediately to its left and right in the row—rather than the eight neighbors that surround each Game of Life cell.

At each step of the rule 110 automaton, the next state of a cell is determined by its own state and the states of its two neighbors. Unlike the Game of Life, whose rules are general and apply to many different arrangements of living and dead cells, the rule 110 automaton has a separate rule for each possibility:

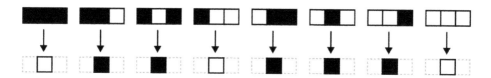

 If we read off the values of the "after" cells from these eight rules, treating a dead cell as the digit 0 and a living cell as 1, we get the binary number 01101110. Converting from binary produces the decimal number 110, which is what gives this cellular automaton its name.

Rule 110 is much simpler than the Game of Life, but again, it's capable of complex behavior. Here are the first few steps of a rule 110 automaton starting from a single live cell:

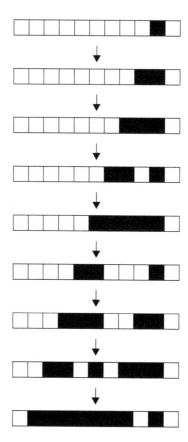

This behavior is already not obviously simple—it's not just generating a solid line of living cells, for instance—and if we run the same automaton for 500 steps we can see interesting patterns begin to emerge:

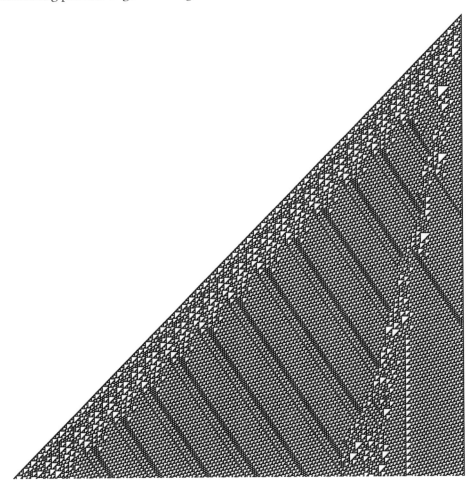

Alternatively, running rule 110 from an initial state consisting of a random pattern of living and dead cells reveals all kinds of shapes moving around and interacting with each other:

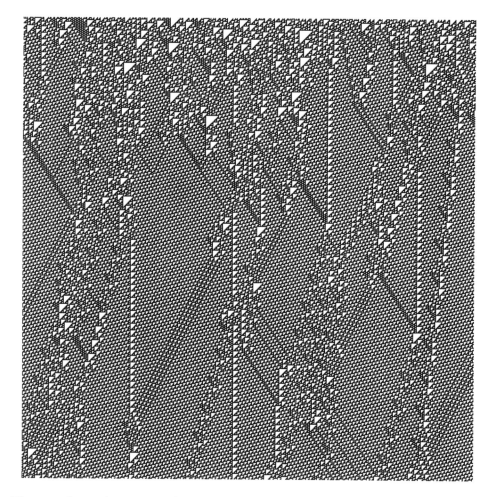

The complexity that emerges from these eight simple rules turns out to be remarkably powerful: in 2004, Matthew Cook published a proof that rule 110 is in fact universal. The proof has a lot of detail (see sections 3 and 4 of *http://www.complex-systems.com/ pdf/15-1-1.pdf*) but, roughly, it introduces several different rule 110 patterns that act as gliders, then shows how to simulate any cyclic tag system by arranging those gliders in a particular way.

This means that rule 110 can run a simulation of a cyclic tag system that is running a simulation of a conventional tag system that is running a simulation of a universal Turing machine—not an efficient way to achieve universal computation, but still an impressive technical result for such a simple cellular automaton.

Wolfram's 2,3 Turing Machine

To complete our whirlwind tour of simple universal systems, here's one that's even simpler than rule 110: *Wolfram's 2,3 Turing machine*. It gets its name from its two states and three characters (a, b, and blank), which means it has only six rules:

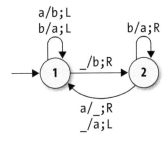

 This Turing machine is unusual in that it doesn't have an accept state, so it never halts, but this is mostly a technical detail. We can still get results out of nonhalting machines by watching for certain behavior—for example, the appearance of a particular pattern of characters on the tape—and treating that as an indication that the current tape contains useful output.

Wolfram's 2,3 Turing machine doesn't seem anywhere near powerful enough to support universal computation, but in 2007, Wolfram Research announced a $25,000 prize to anyone who could prove it was universal, and later that year, Alex Smith claimed the prize by producing a successful proof. As with rule 110, the proof hinges on showing that this machine can simulate any cyclic tag system; again, the proof is very detailed, but can be seen in full at *http://www.wolframscience.com/prizes/tm23/*.

## CHAPTER 8

Impossible Programs

*The most merciful thing in the world, I think, is the in-
ability of the human mind to correlate all its contents.*

—H. P. Lovecraft

In this book, we've explored different models of computers and programming languages, including several kinds of abstract machine. Some of those machines are more
powerful than others, and two varieties in particular come with pretty obvious limitations: finite automata can't solve problems that involve unrestricted counting, like deciding whether a string of brackets is correctly balanced, and pushdown automata can't
handle any problem where information needs to be reused in more than one place, like
deciding whether a string contains the same number of a, b, and c characters.

But the most advanced device we've seen, the Turing machine, seems to have everything
that we need: it's got unlimited storage that can be accessed in any order, arbitrary
loops, conditionals, and subroutines. The extremely minimal programming language
from Chapter 6, the lambda calculus, turned out to be surprisingly powerful too: with
a little ingenuity it allows us to represent simple values and complex data structures as
pure code, as well as implement operations that manipulate those representations. And
in Chapter 7, we saw many other simple systems that, like the lambda calculus, have
the same universal power as Turing machines.

How much further can we push this progression of increasingly powerful systems?
Perhaps not indefinitely: our attempts to make Turing machines more powerful by
adding features didn't get us anywhere, which suggests there may be a hard limit on
computational power. So what are computers and programming languages fundamentally capable of, and is there anything that they can't do? Are there any impossible
programs?

The Facts of Life

These are pretty deep questions, so before we try to tackle them, let's take a tour of some fundamental facts from the world of computation. Some of these facts are obvious, others less so, but they're all important prerequisites for thinking about the capabilities and limitations of computing machines.

Universal Systems Can Perform Algorithms

What, generally speaking, can we do with universal systems like Turing machines, the lambda calculus, and partial recursive functions? If we can properly understand the capabilities of these systems, then we'll be able to investigate their limitations.

The practical purpose of a computing machine is to perform *algorithms*. An algorithm is a list of instructions describing some process for turning an input value into an output value, as long as those instructions fulfill certain criteria:

Finiteness
> There are a finite number of instructions.

Simplicity
> Each instruction is simple enough that it can be performed by a person with a pencil and paper without using any ingenuity.

Termination
> A person following the instructions will finish within a finite number of steps for any input.

Correctness
> A person following the instructions will produce the right answer for any input.

For example, one of the oldest known algorithms is Euclid's algorithm, which dates from around 300 BC. It takes two positive integers and returns the largest integer that will divide them both exactly—their *greatest common divisor*. Here are its instructions:

1. Give the two numbers the names x and y.
2. Decide which of x or y is the larger number.
3. Subtract the smaller number from the larger. (If x is larger, subtract y from it and make this the new value of x; vice versa if y is larger.)
4. Repeat steps 2 and 3 until x and y are equal.
5. When x and y become equal, their value is the greatest common divisor of the original two numbers.

We're happy to recognize this as an algorithm, because it appears to meet the basic criteria. It only contains a few instructions, and they all seem simple enough to be performed with pencil and paper by someone who doesn't have any special insight into the overall problem. With a bit of thought, we can also see that it must finish within a finite number of steps for any input: every repetition of step 3 causes one of the two numbers to get smaller, so they must eventually reach the same value[1] and cause the algorithm to finish. It's not quite so obvious that it'll always give the correct answer, but a few lines of elementary algebra are enough to show that the result must always be the greatest common divisor of the original numbers.

So Euclid's algorithm is worthy of its name, but like any algorithm, it's just a collection of ideas expressed as human-readable words and symbols. If we want to do something useful with it—maybe we'd like to explore its mathematical properties, or design a machine that performs it automatically—we need to translate the algorithm into a stricter, less ambiguous form that's suitable for mathematical analysis or mechanical execution.

We already have several models of computation that we could use for this: we could try to write down Euclid's algorithm as a Turing machine rulebook, or a lambda calculus expression, or a partial recursive function definition, but all of those would involve a lot of housekeeping and other uninteresting detail. For the moment, let's just translate it into unrestricted Ruby:[2]

```ruby
def euclid(x, y)
  until x == y
    if x > y
      x = x - y
    else
      y = y - x
    end
  end

  x
end
```

This #euclid method contains essentially the same instructions as the natural language description of Euclid's algorithm, but this time, they're written in a way that has a strictly defined meaning (according to the operational semantics of Ruby) and therefore can be interpreted by a machine:

```ruby
>> euclid(18, 12)
=> 6
>> euclid(867, 5309)
=> 1
```

In this specific case, it's been easy to take an informal, human-readable description of an algorithm and turn it into unambiguous instructions for a machine to follow. Having Euclid's algorithm in a machine-readable form is very convenient; now we can perform it quickly, repeatedly, and reliably without having to employ manual labor.

---

1. The smallest value x and y can reach is 1, so they'll meet there if all else fails.

2. Ruby already has a built-in version of Euclid's algorithm, Integer#gcd, but that's beside the point.

Hopefully it's clear that we could just as well have implemented this algorithm with the lambda calculus by using similar techniques to the ones we saw in "Numeric Operations" on page 174, or as a partial recursive function built from the operations in "Partial Recursive Functions" on page 210, or as a collection of Turing machine rules like the ones used for simple arithmetic in "Rules" on page 138.

This raises an important question: can *any* algorithm be turned into instructions suitable for execution by a machine? Superficially that seems like a trivial thing to ask—it was pretty obvious how to turn Euclid's algorithm into a program, and as programmers, we have a natural tendency to think of the two things as interchangeable—but there's a real difference between the abstract, intuitive idea of an algorithm and the concrete, logical implementation of that algorithm within a computational system. Could there ever be an algorithm so large, complex, and unusual that its essence can't be captured by an unthinking mechanical process?

Ultimately there can be no rigorous answer, because the question is philosophical rather than scientific. The instructions of an algorithm must be "simple" and "without ingenuity" so that it "can be performed by a person," but those are imprecise ideas about human intuition and capability, not mathematical assertions of the kind that can be used to prove or disprove a hypothesis.

We can still collect evidence one way or the other by coming up with lots of algorithms and seeing whether our computing system of choice—Turing machines, or lambda calculus, or partial recursive functions, or Ruby—can implement them. Mathematicians and computer scientists have been doing exactly that since the 1930s, and so far, nobody has managed to devise a reasonable algorithm that can't be performed by these systems, so we can be pretty confident about our empirical hunch: it certainly *looks* as though a machine can perform any algorithm.

Another strong piece of evidence is the fact that most of these systems were developed independently as attempts to capture and analyze the informal idea of an algorithm, and were only later found to be exactly equivalent to each other. Every historical attempt to model the idea of an algorithm has produced a system whose capabilities are identical to those of a Turing machine, and that's a pretty good hint that a Turing machine adequately represents what an algorithm can do.

The idea that any algorithm can be performed by a machine—specifically a deterministic Turing machine—is called the *Church–Turing thesis*, and although it's just a conjecture rather than a proven fact, it has enough evidence in its favor to be generally accepted as true.

"Turing machines can perform any algorithm" is a philosophical claim about the relationship between the intuitive idea of algorithms and the formal systems that we use to implement them. What it actually means is a matter of interpretation: we could see it as a statement about what can and cannot be computed, or just as a firmer definition of the word "algorithm."

Either way, it's called the "Church–Turing thesis," not the "Church–Turing theorem," because it's an informal claim rather than a provable mathematical assertion—it can't be expressed in purely mathematical language, so there's no way to construct a mathematical proof. It's widely believed to be true because it matches our intuition about the nature of computation and the evidence of what algorithms are capable of, but we still call it a "thesis" to remind ourselves that it has a different status from provable ideas like Pythagoras' theorem.

The Church–Turing thesis implies that Turing machines, despite their simplicity, have all the power required to perform any computation that can in principle be carried out by a person following simple instructions. Many people go further than this and claim that, since all attempts to codify algorithms have led to universal systems that are equivalent in power to Turing machines, it's just not possible to do any better: any real-world computer or programming language can only ever do as much as a Turing machine can do, and no more. Whether it's ultimately possible to build a machine that's more powerful than a Turing machine—that can use exotic laws of physics to perform tasks beyond what we think of as "algorithms"—is not definitively known, but it's definitely true that we don't currently know how to do it.

Programs Can Stand In for Turing Machines

As we saw in Chapter 5, the Turing machine's simplicity makes it cumbersome to design a rulebook for a particular task. To avoid our investigation of computability being overshadowed by the fiddly details of Turing machine programming, we'll use Ruby programs as a substitute, just as we did for Euclid's algorithm.

This sleight of hand is justified by universality: in principle, we can translate any Ruby program into an equivalent Turing machine and vice versa, so a Ruby program is no more or less powerful than a Turing machine, and anything we can discover about the limitations of Ruby's capabilities should apply equally to Turing machines.

A sensible objection is that Ruby has lots of practical functionality that Turing machines don't. A Ruby program can access the filesystem, send and receive messages across the network, accept user input, draw graphics on a bitmapped display, and so on, whereas even the most sophisticated set of Turing machine rules can only ever read and write characters on a tape. But that isn't a fundamental problem, because all of this extra functionality can be *simulated* with a Turing machine: if necessary, we can designate certain parts of the tape as representing "the filesystem" or "the network" or "the display" or whatever, and treat reading and writing to those tape regions as though it was genuine interaction with the outside world. None of these enhancements changes the underlying computational power of a Turing machine; they just provide higher-level interpretations of its activity on the tape.

In practice, we can sidestep the objection completely by restricting ourselves to simple Ruby programs that avoid any controversial language features. For the rest of this chapter, we'll stick to writing programs that read a string from standard input, do some computation, and then write a string to standard output when they're finished; the input string is analogous to the initial contents of a Turing machine's tape, and the output string is like the final tape contents.

Code Is Data

Programs live a double life. As well as being instructions to control a particular system, we can also think of a program as pure data: a tree of expressions, a raw string of characters, or even a single large number. This duality is usually taken for granted by us as programmers, but for general-purpose computers it's vitally important that programs can be represented as data so that they can be used as input to other programs; it's the unification of code and data that makes software possible in the first place.

We've already seen programs-as-data in the case of the universal Turing machine, which expects another Turing machine's rulebook to be written on its tape as a sequence of characters. In fancy *homoiconic* programming languages like Lisp[3] and XSLT, programs are explicitly written as data structures that the language itself can manipulate: every Lisp program is a nested list called an *s-expression*, and every XSLT stylesheet is an XML document.

In Ruby, only the interpreter (which, at least in the case of MRI, is not itself written in Ruby) usually gets to see a structured representation of the program, but the code-as-data principle still applies. Consider this simple Ruby program:

```ruby
puts 'hello world'
```

To an observer who understands the syntax and semantics of Ruby, this is a program that sends a `puts` message to the `main` object with the string `'hello world'`, which results in the `Kernel#puts` method printing `hello world` to standard output. But on a lower level, it's just a sequence of characters, and because characters are represented as bytes, ultimately that sequence can be viewed as a large number:

```ruby
>> program = "puts 'hello world'"
=> "puts 'hello world'"
>> bytes_in_binary = program.bytes.map { |byte| byte.to_s(2).rjust(8, '0') }
=> ["01110000", "01110101", "01110100", "01110011", "00100000", "00100111",
    "01101000", "01100101", "01101100", "01101100", "01101111", "00100000",
```

---

3. Lisp is really a family of programming languages—including Common Lisp, Scheme, and Clojure—that share very similar syntax.

```
   "01110111", "01101111", "01110010", "01101100", "01100100", "00100111"]
>> number = bytes_in_binary.join.to_i(2)
=> 9796543849500706521102980495717740021834791
```

In a sense, puts 'hello world' is Ruby program number 9796543849500706521102980495717740021834791.[4] Conversely, if someone tells us the number of a Ruby program, we can easily turn it back into the program itself and run it:

```
>> number = 9796543849500706521102980495717740021834791
=> 9796543849500706521102980495717740021834791
>> bytes_in_binary = number.to_s(2).scan(/.+?(?=.{8}*\z)/)
=> ["1110000", "01110101", "01110100", "01110011", "00100000", "00100111",
    "01101000", "01100101", "01101100", "01101100", "01101111", "00100000",
    "01110111", "01101111", "01110010", "01101100", "01100100", "00100111"]
>> program = bytes_in_binary.map { |string| string.to_i(2).chr }.join
=> "puts 'hello world'"
>> eval program
hello world
=> nil
```

Of course, this scheme of encoding a program as a large number is what makes it possible to to store it on disk, send it over the Internet, and feed it to a Ruby interpreter (which is itself just a large number on disk!) to make a particular computation happen.

 Since every Ruby program has a unique number, we can automatically generate all possible programs: start by generating program number 1, then generate program number 2, and so on.[5] If we did this for long enough, we'd eventually generate the next hot asynchronous web development framework and retire to a life of leisure.

Universal Systems Can Loop Forever

We've seen that general-purpose computers are universal: we can design a Turing machine that is capable of simulating any other Turing machine, or write a program that can evaluate any other program. Universality is a powerful idea that allows us to use a single adaptable machine for a variety of tasks rather than many specialized devices, but it also has an inconvenient consequence: any system that's powerful enough to be universal will inevitably allow us to construct computations that loop forever without halting.

---

4. It would be more useful to only assign numbers to the *syntactically valid* Ruby programs, but doing that is more complicated.

5. Most of those numbers won't represent syntactically valid Ruby programs, but we can feed each potential program to the Ruby parser and reject it if it has any syntax errors.

Very Long-Running Computations

"All I wanted to say," bellowed the computer, "is that my circuits are now irrevocably committed to calculating the answer to the Ultimate Question of Life, the Universe, and Everything—" he paused and satisfied himself that he now had everyone's attention, before continuing more quietly—"but the program will take me a little while to run."

Fook glanced impatiently at his watch.

"How long?" he said.

"Seven and a half million years," said Deep Thought.

—Douglas Adams, *The Hitchhiker's Guide to the Galaxy*

If we're trying to perform an algorithm—a list of instructions whose purpose is to turn input into output—then looping forever is a bad thing. We want a machine (or program) that will run for a limited time and then halt with some output, not just sit there silently getting warmer. All else being equal, it'd be better to have computers and languages whose every task was guaranteed to finish after a finite number of steps so that we didn't need to worry about whether an answer would eventually emerge.

In some practical applications, though, looping forever is desirable. For example, a web server like Apache or Nginx wouldn't be much use if it accepted a single HTTP request, sent a response and then quit; we want it to run indefinitely, continuing to serve every incoming request until forcibly stopped. But conceptually, we can separate a single-threaded web server into two parts: the code for handling a single request, which *should* always halt so that a response can be sent, and the infinite loop around the outside, which repeatedly calls the request handler as each new request comes in. In this case, looping forever is still a bad thing inside the complex request-handling code, even though the simple wrapper around it needs to run endlessly.

The real world provides many examples of programs that repeatedly perform halting computations inside an infinite loop: web servers, GUI applications, operating systems, and so on. While we generally want algorithmic input-output programs to always halt, the analogous goal for these long-running systems is to be *productive*, namely to always "keep going" and never get stuck in an unresponsive state.

So why must every universal system bring nontermination along for the ride? Isn't there some ingenious way to restrict Turing machines so that they'll always halt, without compromising their usefulness? How do we know we won't someday design a programming language that's just as powerful as Ruby but doesn't have infinite loops in it? There are all sorts of specific examples of why this can't be done, but there's also a more general argument, so let's go through it.

Ruby is a universal programming language, so it must be possible to write Ruby code that evaluates Ruby code. In principle, we can define a method called #evaluate, which takes the source code of a Ruby program and a string to provide to that program on standard input, and returns the result (i.e., the string sent to standard output) of evaluating that program with that input.

The implementation of #evaluate is far too complicated to be contained within this chapter, but here's the broadest possible outline of how it would work:

```
def evaluate(program, input)
  # parse program
  # evaluate program on input while capturing output
  # return output
end
```

#evaluate is essentially a Ruby interpreter written in Ruby. Although we haven't given its implementation, it's certainly possible to write it: first turn program into a sequence of tokens and parse them to build a parse tree (see "Parsing with Pushdown Automata" on page 125), then evaluate that parse tree according to the operational semantics of Ruby (see "Operational Semantics" on page 20). It's a large and complex job, but it can definitely be done; otherwise, Ruby wouldn't qualify as universal.

For simplicity, we'll assume that our imaginary implementation of #evaluate is bug-free and won't crash while it's evaluating program—if we're going to imagine some code, we may as well imagine that it's perfect. Of course it might return some result that indicates that program raised an exception while it was being evaluated, but that's not the same as #evaluate itself actually crashing.

 Ruby happens to have a built-in Kernel#eval method that can evaluate a string of Ruby code, but taking advantage of it here would be a bit of a cheat, not least because (in MRI) it's implemented in C, not Ruby. It's also just unnecessary for the current discussion; we're using Ruby as a representative example of any universal programming language, but many universal languages don't have a built-in eval.

But hey, since it's there, it'd be a shame not to use it to make #evaluate less imaginary. Here's a rough attempt, with apologies for cheating:

```
require 'stringio'

def evaluate(program, input)
  old_stdin, old_stdout = $stdin, $stdout
  $stdin, $stdout = StringIO.new(input), (output = StringIO.new)

  begin
    eval program
  rescue Exception => e
    output.puts(e)
  ensure
    $stdin, $stdout = old_stdin, old_stdout
  end
```

```
      output.string
    end
```

This implementation has many practical and philosophical problems that could all be avoided by writing a pure-Ruby #evaluate. On the other hand, it's short enough to include here and works well enough for demonstration purposes:

```
>> evaluate('print $stdin.read.reverse', 'hello world')
=> "dlrow olleh"
```

The existence of #evaluate allows us to define another method, #evaluate_on_itself, which returns the result of evaluating program with *its own source* as input:

```
def evaluate_on_itself(program)
  evaluate(program, program)
end
```

This might sound like a weird thing to do, but it's totally legitimate; program is just a string, so we're perfectly entitled to treat it both as a Ruby program and as input to that program. Code is data, right?

```
>> evaluate_on_itself('print $stdin.read.reverse')
=> "esrever.daer.nidts$ tnirp"
```

Since we know we can implement #evaluate and #evaluate_on_itself in Ruby, we must therefore be able to write the complete Ruby program *does_it_say_no.rb*:

```
def evaluate(program, input)
  # parse program
  # evaluate program on input while capturing output
  # return output
end

def evaluate_on_itself(program)
  evaluate(program, program)
end

program = $stdin.read

if evaluate_on_itself(program) == 'no'
  print 'yes'
else
  print 'no'
end
```

This program is a straightforward application of existing code: it defines #evaluate and #evaluate_on_itself, then reads another Ruby program from standard input and passes it to #evaluate_on_itself to see what that program does when run with itself as input. If the resulting output is the string 'no', *does_it_say_no.rb* outputs 'yes', otherwise, it outputs 'no'. For example:[6]

---

6. We're using Unix shell syntax here. On Windows, it's necessary to omit the single quotes around the argument to echo, or to put the text in a file and feed it to ruby with the < input redirection operator.

```
$ echo 'print $stdin.read.reverse' | ruby does_it_say_no.rb
no
```

That's the result we expected; as we saw above, when we run `print $stdin.read.reverse` with itself as input, we get the output `esrever.daer.nidts$ tnirp`, which is not equal to no. What about a program that *does* output no?

```
$ echo 'if $stdin.read.include?("no") then print "no" end' | ruby does_it_say_no.rb
yes
```

Again, just as expected.

So here's the big question: what happens when we run *ruby does_it_say_no.rb < does_it_say_no.rb*?[7] Bear in mind that *does_it_say_no.rb* is a real program—one that we could write out in full if we had enough time and enthusiasm—so it must do *something*, but it's not immediately obvious what that is. Let's try to work it out by considering all the possibilities and eliminating the ones that don't make sense.

First, running this particular program with its own source as input can't possibly produce the output yes. By the program's own logic, the output yes can only be produced when running *does_it_say_no.rb* on its own source produces the output no, which contradicts the original premise. So that's not the answer.

Okay, so maybe it outputs no instead. But again, the structure of the program means that it can only output no if exactly the same computation *doesn't* output no—another contradiction.

Is it conceivable that it could output some other string, like maybe, or even the empty string? That would be contradictory too: if `evaluate_on_itself(program, program)` doesn't return no then the program prints no, not something different.

So it can't output yes or no, it can't output something else, and it can't crash unless `#evaluate` contains bugs, which we're assuming it doesn't. The only remaining possibility is that it doesn't produce any output, and that can only happen if the program never finishes: `#evaluate` must loop forever without returning a result.

> In practice it's almost certain that *ruby does_it_say_no.rb < does_it_say_no.rb* will exhaust the finite memory of the host machine, causing *ruby* to crash, rather than actually looping forever. This is a resource constraint imposed from outside the program, though, not a property of the program itself; in principle, we could keep adding more memory to the computer as necessary and let the computation run indefinitely.

---

7. This is the shell command to run *does_it_say_no.rb* with its own source code as input.

This might seem like an unnecessarily complicated way of demonstrating that Ruby lets us write nonhalting programs. After all, `while true do end` is much a simpler example that does the same thing.

But by thinking about the behavior of *does_it_say_no.rb*, we've shown that nonhalting programs are an inevitable consequence of universality, regardless of the specific features of the system. Our argument doesn't rely on any particular abilities of Ruby other than its universality, so the same ideas can be applied to Turing machines, or the lambda calculus, or any other universal system. Whenever we're working with a language that is powerful enough to evaluate itself, we know that it must be possible to use its equivalent of `#evaluate` to construct a program that never halts, without having to know anything else about the language's capabilities.

In particular, it's impossible to remove features (e.g., `while` loops) from a programming language in a way that prevents us from writing nonhalting programs while keeping the language powerful enough to be universal. If removing a particular feature makes it impossible to write a program that loops forever, it must also have made it impossible to implement `#evaluate`.

Languages that have been carefully designed to ensure that their programs must always halt are called *total programming languages*, as opposed to the more conventional *partial programming languages* whose programs sometimes halt with an answer and sometimes don't. Total programming languages are still very powerful and capable of expressing many useful computations, but one thing they can't do is interpret themselves.

That's surprising, since the equivalent of `#evaluate` for a total programming language must by definition always halt, yet it still can't be implemented in that language—if it could, we'd be able to use the *does_it_say_no.rb* technique to make it loop forever.

This gives us our first tantalizing glimpse of an impossible program: we can't write an interpreter for a total programming language in itself, even though there's a perfectly respectable, guaranteed-to-halt algorithm for interpreting it. In fact it's so respectable that we *could* write it in another, more sophisticated total programming language, but that new total language wouldn't be able to implement its own interpreter either.

An interesting curiosity, but total languages are designed to have artificial limits; we were looking for things that *no* computer or programming language could do. We'd better keep going.

Programs Can Refer to Themselves

The self-referential trick used by *does_it_say_no.rb* hinges on our ability to construct a program that can read its own source code, but perhaps it seems a bit like cheating to assume that this will always be possible. In our example, the program received its own source as an explicit input, thanks to functionality provided by the surrounding environment (i.e., the shell); if that hadn't been an option, it could also have read the data directly from disk with `File.read(__FILE__)`, taking advantage of Ruby's filesystem API and the special `__FILE__` constant that always contains the name of the current file.

But we were supposed to be making a general argument that depended only on the universality of Ruby, not on the capabilities of the operating system or the `File` class. What about compiled languages like Java and C that may not have access to their source at runtime? What about JavaScript programs that get loaded into memory over a network connection, and may not be stored locally on a filesystem at all? What about self-contained universal systems like Turing machines and the lambda calculus, where the notions of "filesystem" and "standard input" don't exist?

Fortunately, the *does_it_say_no.rb* argument can withstand this objection, because having a program read its own source from standard input is just a convenient shorthand for something that all universal systems can do, again regardless of their environment or other features. This is a consequence of a fundamental mathematical result called *Kleene's second recursion theorem*, which guarantees that any program can be converted into an equivalent one that is able to calculate its own source code. The recursion theorem provides reassurance that our shorthand was justified: we could have replaced the line `program = $stdin.read` with some code to generate the source of *does_it_say_no.rb* and assign it to `program` without having to do any I/O at all.

Let's see how to do the conversion on a simple Ruby program. Take this one, for example:

```ruby
x = 1
y = 2
puts x + y
```

We want to transform it into a program that looks something like this…

```ruby
program = '…'
x = 1
y = 2
puts x + y
```

…where `program` is assigned a string containing the source of the complete program. But what should the value of `program` be?

A naïve approach is to try to concoct a simple string literal that can be assigned to `program`, but that quickly gets us into trouble, because the literal would be part of the program's source code and would therefore have to appear somewhere inside itself. That would require `program` to begin with the string `'program ='` followed by the value of `program`, which would be the string `'program ='` again followed by the value of `program`, and so on forever:

```ruby
program = %q{program = %q{program = %q{program = %q{program = %q{program = %q{…}}}}}}
x = 1
y = 2
puts x + y
```

Ruby's %q syntax allows us to quote noninterpolated strings with a pair of delimiter characters, in this case curly brackets, instead of single quotes. The advantage is that the string literal can contain unescaped instances of the delimiters as long as they're correctly balanced:

```
>> puts %q{Curly brackets look like { and }.}
Curly brackets look like { and }.
=> nil
>> puts %q{An unbalanced curly bracket like } is a problem.}
SyntaxError: syntax error, unexpected tIDENTIFIER, expecting end-of-input
```

Using %q instead of single quotes helps to avoid character-escaping headaches in strings that contain their own delimiters:

```
program = 'program = \'program = \\\'program = \\\\\\\'…\\\\\\\'\\\'\''
```

The way out of this infinitely deep hole is to take advantage of the fact that a value used by a program doesn't *have* to appear literally in its source code; it can also be computed dynamically from other data. This means we can construct the converted program in three parts:

A. Assign a string literal to a variable (call it data).

B. Use that string to compute the current program's source code and assign it to program.

C. Do whatever other work the program is supposed to do (i.e., the code we originally started with).

So the structure of the program will be more like this:

```
data = '…'
program = …
x = 1
y = 2
puts x + y
```

That sounds plausible as a general strategy, but it's a bit light on specific details. How do we know what string to actually assign to data in part A, and how do we use it in part B to compute program? Here's one solution:

- In part A, create a string literal that contains the source code of parts B and C, and assign that string to data. This string won't need to "contain itself," because it's not the source of the full program, only the section of the program that comes after part A.

- In part B, first compute a string that contains the source code of part A. We can do that because part A mostly consists of a big string literal whose value is available as data, so we just need to prefix data's value with 'data =' to recreate part A's source. Then simply concatenate the result with data to get the source of the entire program (since data contains the source of parts B and C) and assign it to program.

This plan still sounds circular—part A produces the source of part B, and part B produces the source of part A—but it narrowly avoids an infinite regress by ensuring that part B just *computes* the source of part A without having to literally contain it.

We can start making progress by filling in the bits we already know about. We have most of the source of parts B and C already, so we can partially complete the value of data:

```
data = %q{
program = …
x = 1
y = 2
puts x + y
}
program = …
x = 1
y = 2
puts x + y
```

 data needs to contain newline characters. By representing these as actual newlines inside an uninterpolated string literal, rather than as interpolated \n escape sequences, we are able to include the source of parts B and C verbatim without any special encoding or escaping.[8] This straightforward copy-and-paste makes the source of part A easier to compute.

We also know that the source of part A is just the string 'data = %q{…}' with the value of data filling the gap between the curly braces, so we can partially complete the value of program too:

```
data = %q{
program = …
x = 1
y = 2
puts x + y
}
program = "data = %q{#{data}}" + …
x = 1
y = 2
puts x + y
```

Now all that's missing from program is the source code of parts B and C, which is exactly what data contains, so we can append the value of data to program to finish it off:

```
data = %q{
program = …
x = 1
```

8. We can only get away with this because parts B and C happen not to contain any difficult characters like backslashes or unbalanced curly brackets. If they did, we'd have to escape them somehow and then undo that escaping as part of assembling the value of program.

```
y = 2
puts x + y
}
program = "data = %q{#{data}}" + data
x = 1
y = 2
puts x + y
```

Finally, we can go back and fix up the value of data to reflect what part B actually looks like:

```
data = %q{
program = "data = %q{#{data}}" + data
x = 1
y = 2
puts x + y
}
program = "data = %q{#{data}}" + data
x = 1
y = 2
puts x + y
```

And that's it! This program does the same thing as the original, but now it has an extra local variable containing its own source code—an admittedly hollow victory, since it doesn't actually *do* anything with that variable. So what if we convert a program that expects a local variable called program and does something with it? Take the classic example:

```
puts program
```

This is a program that is trying to print its own source code,[9] but it's obviously going to fail in that form, because program is an undefined variable. If we run it through the self-referencing transformation we get this result:

```
data = %q{
program = "data = %q{#{data}}" + data
puts program
}
program = "data = %q{#{data}}" + data
puts program
```

That's a bit more interesting. Let's see what this code does on the console:

```
>> data = %q{
   program = "data = %q{#{data}}" + data
   puts program
   }
=> "\nprogram = \"data = %q{\#{data}}\" + data\nputs program\n"
>> program = "data = %q{#{data}}" + data
=> "data = %q{\nprogram = \"data = %q{\#{data}}\" + data\nputs program\n}\n↵
program = \"data = %q{\#{data}}\" + data\nputs program\n"
>> puts program
data = %q{
```

---

9. Douglas Hofstadter coined the name *quine* for a program that prints itself.

```
program = "data = %q{#{data}}" + data
puts program
}
program = "data = %q{#{data}}" + data
puts program
=> nil
```

Sure enough, the line `puts program` really does print out the source code of the whole program.

Hopefully it's clear that this transformation doesn't depend on any special properties of the program itself, so it will work for any Ruby program, and the use of `$stdin.read` or `File.read(__FILE__)` to read a program's own source can therefore always be eliminated.[10] It also doesn't depend on any special properties of Ruby itself—just the ability to compute new values from old ones, like any other universal system—which implies that any Turing machine can be adapted to refer to its own encoding, any lambda calculus expression can be extended to contain a lambda-calculus representation of its own syntax, and so on.

Decidability

So far we've seen that Turing machines have a lot of power and flexibility: they can execute arbitrary programs encoded as data, perform any algorithm we can think of, run for an unlimited amount of time, and calculate their own descriptions. And in spite of their simplicity, these little imaginary machines have turned out to be representative of universal systems in general.

If they're so powerful and flexible, is there anything that Turing machines—and therefore real-world computers and programming languages—can't do?

Before we can answer that question we need to make it a bit more precise. What kind of thing can we ask a Turing machine to do, and how can we tell whether it's done it? Do we need to investigate every possible kind of problem, or is it enough to consider just some of them? Are we looking for problems whose solutions are merely beyond our current understanding, or problems that we already know we'll *never* be able to solve?

We can narrow the scope of the question by focusing on *decision problems*. A decision problem is any question with a yes or no answer, like "is 2 less than 3?" or "does the regular expression `(a(|b))*` match the string `'abaab'`?" Decision problems are easier to handle than *function problems* whose answer is a number or some other non-Boolean value, like "what is the greatest common divisor of 18 and 12?," but they're still interesting enough to be worth investigating.

---

10. Can you resist the urge to write a Ruby program that can perform this transformation on any Ruby program? If you use `%q{}` to quote `data`'s value, how will you handle backslashes and unbalanced curly brackets in the original source?

A decision problem is *decidable* (or *computable*) if there's an algorithm that's guaranteed to solve it in a finite amount of time for any possible input. The Church–Turing thesis claims that every algorithm can be performed by a Turing machine, so for a problem to be decidable, we have to be able to design a Turing machine that always produces the correct answer and always halts if we let it run for long enough. It's easy enough to interpret a Turing machine's final configuration as a "yes" or "no" answer: we could look to see whether it's written a Y or N character at the current tape location, for example, or we could ignore the tape contents altogether and just check whether its final state is an accept ("yes") or a nonaccept ("no") state.

All the decision problems we've seen in earlier chapters are decidable. Some of them, like "does this finite automaton accept this string?" and "does this regular expression match this string?," are self-evidently decidable because we've written Ruby programs to solve them by simulating finite automata directly. Those programs could be laboriously translated into Turing machines given enough time and energy, and because their execution involves a finite number of steps—each step of a DFA simulation consumes a character of input, and the input has a finite number of characters—they are guaranteed to always halt with a yes-or-no answer, so the original problems qualify as decidable.

Other problems are a bit more subtle. "Does this pushdown automaton accept this string?" might appear to be undecidable, because we've seen that our direct simulation of a pushdown automaton in Ruby has the potential to loop forever and never produce an answer. However, there happens to be a way to calculate exactly how many simulation steps a particular pushdown automaton will need in order to accept or reject an input string of a given length,[11] so the problem is decidable after all: we just calculate the number of steps needed, run the simulation for that many steps, and then check whether or not the input has been accepted.

So, can we do this every time? Is there always a clever way to sneak around a problem and find a way to implement a machine, or a program, that is guaranteed to solve it in a finite amount of time?

Well, no, unfortunately not. There are many decision problems—*infinitely* many—and it turns out that a lot of them are undecidable: there is no guaranteed-to-halt algorithm for solving them. Each of these problems is undecidable not because we just haven't found the right algorithm for it yet, but because the problem itself is fundamentally impossible to solve for some inputs, and we can even prove that no suitable algorithm will ever be found.

---

11. Briefly, for the curious: every pushdown automaton has an equivalent context-free grammar and vice versa; any CFG can be rewritten in *Chomsky normal form*; and any CFG in that form must take exactly $2n - 1$ steps to generate a string of length n. So we can turn the original PDA into a CFG, rewrite the CFG into Chomsky normal form, and then turn that CFG back into a PDA. The resulting pushdown automaton recognizes the same language as the original, but now we know exactly how many steps it'll take to do it.

The Halting Problem

A lot of undecidable problems are concerned with the behavior of machines and programs during their execution. The most famous of these, the *halting problem*, is the task of deciding whether the execution of a particular Turing machine with a particular initial tape will ever halt. Thanks to universality, we can restate the same problem in more practical terms: given a string containing the source code of a Ruby program, and another string of data for that program to read from standard input, will running that program ultimately result in an answer or just an infinite loop?

Building a Halting Checker

It's not obvious why the halting problem should be considered undecidable. After all, it's easy to come up with individual programs for which the question is answerable. Here's a program that will definitely halt, regardless of its input string:

```
input = $stdin.read
puts input.upcase
```

 We'll assume that `$stdin.read` always immediately returns a value— namely, that every program's standard input is finite and nonblocking —because we're interested in the internal behavior of the program, not its interactions with the operating system.

Conversely, a small addition to the source code produces a program that will clearly never halt:

```
input = $stdin.read

while true
  # do nothing
end

puts input.upcase
```

We can certainly write a halting checker to distinguish between only these two cases. Just testing whether the program's source code contains the string `while true` is enough:

```
def halts?(program, input)
  if program.include?('while true')
    false
  else
    true
  end
end
```

This implementation of `#halts?` gives the right answers for the two example programs:

```
>> always = "input = $stdin.read\nputs input.upcase"
=> "input = $stdin.read\nputs input.upcase"
>> halts?(always, 'hello world')
=> true
>> never = "input = $stdin.read\nwhile true\n# do nothing\nend\nputs input.upcase"
=> "input = $stdin.read\nwhile true\n# do nothing\nend\nputs input.upcase"
>> halts?(never, 'hello world')
=> false
```

But #halts? is likely to be wrong for other programs. For example, there are programs whose halting behavior depends on the value of their input:

```
input = $stdin.read

if input.include?('goodbye')
  while true
    # do nothing
  end
else
  puts input.upcase
end
```

We can always extend our halting checker to cope with specific cases like this, since we know what to look for:

```
def halts?(program, input)
  if program.include?('while true')
    if program.include?('input.include?(\'goodbye\')')
      if input.include?('goodbye')
        false
      else
        true
      end
    else
      false
    end
  else
    true
  end
end
```

Now we have a checker that gives the correct answers for all three programs and any possible input strings:

```
>> halts?(always, 'hello world')
=> true
>> halts?(never, 'hello world')
=> false
>> sometimes = "input = $stdin.read\nif input.include?('goodbye')\nwhile true\n↵
# do nothing\nend\nelse\nputs input.upcase\nend"
=> "input = $stdin.read\nif input.include?('goodbye')\nwhile true\n# do nothing\n↵
end\nelse\nputs input.upcase\nend"
>> halts?(sometimes, 'hello world')
=> true
>> halts?(sometimes, 'goodbye world')
=> false
```

We could go on like this indefinitely, adding more checks and more special cases to support an expanding repertoire of example programs, but we'd never get a solution to the full problem of deciding whether *any* program will halt. A brute-force implementation can be made more and more accurate, but it will always have blind spots; the simple-minded approach of looking for specific patterns of syntax can't possibly scale to all programs.

To make `#halts?` work in general, for any possible program and input, seems like it would be difficult. If a program contains any loops at all—whether explicit, like `while` loops, or implicit, like recursive method calls—then it has the potential to run forever, and sophisticated analysis of the program's *meaning* is required if we want to predict anything about how it behaves for a given input. As humans, we can see immediately that this program always halts:

```
input = $stdin.read
output = ''

n = input.length
until n.zero?
  output = output + '*'
  n = n - 1
end

puts output
```

But *why* does it always halt? Certainly not for any straightforward syntactic reason. The explanation is that `IO#read` always returns a `String`, and `String#length` always returns a nonnegative `Integer`, and repeatedly calling `-(1)` on a nonnegative `Integer` always eventually produces an object whose `#zero?` method returns `true`. This chain of reasoning is subtle and highly sensitive to small modifications; if the `n = n - 1` statement inside the loop is changed to `n = n - 2`, the program will only halt for even-length inputs. A halting checker that knew all these facts about Ruby and numbers, as well as how to connect facts together to make accurate decisions about this kind of program, would need to be large and complex.

 The fundamental difficulty is that it's hard to predict what a program will do without actually running it. It's tempting to run the program with `#evaluate` to see whether it halts, but that's no good: if the program doesn't halt, `#evaluate` will run forever and we won't get an answer from `#halts?` no matter how long we wait. Any reliable halting-detection algorithm must find a way to produce a definitive answer in a finite amount of time just by inspecting and analyzing the text of the program, not by simply running it and waiting.

It'll Never Work

Okay, so our intuition tells us that #halts? would be hard to implement correctly, but that doesn't necessarily mean that the halting problem is undecidable. There are plenty of difficult problems (e.g., writing #evaluate) that turn out to be solvable given enough effort and ingenuity; if the halting problem is undecidable, that means #halts? is *impossible* to write, not just extremely difficult.

How do we know that a proper implementation of #halts? can't possibly exist? If it's just an engineering problem, why can't we throw lots of programmers at it and eventually come up with a solution?

Too good to be true

Let's pretend temporarily that the halting problem is decidable. In this imaginary world, it's possible to write a full implementation of #halts?, so a call to halts?(program, input) always comes back with a true or false answer for any program and input, and that answer always correctly predicts whether program would halt if it was run with input on standard input. The rough structure of the #halts? method might be something like this:

```
def halts?(program, input)
  # parse program
  # analyze program
  # return true if program halts on input, false if not
end
```

If we can write #halts?, then we can construct *does_it_halt.rb*, a program that reads another program as input and prints yes or no depending on whether that program halts when it reads the empty string:[12]

```
def halts?(program, input)
  # parse program
  # analyze program
  # return true if program halts on input, false if not
end

def halts_on_empty?(program)
  halts?(program, '')
end

program = $stdin.read

if halts_on_empty?(program)
  print 'yes'
else
```

---

12. The choice of the empty string is unimportant; it's just an arbitrary fixed input. The plan is to run *does_it_halt.rb* on self-contained programs that don't read anything from standard input, so it doesn't matter what input is.

```
  print 'no'
end
```

Once we have *does_it_halt.rb*, we can use it to solve very difficult problems. Consider this famous claim made by Christian Goldbach in 1742:

> Every even integer greater than 2 can be written as the sum of two primes.

This is the *Goldbach conjecture*, and it's famous because nobody has been able to prove whether it's true or false. The evidence suggests that it's true, because an even number picked at random can invariably be broken apart into two primes—12 = 5 + 7, 34 = 3 + 31, 567890 = 7 + 567883 and so forth—and computers have been used to check that this can be done for all even numbers between four and four quintillion (4,000,000,000,000,000,000). But there are infinitely many even numbers, so no computer can check them all, and there's no known proof that every even number must break apart in this way. There is a possibility, however small, that some very large even number is *not* the sum of two primes.

Proving the Goldbach conjecture is one of the holy grails of number theory; in the year 2000, the publisher Faber and Faber offered a million-dollar prize to anyone who could produce a proof. But wait: we already have the tools to discover whether the conjecture is true! We just need to write a program that searches for a counterexample:

```
require 'prime'

def primes_less_than(n)
  Prime.each(n - 1).entries
end

def sum_of_two_primes?(n)
  primes = primes_less_than(n)
  primes.any? { |a| primes.any? { |b| a + b == n } }
end

n = 4

while sum_of_two_primes?(n)
  n = n + 2
end

print n
```

This establishes a connection between the truth of the Goldbach conjecture and the halting behavior of a program. If the conjecture is true, this program will never find a counterexample no matter how high it counts, so it will loop forever; if the conjecture's false, n will eventually be assigned the value of an even number that isn't the sum of two primes, and the program will halt. So we just have to save it as *goldbach.rb* and run *ruby does_it_halt.rb < goldbach.rb* to find out whether it's a halting program, and that will tell us whether the Goldbach conjecture is true. A million dollars is ours![13]

Well, obviously this is too good to be true. To write a program that can accurately predict the behavior of *goldbach.rb* would require a proficiency in number theory beyond our current understanding. Mathematicians have been working for hundreds of years to try to prove or disprove the Goldbach conjecture; it's unlikely that a bunch of avaricious software engineers could construct a Ruby program that can miraculously solve not only this problem but *any* unsolved mathematical conjecture that can be expressed as a looping program.

Fundamentally impossible

So far we've seen strong evidence that the halting problem is undecidable, but not conclusive proof. Our intuition may say it's unlikely that we can prove or disprove the Goldbach conjecture just by turning it into a program, but computation can be pretty counterintuitive at times, so we shouldn't allow ourselves to be convinced solely by arguments about how improbable something is. If the halting problem really is undecidable, as opposed to simply very difficult, we should be able to prove it.

Here's why #halts? can never work. If it *did* work, we'd be able to construct a new method #halts_on_itself? that calls #halts? to determine what a program does when run with its own source code as input:[14]

```ruby
def halts_on_itself?(program)
  halts?(program, program)
end
```

Like #halts?, the #halts_on_itself? method will always finish and return a Boolean value: true if program halts when run with itself as input, false if it loops forever.

Given working implementations of #halts? and #halts_on_itself?, we can write a program called *do_the_opposite.rb*:

```ruby
def halts?(program, input)
  # parse program
  # analyze program
  # return true if program halts on input, false if not
end

def halts_on_itself?(program)
  halts?(program, program)
end

program = $stdin.read

if halts_on_itself?(program)
  while true
    # do nothing
  end
end
```

---

13. Faber's million-dollar prize expired in 2002, but anyone who produced a proof today would still be in for some serious fortune and glory on the rock star mathematician circuit.

14. This is reminiscent of #evaluate_on_itself from "Universal Systems Can Loop Forever" on page 259, with #halts? in place of #evaluate.

This code reads `program` from standard input, finds out whether it would halt if run on itself, and promptly does the exact opposite: if `program` would halt, *do_the_opposite.rb* loops forever; if `program` would loop forever, *do_the_opposite.rb* halts.

Now, what does *ruby do_the_opposite.rb < do_the_opposite.rb* do?[15] Just as we saw earlier with *does_it_say_no.rb*, this question creates an inescapable contradiction.

`#halts_on_itself?` must return either `true` or `false` when given the source of *do_the_opposite.rb* as an argument. If it returns `true` to indicate a halting program, then *ruby do_the_opposite.rb < do_the_opposite.rb* will loop forever, which means `#halts_on_itself?` was wrong about what would happen. On the other hand, if `#halts_on_itself?` returns `false`, that'll make *do_the_opposite.rb* immediately halt, again contradicting `#halts_on_itself?`'s prediction.

It's wrong to pick on `#halts_on_itself?` here—it's just an innocent one-liner that delegates to `#halts?` and relays its answer. What we've really shown is that it's not possible for `#halts?` to return a satisfactory answer when called with *do_the_opposite.rb* as both `program` and `input` arguments; no matter how hard it works, any result it produces will automatically be wrong. That means there are only two possible fates for any real implementation of `#halts?`:

- It sometimes gives the wrong answer, e.g., predicting that *do_the_opposite.rb* will loop forever even though it halts (or vice versa).
- It sometimes loops forever and never returns any answer, just like `#evaluate` does in *ruby does_it_say_no.rb < does_it_say_no.rb*.

So a fully correct implementation of `#halts?` can never exist: there must be inputs for which it makes either an incorrect prediction or no prediction at all.

Remember the definition of decidability:

> A decision problem is decidable if there's an algorithm that's guaranteed to solve it in a finite amount of time for any possible input.

We've proved it's impossible to write a Ruby program that completely solves the halting problem, and since Ruby programs are equivalent in power to Turing machines, it must be impossible with a Turing machine too. The Church–Turing thesis says that *every* algorithm can be performed by a Turing machine, so if there's no Turing machine for solving the halting problem, there's no algorithm either; in other words, the halting problem is undecidable.

Other Undecidable Problems

It's discouraging that there's an easily defined problem ("does this program halt?") that computers can't reliably solve. However, that specific problem is relatively abstract,

---

15. Or equivalently: what does `#halts_on_itself?` return if we call it with *do_the_opposite.rb*'s source code as its argument?

and the *do_the_opposite.rb* program we used to illustrate it is impractical and contrived; it doesn't seem likely that we'll ever want to actually implement #halts?, or write a program like *do_the_opposite.rb*, as part of a real-world application. Perhaps we can disregard undecidability as an academic curiosity and get on with our lives.

Unfortunately it's not that simple, because the halting problem is not the only undecidable problem. There are plenty of others that we might realistically want to solve in our day-to-day work of building software, and their undecidability has real consequences for the practical limitations of automated tools and processes.

Let's look at a toy example. Suppose we've been given the job of developing a Ruby program to print the string 'hello world'. That sounds simple enough, but in our capacity as inveterate procrastinators[16] we're also going to develop an automated tool that can reliably decide whether or not a particular program prints hello world when supplied with a particular input.[17] Armed with this tool, we can analyze our final program and check that it does what it's supposed to.

Now, imagine we succeed in developing a method #prints_hello_world? that can correctly make that decision about any program. Omitting implementation details, the method has this general form:

```
def prints_hello_world?(program, input)
  # parse program
  # analyze program
  # return true if program prints "hello world", false if not
end
```

Once we've finished writing our original program, we can use #prints_hello_world? to verify that it does the right thing; if it does, we'll check it into source control, email the boss, and everyone's happy. But the situation is even better than that, because we can also use #prints_hello_world? to implement another interesting method:

```
def halts?(program, input)
  hello_world_program = %Q{
    program = #{program.inspect}
    input = $stdin.read
    evaluate(program, input) # evaluate program, ignoring its output
    print 'hello world'
  }

  prints_hello_world?(hello_world_program, input)
end
```

---

16. Surely "responsible software engineering professionals"?

17. Again, that input might be irrelevant if the program doesn't actually read anything from $stdin, but we're including it for the sake of completeness and consistency.

The %Q syntax quotes a string in the same way as %q and then performs interpolation, so #{program.inspect} gets replaced with a Ruby string literal containing the value of program.

Our new version of #halts? works by constructing a special program, hello_world_program, which does two main things:

1. Evaluates program with input available on its standard input
2. Prints hello world

hello_world_program is constructed so that its execution has only two possible outcomes: either evaluate(program, input) will finish successfully, in which case hello world will be printed, or evaluate(program, input) will loop forever and there'll be no output at all.

This special program is fed into #prints_hello_world? to find out which of those two outcomes will happen. If #prints_hello_world? returns true, that means evaluate(program, input) will eventually finish and allow hello world to be printed, so #halts? returns true to indicate that program halts on input. If #prints_hello_world? instead returns false, that must be because hello_world_program will never reach its final line, so #halts? returns false to say that evaluate(program, input) loops forever.

Our new implementation of #halts? shows that the halting problem is *reducible* to the problem of checking whether a program prints hello world. In other words, any algorithm that computes #prints_hello_world? can be adapted to make an algorithm that computes #halts?.

We already know that a working #halts? can't exist, so the obvious conclusion is that a complete implementation of #prints_hello_world? can't exist either. And if it's impossible to implement, the Church–Turing thesis says there's no algorithm for it, so "does this program print hello world?" is another undecidable problem.

In reality, nobody cares about automatically detecting whether a program prints a particular string, but the structure of this undecidability proof points to something larger and more general. We only had to construct a program that exhibits the "prints hello world" property whenever some other program halts, and that was enough to show undecidability. What stops us from reusing this argument for *any* property of program behavior, including properties that we actually do care about?

Well, nothing does. This is *Rice's theorem*: any nontrivial property of program behavior is undecidable, because the halting problem can always be reduced to the problem of deciding whether that property is true; if we could invent an algorithm for deciding that property, we'd be able to use it to build another algorithm that decides the halting problem, and that's impossible.

Roughly speaking, a "nontrivial property" is a claim about *what* a program does, not *how* it does it. For example, Rice's theorem doesn't apply to a purely syntactic property like "does this program's source code contain the string `'reverse'`?," because that's an incidental implementation detail that can be refactored away without changing the program's externally visible behavior. On the other hand, a semantic property like "does this program output the reverse of its input?" is within the scope of Rice's theorem and therefore undecidable.

Rice's theorem tells us there are a huge number of undecidable problems that are concerned with what a program will do when it's executed.

Depressing Implications

Undecidability is an inconvenient fact of life. The halting problem is disappointing, because it shows we can't have everything: we want the unrestricted power of a universal programming language, but we also want to write programs that produce a result without getting stuck in an infinite loop, or at least programs whose *subroutines* halt as part of some larger long-running task (see "Very Long-Running Computations" on page 260).

This disappointment is bleakly summarized in a classic paper from 2004:

> There is a dichotomy in language design, because of the halting problem. For our programming discipline we are forced to choose between
>
> A. Security—a language in which all programs are known to terminate.
> B. Universality—a language in which we can write
>   i. all terminating programs
>   ii. silly programs which fail to terminate
>
> and, given an arbitrary program we cannot in general say if it is (i) or (ii).
>
> Five decades ago, at the beginning of electronic computing, we chose (B).
>
> —David Turner, *Total Functional Programming* (*http://www.jucs.org/jucs_10_7/total _functional_programming*)

Yes, we'd all like to avoid writing silly programs, but that's just tough luck. There's no way to tell whether an arbitrary program is silly, so we can't completely avoid writing them without sacrificing universality.[18]

The implications of Rice's theorem are depressing too: not only is the question "does this program halt?" undecidable, but so is "does this program do what I want it to do?" We live in a universe where there's no way to build a machine that can accurately predict

---

18. Total programming languages are a potential solution to this problem, but so far they haven't taken off, perhaps because they can be more difficult to understand than conventional languages.

whether a program will print `hello world`, calculate a particular mathematical function, or make a particular operating system call, and that's just the way it is.

That's frustrating, because it would be really useful to be able to check program properties mechanically; the reliability of modern software would be improved by a tool that decides whether a program conforms to its specification or contains any bugs. Those properties might be mechanically checkable for individual programs, but unless they're checkable in general, then we'll never be able to trust machines to do the job for us.

For example, say we invent a new software platform and decide to make money by selling compatible programs from an online shop—an "application superstore," if you like—on behalf of our platform's third-party developers. We want our customers to be able to shop with confidence, so we decide to only sell programs that meet certain criteria: they must not crash, they must not call private APIs, and they must not execute arbitrary code downloaded from the Internet.

When thousands of developers start submitting programs to us, how do we review each one to see whether it falls within our guidelines? It would save a lot of time and money if we could use an automated system to check every submission for compliance, but thanks to undecidability, it's not possible to build a system that does the job accurately. We have no choice but to hire a small army of human beings to manually test those programs by running them, disassembling them, and instrumenting the operating system to profile their dynamic behavior.

Manual review is slow, expensive, and error-prone, with the added drawback that each program can only be run for a short amount of time, providing a limited snapshot of its dynamic behavior. So even if nobody makes a mistake, occasionally something undesirable will slip through the net and we'll have a load of angry customers on our hands. Thanks a lot, undecidability.

Beneath all this inconvenience are two fundamental problems. The first is that we don't have the power to look into the future and see what will happen when a program is executed; the only general way to find out what a program does is to run it for real. While some programs are simple enough to have behavior that's straightforwardly predictable, a universal language will always permit programs whose behavior can't be predicted just by analyzing their source code.[19]

The second problem is that, when we do decide to run a program, there's no reliable way to know how long it will take to finish. The only general solution is to run it and wait, but since we know that programs in a universal language can loop forever without halting, there will always be some programs for which no finite amount of waiting is long enough.

---

19. Stephen Wolfram coined the name *computational irreducibility* (*http://mathworld.wolfram.com/ComputationalIrreducibility.html*) for the idea that a program's behavior can't be predicted without running it.

Why Does This Happen?

In this chapter, we've seen that all universal systems are powerful enough to refer to themselves. Programs operate on numbers, numbers can represent strings, and strings are how the instructions of a program are written down, so programs are perfectly capable of operating on their own source code.

This capacity for self-reference makes it impossible to write a program that can reliably predict program behavior. Once a particular behavior-checking program has been written, we are always able to construct a larger program that defeats it: the new program incorporates the checker as a subroutine, checks its own source code, and then immediately does the exact opposite of whatever the checker said it would do. These self-contradictory programs are curiosities rather than something we'd ever write in practice, but they're just a symptom, not the cause, of the underlying problem: in general, program behavior is too powerful to be accurately predicted.

 Human language has similar power and similar problems. "This sentence is a lie" (the *liar paradox*) is an English sentence that can't be true or false. But the liar paradox depends on the special self-referential word "this"; as we saw in "Programs Can Refer to Themselves" on page 264, any computer program can be made self-referential *by construction*, without requiring any special language features.

When it comes down to it, there are two basic reasons why the behavior of programs is so hard to predict:

1. Any system with enough power to be self-referential can't correctly answer every question about itself.[20] We will always be able to construct a program like *do_the_opposite.rb* whose behavior can't be predicted by the system. To avoid this problem, we need to step outside the self-referential system and use a different, *more powerful* system to answer questions about it.

2. But in the case of universal programming languages, there *is* no more powerful system for us to upgrade to. The Church–Turing thesis tells us that any usable algorithm we invent for making predictions about the behavior of programs can itself be performed by a program, so we're stuck with the capabilities of universal systems.

---

20. This is roughly the content of Gödel's first incompleteness theorem (*http://en.wikipedia.org/wiki/G%C3 %B6del%27s_incompleteness_theorems*).

Coping with Uncomputability

The whole point of writing a program is to get a computer to do something useful. As programmers, how are we supposed to cope with a world where checking that a program works properly is an unsolvable problem?

Denial is a tempting response: *Ignore the whole issue. It would be nice if we could automatically verify program behavior, but we can't, so let's just hope for the best and never try to check that a program does its job correctly.*

But that would be an overreaction, because the situation isn't as bad as it sounds. Rice's theorem doesn't mean that program analysis is impossible, just that we can't write a nontrivial analyzer that will *always* halt and produce the right answer. As we saw in "Building a Halting Checker" on page 271, there's nothing to stop us from writing a tool that gives the right answer for *some* programs, as long as we can tolerate the fact that there will always be *other* programs for which it either gives the wrong answer or loops forever without returning anything.

Here are some practical ways of analyzing and predicting program behavior, in spite of undecidability:

- Ask undecidable questions, but give up if an answer can't be found. For example, to check whether a program prints a particular string, we can run it and wait; if it doesn't print that string within a particular period of time, say 10 seconds, we just terminate the program and assume it's no good. We might accidentally throw out a program that produces the expected output after 11 seconds, but in many cases that's an acceptable risk, especially since slow programs can be undesirable in their own right.

- Ask several small questions whose answers, when taken together, provide empirical evidence for the answer to a larger question. When performing automated acceptance testing, we're usually not able to check that a program does the right thing for every possible input, but we can try running it for a limited number of *example* inputs to see what happens. Each test run gives us information about how the program behaves in that specific case, and we can use that information to become more confident of how it's likely to behave in general. This leaves open the possibility that there are other untested inputs that cause wildly different behavior, but we can live with that as long as our test cases do a good job of representing most kinds of realistic input.

  Another example of this approach is the use of unit tests to verify the behavior of small pieces of a program individually rather than trying to verify the program as a whole. A well-isolated unit test concentrates on checking the properties of a simple unit of code, and makes assumptions about other parts of the program by representing them with test doubles (i.e., stubs and mocks). Individual unit tests that exercise small pieces of well-understood code can be simple and fast, minimizing the danger that any one test will run forever or give a misleading answer.

By unit testing all the program's pieces in this way, we can set up a chain of assumptions and implications that resembles a mathematical proof: "if piece A works, then piece B works, and if piece B works, then piece C works." Deciding whether all of these assumptions are justified is the responsibility of human reasoning rather than automated verification, although integration and acceptance testing can improve our confidence that the entire system does what it's supposed to do.

- Ask decidable questions by being conservative where necessary. The above suggestions involve actually running parts of a program to see what happens, which always introduces the risk of hitting an infinite loop, but there are useful questions that can be answered just by inspecting a program's source code statically. The most obvious example is "does this program contain any syntax errors?," but we can answer more interesting questions if we're prepared to accept safe approximations in cases where the real answer is undecidable.

  A common analysis is to look through a program's source to see if it contains *dead code* that computes values that are never used, or *unreachable code* that never gets evaluated. We can't always tell whether code is truly dead or unreachable, in which case we have to be conservative and assume it isn't, but there are cases where it's obvious: in some languages, we know that an assignment to a local variable that's never mentioned again is definitely dead, and that a statement that immediately follows a **return** is definitely unreachable.[21] An optimizing compiler like GCC uses these techniques to identify and eliminate unnecessary code, making programs smaller and faster without affecting their behavior.

- Approximate a program by converting it into something simpler, then ask decidable questions about the approximation. This important idea is the subject of the next chapter.

---

21. The Java language specification requires the compiler to reject any program that contains unreachable code. See *http://docs.oracle.com/javase/specs/jls/se7/html/jls-14.html#jls-14.21* for a lengthy explanation of how a Java compiler is meant to decide which parts of a program are potentially reachable without running any of it.

## CHAPTER 9

Programming in Toyland

Programming is about using syntax to communicate ideas to a machine. When we write a program, we have an idea of what we want the machine to do when it executes that program, and knowing the semantics of our programming language gives us some confidence that the machine is going to understand what each small piece of the program means.

But a complex computer program is greater than the sum of its individual statements and expressions. Once we've plugged together many small parts to make a larger whole, it would be useful to be able to check whether the overall program actually does what we originally wanted it to do. We might want to know that it always returns certain results, for example, or that running it will have certain side effects on the filesystem or network, or just that it doesn't contain obvious bugs that will make it crash on unexpected inputs.

In fact, there are all sorts of properties that we might want our programs to have, and it would be really convenient if we could just check the syntax of a particular program to see whether or not it has those properties, but we know from Rice's theorem that predicting a program's behavior by looking at its source code can't always give us the right answer. Of course, the most direct way to find out what a program will do is just to run it, and sometimes that's okay—a lot of software testing is done by running programs on known inputs and checking the actual outputs against the expected ones —but there are a few reasons why running code might not be an acceptable way of investigating it either.

For one thing, any useful program is likely to deal with information that won't be known until run time: interactive input from the user, files passed in as arguments, data read from the network, that sort of thing. We can certainly try running a program with dummy inputs to get some sense of what it does, but that just tells us about the program's behavior for those inputs; what happens when the real inputs are different? Running a program on all possible combinations of inputs is often impractical or impossible, and trying the program once with a specific set of inputs, however realistic they are, doesn't necessarily tell us very much about how it will behave in general.

Another problem, which we explored in "Universal Systems Can Loop For-ever" on page 259, is that programs written in sufficiently powerful[1] languages are perfectly capable of running forever without ever producing a result. This makes it impossible to reliably investigate arbitrary programs by running them, because it's sometimes impossible to tell in advance whether a program is going to run indefinitely (see "The Halting Problem" on page 271), so any automatic checker that tried to run a candidate program would be at risk of never coming back with an answer.

And lastly, even in the case of a program that does have all its input data available in advance and that will, for whatever reason, always eventually terminate instead of looping forever, it might just be expensive or inconvenient to run that program to see what happens. It could take a long time to finish, or have irreversible side effects—sending emails, transferring money, launching missiles—which are undesirable for testing purposes.

All these reasons make it useful to be able to discover information about a program without actually running it. One way of doing this is to use *abstract interpretation*, an analysis technique in which we execute a simplified version of the program and use the results to deduce properties of the original.

Abstract Interpretation

Abstract interpretation gives us a way of approaching a problem that's somehow too difficult to handle, perhaps because it's too large, too complex, or has too many un-knowns to be tackled directly. The main idea of abstract interpretation is to use an *abstraction*, a model of the real problem that discards enough detail to make it man-ageable—perhaps by making it smaller, simpler, or by eliminating unknowns—but that also retains enough detail to make its solution relevant to the original problem.

To make this vague idea more concrete, let's look at a simple application of abstract interpretation.

Route Planning

Suppose you're a tourist in an unfamiliar country and want to plan a road trip to another town. How will you decide which route to take? A direct solution is to jump into your rental car and drive in whichever direction seems the most promising. Depending on how lucky you are, and on how much help the foreign road signs give you, this brute-force exploration of an unknown road network might eventually get you to your des-tination. But it's an expensive strategy, and it's likely that you'll just get more and more lost until you give up completely.

---

1. "Sufficiently powerful" means "universal" here. See "Universal Systems Can Loop Forever" on page 259 for more.

Using a map to plan your trip is a much more sensible idea. A printed road atlas is an abstraction that sacrifices a lot of the detail of the physical road network. It doesn't tell you what the traffic is like, which roads are currently closed, where individual buildings are, or anything at all about the third dimension; it is, crucially, much smaller and flatter than the real thing. But a map does retain the most important information required for journey planning: the relative positions of all the towns, which roads lead to each town, and how those roads are connected to each other.

Despite all of this missing detail, an accurate map is useful, because the route you plan with it is likely to be valid in reality, not just in the abstract world of the map. A cartographer has done the expensive work of creating a model of reality, giving you the opportunity to perform a computation on that model by looking at a simplified representation of the road network and planning your route on it. You can then transfer the result of that computation back into the real world when you actually get in your car and drive to your destination, allowing cheap decisions made in the abstract world of the map to prevent you from having to make expensive decisions on the physical roads.

The approximations used by a map make navigational computations much easier without fatally compromising the fidelity of their results. There are plenty of circumstances in which decisions made with a map might turn out to be wrong—there is no guarantee that a map has told you absolutely *everything* you need to know about your journey—but planning your route in advance lets you rule out particular kinds of mistakes and makes the whole problem of getting from one place to another much more manageable.

Abstraction: Multiplying Signs

Planning a route with a printed map is a real application of abstract interpretation, but it's also very informal. For a more formal example, we can look at the multiplication of numbers; although it's still only a toy example, multiplication gives us a chance to start writing code to investigate these ideas.

Pretend for a moment that multiplying two numbers is a difficult or expensive operation, and that we're interested in finding out some information about the result of a multiplication without having to actually perform it. Specifically: what is the *sign* of the result? Is it a negative number, zero, or a positive number?

The notionally expensive way of finding out is to compute in the *concrete* world, using the *standard interpretation* of multiplication: multiply the numbers for real, look at the resulting number, and decide whether that result is negative, zero, or positive. In Ruby, for example:

```
>> 6 * -9
=> -54
```

-54 is negative, so we've learned that the product of 6 and -9 is a negative number. Job done.

However, it's also possible to discover the same information by computing in an *abstract* world, using an *abstract interpretation* of multiplication. Just as a map uses lines on a flat page to represent roads in the real world, we can use abstract values to represent numbers; we can plan a route on a map instead of finding our way by trial and error on real roads, and we can define an abstract multiplication operation on abstract values instead of using concrete multiplication on concrete numbers.

To do this, we need to design abstract values that make the calculation simpler while still retaining enough information to be a useful answer. We can take advantage of the fact that the absolute values[2] of two multiplied numbers don't make any difference to the sign of the result:

```
>> (6 * -9) < 0
=> true
>> (1000 * -5) < 0
=> true
>> (1 * -1) < 0
=> true
```

As young children, we're taught that it's only the signs of the arguments that matter: the product of two positive numbers, or two negative numbers, is always a positive number; the product of one positive and one negative number is always negative; and the product of zero with any other number is always zero.

So let's use these different kinds of number—"negative," "zero," and "positive"—as our abstract values. We can do this in Ruby by defining a `Sign` class and creating three instances of it:

```
class Sign < Struct.new(:name)
  NEGATIVE, ZERO, POSITIVE = [:negative, :zero, :positive].map { |name| new(name) }

  def inspect
    "#<Sign #{name}>"
  end
end
```

This gives us Ruby objects that we can use as our abstract values: `Sign::NEGATIVE` represents "any negative number," `Sign::ZERO` represents "the number zero," and `Sign::POSITIVE` represents "any positive number." These three `Sign` objects make up the tiny abstract world where we'll perform abstract calculations, while our concrete world consists of the virtually unlimited supply of Ruby integers.[3]

We can define abstract multiplication for `Sign` values by implementing just the sign-related aspect of concrete multiplication:

```
class Sign
  def *(other_sign)
```

2. A number's *absolute value* is what we get when we take the sign away. The absolute value of –10, for example, is 10.

3. Ruby's `Bignum` objects can represent integers of any size, limited only by available memory.

```
      if [self, other_sign].include?(ZERO)
        ZERO
      elsif self == other_sign
        POSITIVE
      else
        NEGATIVE
      end
    end
end
```

Instances of Sign can now be "multiplied" together just like numbers, and our implementation of Sign#* produces answers that are consistent with multiplication of actual numbers:

```
>> Sign::POSITIVE * Sign::POSITIVE
=> #<Sign positive>
>> Sign::NEGATIVE * Sign::ZERO
=> #<Sign zero>
>> Sign::POSITIVE * Sign::NEGATIVE
=> #<Sign negative>
```

For example, the last line above asks the question: what do we get when we multiply any positive number by any negative number? The answer comes back: a negative number. This is still a kind of multiplication, but it's much simpler than the kind we're used to, and it only works on "numbers" that have had almost all of their identifying information removed. If we're still imagining that real multiplication is expensive, this seems like a cut-down version of multiplication that could be considered cheap.

Armed with our abstract world of numbers and an abstract interpretation of multiplication for those numbers, we can tackle the original problem in a different way. Rather than multiplying two numbers directly to find out the sign of their result, we can convert the numbers into their abstract counterparts and multiply those instead. First we need a way to convert concrete numbers into abstract ones:

```
class Numeric
  def sign
    if self < 0
      Sign::NEGATIVE
    elsif zero?
      Sign::ZERO
    else
      Sign::POSITIVE
    end
  end
end
```

Now we can convert two numbers and do the multiplication in the abstract world:

```
>> 6.sign
=> #<Sign positive>
>> -9.sign
=> #<Sign negative>
>> 6.sign * -9.sign
=> #<Sign negative>
```

Again we've calculated that 6 * -9 produces a negative number, but this time we've done it without any multiplication of actual numbers. Stepping up into the abstract world gives us an alternative way of performing the computation, and crucially, the abstract result can be translated back down into the concrete world so we can make sense of it, although we can only get an approximate concrete answer because of the detail we sacrificed in making the abstraction. In this case, the abstract result `Sign::NEG ATIVE` tells us that any of the concrete numbers -1, -2, -3, etc., might be the answer to 6 * -9, but that the answer is definitely not 0 or any positive number like 1 or 500.

Note that, because Ruby values are objects—data structures that carry their operations with them—we can use the same Ruby expression to perform either a concrete or an abstract computation depending on whether we provide concrete (`Fixnum`) or abstract (`Sign`) objects as arguments. Take a `#calculate` method that multiplies three numbers in a particular way:

```
def calculate(x, y, z)
  (x * y) * (x * z)
end
```

If we call `#calculate` with `Fixnum` objects, the calculation will be done by `Fixnum#*` and we'll get a concrete `Fixnum` result. If we call it with `Sign` instances instead, the `Sign#*` operation will be used and produce a `Sign` result.

```
>> calculate(3, -5, 0)
=> 0
>> calculate(Sign::POSITIVE, Sign::NEGATIVE, Sign::ZERO)
=> #<Sign zero>
```

This gives us a limited opportunity to perform abstract interpretation within real Ruby programs by replacing concrete arguments with their abstract counterparts and running the rest of the code without modification.

> This technique is reminiscent of the way that *test doubles* (e.g., *stubs* and *mocks*) are used in automated unit testing. Test doubles are special placeholder objects that get injected into code as a way to control and verify its behavior. They're useful in any situation where using more realistic objects as test data would be too inconvenient or expensive.

Safety and Approximation: Adding Signs

So far we've seen that a computation in the abstract world will produce less precise results than its concrete counterpart, because an abstraction throws away detail: a route we plan on a map will tell us which way to turn but not which lane to drive in, and a multiplication between two `Sign` objects will tell us which side of zero the answer lies on but not its actual value.

A lot of the time, it's fine for a result to be imprecise, but for an abstraction to be useful, it's important that this imprecision is *safe*. Safety means that the abstraction always tells the truth: the result of an abstract computation must agree with the result of its concrete counterpart. If not, the abstraction is giving us unreliable information and is probably worse than useless.

Our `Sign` abstraction is safe because converting numbers into `Sign`s and multiplying them together always gives us the same result as calculating with the numbers themselves and just converting the final result into a `Sign`:

```
>> (6 * -9).sign == (6.sign * -9.sign)
=> true
>> (100 * 0).sign == (100.sign * 0.sign)
=> true
>> calculate(1, -2, -3).sign == calculate(1.sign, -2.sign, -3.sign)
=> true
```

In this respect, our `Sign` abstraction is actually quite precise. It retains exactly the right amount of information and preserves it perfectly throughout abstract computations. The safety issue becomes more significant when the abstraction doesn't match up quite so perfectly with the computations we want to perform, as we can see by experimenting with abstract addition.

There are *some* rules about how the signs of two numbers can determine the sign of the number we get when we add them together, but they don't work for all possible combinations of signs. We know that the sum of two positive numbers must be positive, and that the sum of a negative number and zero must be negative, but what about when we add a negative and a positive number? In that case, the sign of the result depends on the relationship between the two numbers' absolute values: if the positive number has a larger absolute value than the negative number, we'll get a positive answer (−20 + 30 = 10), if the negative number's absolute value is larger, then we'll get a negative answer (−30 + 20 = −10), and if they are exactly equal, we'll get zero. But of course the absolute value of each number is precisely the information that our abstraction has discarded, so we can't make this sort of decision in the abstract world.

This is a problem for our abstraction because it's *too* abstract to be able to compute addition accurately in every situation. How do we handle this? We could botch the definition of abstract addition just to get it to return some result—return `Sign::ZERO`, say, whenever we don't know what the right answer is—but that would be unsafe, because it would mean the abstract computation was giving an answer that might actively disagree with the one we'd get by doing the concrete computation instead.

The solution is to expand the abstraction to accommodate this uncertainty. Just as we have `Sign` values that mean "any positive number" and "any negative number," we can introduce a new one that simply means "any number." This is really the only honest answer that we can give when we're asked a question that we don't have enough detail to answer: the result could be negative, zero, or positive, no guarantees either way. Let's call this new value `Sign::UNKNOWN`:

```
class Sign
  UNKNOWN = new(:unknown)
end
```

This gives us what we need to implement abstract addition safely. The rules for calculating the sign of the sum of two numbers x and y are:

- If x and y have the same sign (both positive, both negative, or both zero), then that's also the sign of their sum.
- If x is zero, their sum has the same sign as y, and vice versa.
- Otherwise, the sign of their sum is unknown.

We can turn that into an implementation of Sign#+ easily enough:

```
class Sign
  def +(other_sign)
    if self == other_sign || other_sign == ZERO
      self
    elsif self == ZERO
      other_sign
    else
      UNKNOWN
    end
  end
end
```

This gives us the behavior we want:

```
>> Sign::POSITIVE + Sign::POSITIVE
=> #<Sign positive>
>> Sign::NEGATIVE + Sign::ZERO
=> #<Sign negative>
>> Sign::NEGATIVE + Sign::POSITIVE
=> #<Sign unknown>
```

In fact, this implementation happens to do the right thing when the sign of one of the *inputs* is unknown:

```
>> Sign::POSITIVE + Sign::UNKNOWN
=> #<Sign unknown>
>> Sign::UNKNOWN + Sign::ZERO
=> #<Sign unknown>
>> Sign::POSITIVE + Sign::NEGATIVE + Sign::NEGATIVE
=> #<Sign unknown>
```

We do need to go back and fix up our implementation of Sign#*, though, so that it handles Sign::UNKNOWN correctly:

```
class Sign
  def *(other_sign)
    if [self, other_sign].include?(ZERO)
      ZERO
    elsif [self, other_sign].include?(UNKNOWN)
      UNKNOWN
    elsif self == other_sign
      POSITIVE
```

```
      else
        NEGATIVE
      end
    end
  end
```

This gives us two abstract operations to play around with. Notice that Sign::UNKNOWN isn't totally contagious; even an unknown number multiplied by zero is still zero, so any uncertainty that creeps in partway through a computation may get swallowed up by the time it finishes:

```
>> (Sign::POSITIVE + Sign::NEGATIVE) * Sign::ZERO + Sign::POSITIVE
=> #<Sign positive>
```

We also need to adjust our idea of correctness to deal with the imprecision introduced by Sign::UNKNOWN. Because our abstraction sometimes doesn't have enough information to give a precise answer, it's no longer true that the abstract and concrete versions of a computation always give exactly matching results:

```
>> (10 + 3).sign == (10.sign + 3.sign)
=> true
>> (-5 + 0).sign == (-5.sign + 0.sign)
=> true
>> (6 + -9).sign == (6.sign + -9.sign)
=> false
>> (6 + -9).sign
=> #<Sign negative>
>> 6.sign + -9.sign
=> #<Sign unknown>
```

So what's going on here? Is our abstraction still safe? Well, yes, because in the cases where it loses precision and returns Sign::UNKNOWN, the abstract computation is still telling us something true: "the result is a negative number, zero, or a positive number." It's not as useful as the answer we can get by doing the concrete computation, but it's not *wrong*, and it's as good as we're going to get without adding more information to our abstract values and making abstract computations more complex.

We can express this in code by having a better way of comparing Signs than #==, which is now too unforgiving for the safety check. What we want to know is: does the result of the concrete computation *fall within* the result predicted by the abstract one? If the abstract computation says that a few different results are possible, does the concrete computation actually produce one of those results, or something else entirely?

Let's define an operation on Signs that can tell us whether two abstract values relate to each other in this way. Since what we're testing is whether one Sign value "fits inside" another, let's make it the #<= method:

```
class Sign
  def <=(other_sign)
    self == other_sign || other_sign == UNKNOWN
  end
end
```

This gives us the test we want:

```
>> Sign::POSITIVE <= Sign::POSITIVE
=> true
>> Sign::POSITIVE <= Sign::UNKNOWN
=> true
>> Sign::POSITIVE <= Sign::NEGATIVE
=> false
```

Now we can check for safety by seeing whether each concrete computation's result falls within the abstract computation's prediction:

```
>> (6 * -9).sign <= (6.sign * -9.sign)
=> true
>> (-5 + 0).sign <= (-5.sign + 0.sign)
=> true
>> (6 + -9).sign <= (6.sign + -9.sign)
=> true
```

This safety property holds for any computation involving addition and multiplication, because we've designed an abstraction that falls back to a safe approximation when it can't give a precise answer.

Incidentally, having access to this abstraction lets us do simple analysis of Ruby code that adds and multiplies numbers. As an example, here's a method that sums the squares of its arguments:

```
def sum_of_squares(x, y)
  (x * x) + (y * y)
end
```

If we want to automatically analyze this method to learn something about how it behaves, we have a choice: we can treat it as a black box and run it for all possible arguments, which would take forever, or we can inspect its source code and try to use mathematical reasoning to deduce some of its properties, which is complicated. (And, in the general case, doomed to failure because of Rice's theorem.) Abstract interpretation gives us the third option of calling the method with abstract values to see what outputs are produced by an abstract version of the computation, and it's practical to do this for all possible inputs, because there are only a small number of potential combinations of abstract values.

Each of the arguments x and y can be a negative, zero, or positive number, so let's see what the possible outputs can be:

```
>> inputs = Sign::NEGATIVE, Sign::ZERO, Sign::POSITIVE
=> [#<Sign negative>, #<Sign zero>, #<Sign positive>]
>> outputs = inputs.product(inputs).map { |x, y| sum_of_squares(x, y) }
=> [
     #<Sign positive>, #<Sign positive>, #<Sign positive>,
     #<Sign positive>, #<Sign zero>, #<Sign positive>,
     #<Sign positive>, #<Sign positive>, #<Sign positive>
   ]
>> outputs.uniq
=> [#<Sign positive>, #<Sign zero>]
```

Without having done any clever analysis, this tells us that `#sum_of_squares` can only produce zero or positive numbers, never negative numbers—a fairly boring property that's obvious to an educated human reading the source code, but not something that would be immediately evident to a machine. Of course, this kind of trick only works for very simple code, but despite being a toy, it shows how abstraction can make a difficult problem more tractable.

Static Semantics

So far we've seen toy examples of how to discover approximate information about computations without actually performing them. We could learn more by doing those computations for real, but approximate information is better than nothing, and for some applications (like route planning), it might be all we really need.

In the multiplication and addition examples, we were able to turn a small program into a simpler, more abstract version just by feeding it abstract values as input instead of concrete numbers, but we can only get so far with this technique if we want to investigate larger and more elaborate programs. It's easy to create values that supply their own implementations of multiplication and addition, but Ruby doesn't allow values to control their own behavior more generally—when they're used in an `if` statement, for example—because it has hardcoded rules[4] about how particular pieces of syntax should work. Besides, we still have the problem that it's not feasible in general to learn about programs by running them and waiting for their output, because some programs loop forever without returning a result.

Another downside of the multiplication and addition examples is that they're not very interesting: nobody cares about whether their program returns positive or negative numbers. In practice, the interesting questions are ones like "will my program crash when I run it?" and "can my program be transformed to make it more efficient?"

We can answer more interesting questions about programs by considering their *static semantics*. In Chapter 2, we looked at the *dynamic semantics* of programming languages, a way of specifying the meaning of code when it's executed; a language's static semantics tells us about properties of programs that we can investigate without executing them. The classic example of static semantics is a *type system*: a collection of rules that can be used to analyze a program and check that it doesn't contain certain kinds of bug. In "Correctness" on page 41, we considered SIMPLE programs like «x = true; x = x + 1», which are syntactically valid but cause a problem for the dynamic semantics when they're executed. A type system can anticipate these mistakes ahead of time, allowing some bad programs to be automatically rejected before anyone tries to run them.

---

4. Unlike, say, Smalltalk.

Abstract interpretation gives us a way of thinking about the static semantics of a program. Programs are meant to be run, so our standard interpretation of a program's meaning is the one given by its dynamic semantics: «x = 1 + 2; y = x * 3» is a program that manipulates numbers by doing arithmetic on them and storing them somewhere in memory. But if we have an alternative, more abstract semantics for the language, we can "execute" the same program according to different rules, and get more abstract results that give us partial information about what will happen when the program is interpreted normally.

Implementation

Let's make these ideas concrete by building a type system for the SIMPLE language from Chapter 2. Superficially, this will look like a big-step operational semantics from "Big-Step Semantics" on page 42: we'll implement a method on each of the classes representing the syntax of SIMPLE programs (Number, Add, and so on), and calling the method will return a final result. In the dynamic semantics, that method is called #evaluate, and its result is either a fully evaluated SIMPLE value or an environment associating names with SIMPLE values, depending on whether we evaluate an expression or a statement:

```
>> expression = Add.new(Variable.new(:x), Number.new(1))
=> «x + 1»
>> expression.evaluate({ x: Number.new(2) })
=> «3»
>> statement = Assign.new(:y, Number.new(3))
=> «y = 3»
>> statement.evaluate({ x: Number.new(1) })
=> {:x=>«1», :y=>«3»}
```

For our static semantics, we'll implement a different method that does less work and returns a more abstract result. Instead of concrete values and environments, our abstract values will be *types*. A type represents many possible values: a SIMPLE expression can evaluate to a number or a Boolean, so for expressions, our types will be "any number" and "any Boolean." These types are similar to the Sign values we saw earlier, especially Sign::UNKNOWN, which really does mean "any number." As with Sign, we can introduce types by defining a class called Type and creating some instances:

```
class Type < Struct.new(:name)
  NUMBER, BOOLEAN = [:number, :boolean].map { |name| new(name) }

  def inspect
    "#<Type #{name}>"
  end
end
```

Our new method will return a type, so let's call it #type. It's supposed to answer a question: when this SIMPLE syntax is evaluated, what type of value will it return? This is very easy to implement for SIMPLE's Number and Boolean syntax classes, because numbers and Booleans evaluate to themselves, so we know exactly what type of value we'll get:

```
class Number
  def type
    Type::NUMBER
  end
end

class Boolean
  def type
    Type::BOOLEAN
  end
end
```

For operations like Add, Multiply, and LessThan, it's slightly more complicated. We know that evaluating Add returns a number, for example, but we also know that evaluation will only succeed if both arguments to Add also evaluate to a number, otherwise the SIMPLE interpreter will fail with an error:

```
>> Add.new(Number.new(1), Number.new(2)).evaluate({})
=> «3»
>> Add.new(Number.new(1), Boolean.new(true)).evaluate({})
TypeError: true can't be coerced into Fixnum
```

How can we find out whether an argument will evaluate to a number? That's what its type tells us. So for Add, the rule is something like: if the type of both arguments is Type::NUMBER, the type of the overall result is Type::NUMBER; otherwise, the result is no type at all, because the evaluation of any expression that tries to add nonnumeric values will fail before it can return anything. For simplicity, we'll let the #type method return nil to indicate this failure, although in other circumstances, we might have chosen to raise an exception or return some special error value instead (Type::ERROR, for instance) if that made the overall implementation more convenient.

The code for Add looks like this:

```
class Add
  def type
    if left.type == Type::NUMBER && right.type == Type::NUMBER
      Type::NUMBER
    end
  end
end
```

The implementation of Multiply#type is identical, and LessThan#type is very similar, except that it returns Type::BOOLEAN instead of Type::NUMBER:

```
class LessThan
  def type
    if left.type == Type::NUMBER && right.type == Type::NUMBER
      Type::BOOLEAN
    end
  end
end
```

On the console, we can see that this is enough to distinguish between expressions that will evaluate successfully and those that won't, even though the syntax of SIMPLE allows both:

```
>> Add.new(Number.new(1), Number.new(2)).type
=> #<Type number>
>> Add.new(Number.new(1), Boolean.new(true)).type
=> nil
>> LessThan.new(Number.new(1), Number.new(2)).type
=> #<Type boolean>
>> LessThan.new(Number.new(1), Boolean.new(true)).type
=> nil
```

 We're assuming that the abstract syntax tree is at least *syntactically* valid. The actual values stored at the leaves of the tree are ignored by the static semantics, so #type might incorrectly predict the evaluation behavior of a badly formed expression:

```
>> bad_expression = Add.new(Number.new(true), Number.new(1)) ❶
=> «true + 1»
>> bad_expression.type
=> #<Type number> ❷
>> bad_expression.evaluate({})
NoMethodError: undefined method `+' for true:TrueClass ❸
```

❶ The high-level structure of this AST looks correct (an Add containing two Numbers), but the first Number object is malformed, because its value attribute is true instead of a Fixnum.

❷ The static semantics assumes that adding two Numbers together will always produce another Number, so #type says that evaluation will succeed...

❸ ...but if we actually evaluate the expression, we get an exception when Ruby tries to add 1 to true.

Badly formed expressions should never be produced by a SIMPLE parser, so this is unlikely to be a problem in practice.

This is a more general version of the earlier trick with addition, multiplication, and Sign. Even though we're not doing any actual addition or comparison of numbers, the static semantics gives us an alternative way of "executing" the program that still returns a useful result.

Instead of interpreting the expression «1 + 2» as a program about *values*, we're throwing away some detail and interpreting it as a program about *types*, and the static semantics provides the alternative interpretations of «1», «2», and «+», which let us run this program-about-types to see what its result is. That result is less specific—more abstract— than the one we'd get by running the program normally according to the dynamic semantics, but it's nonetheless a useful result, because we have a way of translating it into something meaningful in the concrete world: Type::NUMBER means "calling #eval uate on this expression will return a `Number`," and `nil` means "calling `#evaluate` may cause an error."

We almost have the complete static semantics of SIMPLE expressions now, but we haven't looked at variables. What should `Variable#type` return? It depends what value the variable contains: in a program like «x = 5; y = x + 1» the variable y has the type `Type::NUMBER`, but in «x = 5; y = x < 1» it has the type `Type::BOOLEAN`. How can we handle this?

We saw in "Small-Step Semantics" on page 21 that the dynamic semantics of `Variable` uses an environment hash to map variable names onto their values, and the static semantics needs something similar: a mapping from variable names onto *types*. We could call this a "type environment," but let's use the name *type context* to avoid getting the two kinds of environment mixed up. If we pass a type context into `Variable#type`, all it has to do is look up that variable in the context:

```
class Variable
  def type(context)
    context[name]
  end
end
```

 Where does this type context come from? For the moment, we'll just assume that it gets provided somehow, by some external mechanism, whenever we need it. For example, perhaps each SIMPLE program has an accompanying header file that declares the types of all the variables that will be used; this file would have no effect when the program was run, but could be used to automatically check it against the static semantics during development.

Now that `#type` expects a `context` argument, we need to go back and revise the other implementations of `#type` to accept a type context:

```
class Number
  def type(context)
    Type::NUMBER
  end
end

class Boolean
  def type(context)
    Type::BOOLEAN
  end
end

class Add
  def type(context)
    if left.type(context) == Type::NUMBER && right.type(context) == Type::NUMBER
      Type::NUMBER
    end
  end
```

```
      end

    class LessThan
      def type(context)
        if left.type(context) == Type::NUMBER && right.type(context) == Type::NUMBER
          Type::BOOLEAN
        end
      end
    end
```

This lets us ask for the type of expressions that involve variables, as long as we provide a context that gives them the right types:

```
>> expression = Add.new(Variable.new(:x), Variable.new(:y))
=> «x + y»
>> expression.type({})
=> nil
>> expression.type({ x: Type::NUMBER, y: Type::NUMBER })
=> #<Type number>
>> expression.type({ x: Type::NUMBER, y: Type::BOOLEAN })
=> nil
```

That gives us implementations of #type for all forms of expression syntax, so what about statements? Evaluating a SIMPLE statement returns an environment, not a value, so how do we express that in the static semantics?

The easiest way to handle statements is to treat them as a kind of inert expression: assume that they don't return a value (which is true) and ignore the effect they have on the environment. We can come up with a new type that means "doesn't return a value" and associate that type with any statement as long as all its subparts have the right types. Let's give this new type the name Type::VOID:

```
    class Type
      VOID = new(:void)
    end
```

Implementations of #type for DoNothing and Sequence are easy. Evaluation of DoNothing will always succeed, and evaluation of Sequence will succeed as long as the statements it's connecting don't have anything wrong with them:

```
    class DoNothing
      def type(context)
        Type::VOID
      end
    end

    class Sequence
      def type(context)
        if first.type(context) == Type::VOID && second.type(context) == Type::VOID
          Type::VOID
        end
      end
    end
```

If and While are slightly more discerning. They both contain an expression that acts as a condition, and for the program to work properly, the condition has to evaluate to a Boolean:

```
class If
  def type(context)
    if condition.type(context) == Type::BOOLEAN &&
        consequence.type(context) == Type::VOID &&
        alternative.type(context) == Type::VOID
      Type::VOID
    end
  end
end

class While
  def type(context)
    if condition.type(context) == Type::BOOLEAN && body.type(context) == Type::VOID
      Type::VOID
    end
  end
end
```

This lets us distinguish between a statement that will go wrong during evaluation and one that won't:

```
>> If.new(
     LessThan.new(Number.new(1), Number.new(2)), DoNothing.new, DoNothing.new
   ).type({})
=> #<Type void>
>> If.new(
     Add.new(Number.new(1), Number.new(2)), DoNothing.new, DoNothing.new
   ).type({})
=> nil
>> While.new(Variable.new(:x), DoNothing.new).type({ x: Type::BOOLEAN })
=> #<Type void>
>> While.new(Variable.new(:x), DoNothing.new).type({ x: Type::NUMBER })
=> nil
```

 Type::VOID and nil have different meanings here. When #type returns Type::VOID, that means "this code is fine but intentionally returns no value"; nil means "this code contains a mistake."

The only method left to implement is Assign#type. We know it should return Type::VOID, but under what circumstances? How do we decide if an assignment is well-behaved or not? We'll want to check that the expression on the righthand side of the assignment is sensible according to the static semantics, but do we care what type it is?

These questions lead us to make some design decisions about what should be considered valid SIMPLE programs. For example, is «x = 1; y = 2; x = x < y» okay? It's certainly fine according to the dynamic semantics—nothing bad happens when it's executed—but we might (or might not!) be uncomfortable with allowing programs where the variables change from holding one type of value to another during execution. That kind of flexibility might be valuable to some programmers, but for others, it could act as a source of accidental errors.

From the perspective of someone designing the static semantics, it's also more difficult to handle a language where variables can change their types. At the moment, we're assuming that the type context arrives from some external source and remains unchanged throughout the program, but we could opt for a more sophisticated system where the context is empty at the beginning of the program and gradually builds up as variables are declared or assigned, in the same way that the dynamic semantics gradually builds up the value environment as the program executes. But this gets complicated: if statements could modify the type context, then we'd need the #type method to return both a type and a context, in the same way that the dynamic semantics' #reduce method returns a reduced program and an environment, so that an earlier statement can pass an updated context to a later one. We'd also have to deal with situations like «if (b) { x = 1 } else { y = 2 }» where different execution paths produce different type contexts, as well as ones like «if (b) { x = 1 } else { x = true }» where those different contexts actively contradict each other.[5]

Fundamentally, there is a tension between the restrictiveness of a type system and the expressiveness of the programs we can write within it. A restrictive type system can be good, because it provides strong guarantees that rule out lots of possible errors, but it's bad when it prevents us from writing the programs we want to write. A good type system finds an acceptable compromise between restrictiveness and expressiveness, ruling out enough problems to be worthwhile without getting in the way, while being simple enough for programmers to understand.

We'll resolve this tension by sticking with the uncomplicated idea of a type context that's provided by something outside the program itself and doesn't get updated by individual statements. This does rule out certain kinds of program, and definitely avoids the problem of how and where this type context originates, but it keeps the static semantics simple and gives us a rule we can easily work with.

For assignment statements, then, let's say that the type of the expression should match the type of the variable to which its value is being assigned:

```
class Assign
  def type(context)
    if context[name] == expression.type(context)
      Type::VOID
    end
  end
end
```

---

5. An easy solution would be to say that the type system rejects a statement unless all of its execution paths produce the same context.

This rule is good enough for all programs where we can decide the type of each variable upfront and have it stay the same, which is a tolerable constraint. For example, we can check the `While` loop whose dynamic semantics we implemented in Chapter 2:

```
>> statement =
    While.new(
      LessThan.new(Variable.new(:x), Number.new(5)),
      Assign.new(:x, Add.new(Variable.new(:x), Number.new(3)))
    )
=> «while (x < 5) { x = x + 3 }»
>> statement.type({})
=> nil
>> statement.type({ x: Type::NUMBER })
=> #<Type void>
>> statement.type({ x: Type::BOOLEAN })
=> nil
```

Benefits and Limitations

The type system we've built can prevent basic errors. By running a toy version of a program according to these static semantics, we can find out what types of value can appear at each point in the original program, and check that these types match up correctly with what the dynamic semantics is going to try to do when we run it. The simplicity of this toy interpretation means that we get only limited information about what might happen when the program is evaluated, but it also means that we can do our checking easily and without complications. For example, we can check a program that runs forever:

```
>> statement =
    Sequence.new(
      Assign.new(:x, Number.new(0)),
      While.new(
        Boolean.new(true),
        Assign.new(:x, Add.new(Variable.new(:x), Number.new(1)))
      )
    )
=> «x = 0; while (true) { x = x + 1 }»
>> statement.type({ x: Type::NUMBER })
=> #<Type void>
>> statement.evaluate({})
SystemStackError: stack level too deep
```

That program is definitely stupid, but it doesn't contain any type errors: the loop condition is a Boolean, and the variable x is consistently used to store a number. Of course, the type system isn't clever enough to tell us whether a program is doing what we meant it to do, or even doing anything useful at all, only whether its parts match up in the right way. And because it needs to be safe, just like our `Sign` abstraction, it will sometimes give us an overly pessimistic answer about whether a program contains any errors. We can see this if we extend the above program with an extra statement:

```
>> statement = Sequence.new(statement, Assign.new(:x, Boolean.new(true)))
=> «x = 0; while (true) { x = x + 1 }; x = true»
>> statement.type({ x: Type::NUMBER })
=> nil
```

The #type method returns nil to indicate an error because there's a statement that
assigns a Boolean value to x, but there's no way this could actually cause a problem at
runtime, because this statement will never get executed. Our type system isn't clever
enough to spot this, but it gives us a safe answer, "this program *might* go wrong," which
is overly cautious but not incorrect. Something in the program tries to assign a Boolean
value to a numeric variable, so part of it has the potential to go wrong, but *for other
reasons* it never actually will.

It's not just infinite loops that cause problems. The dynamic semantics has no problem
with a program like this:

```
>> statement =
     Sequence.new(
       If.new(
         Variable.new(:b),
         Assign.new(:x, Number.new(6)),
         Assign.new(:x, Boolean.new(true))
       ),
       Sequence.new(
         If.new(
           Variable.new(:b),
           Assign.new(:y, Variable.new(:x)),
           Assign.new(:y, Number.new(1))
         ),
         Assign.new(:z, Add.new(Variable.new(:y), Number.new(1)))
       )
     )
=> «if (b) { x = 6 } else { x = true }; if (b) { y = x } else { y = 1 }; z = y + 1»
>> statement.evaluate({ b: Boolean.new(true) })
=> {:b=>«true», :x=>«6», :y=>«6», :z=>«7»}
>> statement.evaluate({ b: Boolean.new(false) })
=> {:b=>«false», :x=>«true», :y=>«1», :z=>«2»}
```

The variable x is used to store a number or a Boolean depending on whether b is true
or false, which is never a problem during evaluation, because the program consistently
uses either one or the other; there's no possible execution path where x is treated as
both a number and a Boolean. But the abstract values used by the static semantics don't
have enough detail to be able to show that this is okay,[6] so the safe approximation is
to always say "this program might go wrong":

```
>> statement.type({})
=> nil
>> context = { b: Type::BOOLEAN, y: Type::NUMBER, z: Type::NUMBER }
=> {:b=>#<Type boolean>, :y=>#<Type number>, :z=>#<Type number>}
```

---

6. In this case, the detail is that the type of x depends upon the value of b. Our types don't contain any
   information about the specific values of variables, and they can't express dependencies between types
   and values.

```
>> statement.type(context)
=> nil
>> statement.type(context.merge({ x: Type::NUMBER }))
=> nil
>> statement.type(context.merge({ x: Type::BOOLEAN }))
=> nil
```

This is a *static type system*, designed for checking the program before it's run; in a statically typed language, each *variable* has an associated type. Ruby's *dynamic type system* works differently: variables don't have types, and the types of *values* are only checked when they're actually used during the execution of a program. This allows Ruby to handle values of different types being assigned to the same variable, at the cost of not being able to detect typing bugs before the program is executed.

This system is focused on programs going wrong in a specific way: the dynamic semantics of each piece of syntax has certain expectations about what types of values it will be handling, and the type system checks those expectations to make sure that a number won't show up where a Boolean is expected and vice versa. But there are other ways for a program to go wrong, and this static semantics doesn't check for them. For example, the type system pays no attention to whether a variable has actually been given a value before it's used, so any program containing uninitialized variables will pass the type checker and still fail during evaluation:

```
>> statement = Assign.new(:x, Add.new(Variable.new(:x), Number.new(1)))
=> «x = x + 1»
>> statement.type({ x: Type::NUMBER })
=> #<Type void>
>> statement.evaluate({})
NoMethodError: undefined method `value' for nil:NilClass
```

Any information we get from the type system has to be taken with a pinch of salt, and we have to pay attention to its limitations when deciding how much faith to put in it. A successful execution of a program's static semantics doesn't mean "this program will definitely work," only "this program definitely won't fail in a particular way." It would be great to have an automated system that can tell us that a program is free of any conceivable kind of bug or error, but as we saw in Chapter 8, the universe just isn't that convenient.

Applications

This chapter has sketched the basic idea of abstract interpretation—using cheap approximations to learn about the behavior of expensive computations—and showed a simple type system as an example of how approximations can be useful for analyzing programs.

Our discussion of abstract interpretation was very informal. Formally, abstract interpretation is a mathematical technique where different semantics for the same language are connected together by functions that convert collections of concrete values into abstract ones and vice versa, allowing the results and properties of abstract programs to be understood in terms of concrete ones.

A notable industrial application of this technique is the Astrée static analyzer (*http://www.astree.ens.fr/*), which uses abstract interpretation to automatically prove that a C program is free of runtime errors like division by zero, out-of-bounds array indexing, and integer overflow. Astrée has been used to verify the flight control software of Airbus A340 and A380 airplanes, as well as the automatic docking software for the *Jules Verne* ATV-001 mission that transported supplies to the International Space Station. Abstract interpretation respects Rice's theorem by providing safe approximations rather than guaranteed answers, so Astrée has the potential to report a possible runtime error where none actually exists (a *false alarm*); in practice, its abstractions were precise enough to avoid any false alarms when verifying the A340 software.

Programs written in the SIMPLE language can only manipulate rudimentary values—numbers and Booleans—so the types seen in this chapter are very basic. Real programming languages handle a wider variety of possible values, so real static type systems are more sophisticated. For example, statically typed functional programming languages like ML and Haskell have values that are functions (like Ruby's procs), so their type systems support *function types* with meanings like "a function that takes two numeric arguments and returns a Boolean," allowing the type checker to verify that the arguments used in a function call match up with that function's definition.

Type systems can carry other information too: Java has a *type and effect system* that tracks not only the types of methods' arguments and return values but also which *checked exceptions* can be thrown by the body of the method (throwing an exception is an *effect*), which is used to ensure that all possible exceptions are either handled or explicitly propagated.

Afterword

Well, that's the end of our journey through the theory of computation. We've designed languages and machines with various capabilities, teased computation out of unusual systems, and crashed headlong into the theoretical limits of computer programming.

Aside from exploring specific machines and techniques, we've seen some more general ideas along the way:

- Anyone can design and implement a programming language. The basic ideas of syntax and semantics are simple, and tools like Treetop can take care of the uninteresting details.

- Every computer program is a mathematical object. Syntactically a program is just a large number; semantically it can represent a mathematical function, or a hierarchical structure which can be manipulated by formal reduction rules. This means that many techniques and results from mathematics, like Kleene's recursion theorem or Gödel's incompleteness theorem, can equally be applied to programs.

- Computation, which we initially described as just "what a computer does," has turned out to be something of a force of nature. It's tempting to think of computation as a sophisticated human invention that can only be performed by specially-designed systems with many complicated parts, but it also shows up in systems that don't seem complex enough to support it. So computation isn't a sterile, artificial process that only happens inside a microprocessor, but rather a pervasive phenomenon that crops up in many different places and in many different ways.

- Computation is not all-or-nothing. Different machines have different amounts of computational power, giving us a continuum of usefulness: DFAs and NFAs have limited capabilities, DPDAs are more powerful, NPDAs more powerful still, and Turing machines are the most powerful we know of.

- Encodings and levels of abstraction are essential to harnessing the power of computation. Computers are machines for maintaining a tower of abstractions, beginning at the very low level of semiconductor physics and rising to the much higher level of multitouch graphical user interfaces. To make computation useful, we need to be able to encode complex ideas from the real world in a simpler form that machines can manipulate, and then be able to decode the results back into a meaningful high-level representation.

- There are limits to what computation can do. We don't know how to build a computer that is fundamentally more capable than a Turing machine, but there are well-defined problems that a Turing machine can't solve, and a lot of those problems involve discovering information about the programs we write. We can cope with these limitations by learning to make use of vague or incomplete answers to questions about our programs' behavior.

These ideas may not immediately change the way you work, but I hope they've satisfied some of your curiosity, and that they'll help you to enjoy the time you spend making computation happen in the universe.

Index

Symbols
* operator, 9, 83
. (dot), 3, 5
: (colon), 2
=> prompt, 1
>> prompt, 1
[ ] (square brackets), 3, 4
{ } (curly brackets), 3, 9

A
absolute value, 288
abstract interpretation
    about, 286
    adding signs, 290–295
    applications, 305
    multiplying signs, 287–290
    route planning, 286
abstract machines, 20
abstract syntax tree (AST)
    about, 19
    building by hand, 23
    reduction relation, 22
accept states, 65, 74, 90
Adams, Douglas, 260
algorithms, 254–257
Analytical Engine, 57
applications
    abstract interpretation, 305
    big-step semantics, 47
    denotational semantics, 55
    small-step semantics, 42
arguments
    blocks of code and, 10
    messages and, 5

    passing to methods, 31
    procs and, 163
    variable number of, 9
Array class
    #<< method, 58
    about, 10
    #push method, 185
assignment statements, 33
assignments
    local variables and, 7
    parallel, 8, 9
AST (abstract syntax tree)
    about, 19
    building by hand, 23
    reduction relation, 22
Astrée static analyzer, 306
axiomatic semantics, 57

B
Babbage, Charles, 57
balanced brackets example, 105–108
big-step semantics
    about, 42
    applications, 47
    comparing styles, 54
    expressions, 43–45
    statements, 45–47
Bignum object, 288
binary representation, 157
blocks of code
    about, 9
    arguments and, 10
Booleans in FizzBuzz example, 169–172
Brzozowski's algorithm, 102

We'd like to hear your suggestions for improving our indexes. Send email to *index@oreilly.com*.

About the Author

Tom Stuart is a computer scientist and programmer, and the founder of Codon, a digital product consultancy in London. He works as a consultant, mentor, and trainer, helping companies to improve the quality and clarity of their approach to creating software products, usually on the Web. He has lectured on optimizing compilers at the University of Cambridge, co-organizes the Ruby Manor conference, and is a member of the London Ruby User Group.

Colophon

The animal on the cover of *Understanding Computation* is the bear paw clam (*Hippopus hippopus*). The bear paw clam, also known as the horse's hoof clam because of its shape and the strawberry clam for its reddish color, is part of the giant clam subfamily Tridacnidae, which in turn is part of the family Cardiidae. The bear paw clam mostly lives in reefs in the Indo-Pacific area.

The bear paw clam has two identical and symmetrical hinged sections. It also has deep ridges and a distinctive red-white color pattern. It feeds on plankton in the surrounding area by staying in one location and filtering surrounding water using its siphons.

The cover image is from a loose plate, source unknown. The cover font is Adobe ITC Garamond. The text font is Adobe Minion Pro; the heading font is Adobe Myriad Condensed; and the code font is Dalton Maag's Ubuntu Mono.

Get even more for your money.

Join the O'Reilly Community, and register the O'Reilly books you own. It's free, and you'll get:

- $4.99 ebook upgrade offer
- 40% upgrade offer on O'Reilly print books
- Membership discounts on books and events
- Free lifetime updates to ebooks and videos
- Multiple ebook formats, DRM FREE
- Participation in the O'Reilly community
- Newsletters
- Account management
- 100% Satisfaction Guarantee

Signing up is easy:

1. **Go to: oreilly.com/go/register**
2. **Create an O'Reilly login.**
3. **Provide your address.**
4. **Register your books.**

Note: English-language books only

To order books online:
oreilly.com/store

For questions about products or an order:
orders@oreilly.com

To sign up to get topic-specific email announcements and/or news about upcoming books, conferences, special offers, and new technologies:
elists@oreilly.com

For technical questions about book content:
booktech@oreilly.com

To submit new book proposals to our editors:
proposals@oreilly.com

O'Reilly books are available in multiple DRM-free ebook formats. For more information:
oreilly.com/ebooks

Spreading the knowledge of innovators   oreilly.com

Have it your way.

Milton Keynes UK
Ingram Content Group UK Ltd.
UKHW052311010824
446337UK00017B/103

9 781449 329273